D0405073

LANDLORDING & PROPERTY MANAGEMENT

LANDLORDING & PROPERTY MANAGEMENT

Insider's Advice
on How to Own
Real Estate and
Manage It Profitably

by Mark B. Weiss, C.C.I.M.,
& Dan Baldwin

Adams Media Corporation
Avon, Massachusetts

A Streetwise® Publication.
Streetwise® is a registered trademark of Adams Media Corporation.

Published by Adams Media Corporation
57 Littlefield Street, Avon, MA 02322 U.S.A
www.adamsmedia.com

ISBN: 1-58062-766-8

Printed in the United States of America.

J I H G F E D C B A

Library of Congress Cataloging-in-Publication Data
Weiss, Mark B.
Streetwise landlording and property management / written by
Mark B. Weiss and Dan Baldwin.
p.   cm.
Includes index.
ISBN 1-58062-766-8
1. Real estate management–United States. 2. Landlord and tenant–United States.
3. Rental housing–United States–Management 4. Real estate investment–United States.
I. Title: Landlording and property management. II. Baldwin, Dan. III. Title.
HD1394.5.U6 W45 2002
333.33'8–dc21
2002011426

This publication is designed to provide accurate and authoritative information with regard to the subject matter covered. It is sold with the understanding that the publisher is not engaged in rendering legal, accounting, or other professional advice. If legal advice or other expert assistance is required, the services of a competent professional person should be sought.
— From a *Declaration of Principles* jointly adopted by a Committee of the American Bar Association and a Committee of Publishers and Associations

This publication is intended to provide current and prospective business owners with useful information that may assist them in preparing for and obtaining business capital loans and investment funding. This information is general in nature and is not intended to provide specific advice for any individual or business entity. While the information contained herein should be helpful to the reader, appropriate financial, accounting, tax, or legal advice should always be sought from a competent professional engaged for any specific situation regarding your enterprise.

Cover illustration by Eric Mueller.

This book is available at quantity discounts for bulk purchases.
For information, call 1-800-872-5627.

Visit our exciting small business Web site: www.businesstown.com

CONTENTS

PART I: IS PROPERTY MANAGEMENT RIGHT FOR YOU?

PART II: WHAT YOU NEED TO KNOW TO GET STARTED

PART III: THE INS AND OUTS OF MANAGING PROPERTY

CONTENTS

PART IV: ENLISTING PROFESSIONAL HELP

PART V: OTHER ISSUES TO CONSIDER

Acknowledgments

I thank my wife, Marilyn, without whose support I would not have gained the recognition, knowledge, and experience to write this book; my son, Daniel, who has been patient and understanding; Paul Egel, my father-in-law, who has been a mentor and supportive with wisdom, gentility, patience, and spirit; and Kathy Welton, who had the confidence in me as a real-estate professional to undertake this project.

—Mark B. Weiss

This book would never have come into existence without the incredible encouragement and support of my parents, Dan and Laura Baldwin; my wife, Mary Baldwin; George Sewell and Micah Hackler (The Factory); and Kathy Welton, the National Realtors Association, and their Web site, *www.Realtor.org.*

—Dan Baldwin

Introduction

Ownership and/or property management of real estate offers a genuine opportunity for virtually anyone to achieve the American dream—in whatever way a particular individual, family, or group might define it.

Owning property has proven to be a key element in the financial success of people in all walks of life throughout the country. Why? Mark Twain had an answer: "Because they're not making any more of it." This lack of any new property supply can be your route to wealth, stability, and happiness.

If you look up for a moment, you will see that you are surrounded by property, whether you are sitting at home or on a park bench. Somebody somewhere owns what you're looking at. We live in property. Shop in property. Go to school, work, and vacation in property. Even undeveloped land is property. And somebody has to manage it.

Property management is serious business. It can be tough. It can be brutal. It can also be richly rewarding and a lot of fun. Which experience will be yours depends mostly on how you apply yourself to the principles and guidelines in this book. Success in real estate requires education, experience, hard work, dedication, and a vision, though a touch of good luck now and then doesn't hurt either. This book is primarily about these first five elements. If you master education, experience, hard work, and dedication, and if you can apply a little vision now and then, you should be in a pretty good position to earn and enjoy your own luck.

Is it time for you to get serious about property management? Only you can answer that question. Maybe you'd prefer to do a little in-depth research before making your decision. You might like to get a pretty good idea of what you might be getting into, or you might want a leg up and a head start on the competition. In any of those cases, this book is for you. It evaluates the ups and downs of the business, provides the pros and cons of some property-management particulars, and separates wise actions from the foolish or downright "are you crazy?" ones.

> Success in real estate requires education, experience, hard work, dedication, and a vision.

Managing property is not a course to be taken lightly. It's a business, and it's a demanding one. You have to think of it that way. When you purchase a building, a home, a shopping center, or land, you're opening a business. Your survival and success will depend on your ability to manage that business to the best of your ability. Among the topics you'll need to master are the following:

- Monitoring cash flow.
- Controlling expenses.
- Filing tax returns.
- Working with local, state, and federal bureaucracies.
- Tenant's rights.
- Disclosures.
- Maintenance and repair.
- Legal matters.
- Finding reliable suppliers and contractors.
- Marketing, advertising, and public relations.
- Accounting.
- Dealing with people.

> The way people react to your property management style can have a significant impact on your profit and loss columns.

That last item could well become your greatest challenge. If you can't deal effectively with people, most deals will prove to be bad deals in one way or another. You'll always have some headaches in business, but when you deal with people effectively and professionally, you have fewer of them. You'll also find that the headaches are of shorter duration and that their effects are smaller. The way people react to your property management style can have a significant impact on your profit and loss columns.

Use this book to help you anticipate problems as well as to solve those that you cannot avoid. You can learn from the experience of those who have gone before you—especially from their unfortunate experiences. Of course you'll make mistakes, but why make the mistakes of others when you can learn from them instead? Follow the proven path, as mapped out in this book, and you'll be able to develop the skills necessary to accumulate wealth, enhance your security, enjoy life, and acquire your share of the American dream.

PART I

Is Property Management Right for You?

Topics covered in this part:

- **What it takes to be a successful landlord.**
- **How to assess your property-management skills and experience.**
- **The pros and cons of getting involved in real estate.**

CHAPTER 1 DO YOU HAVE WHAT IT TAKES?
CHAPTER 2 THE PROS AND CONS OF BEING A LANDLORD

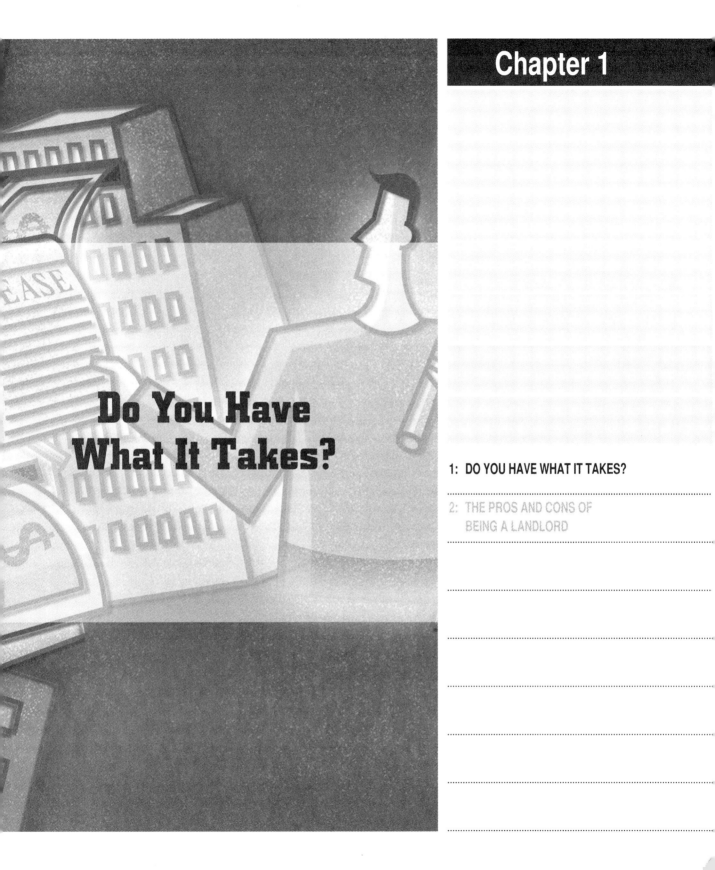

Chapter 1

Do You Have What It Takes?

Managing a property is no piece of cake. Before you get into it, it's important to evaluate your capacity for becoming a landlord. The ultimate rule for success in any part of life is to "know thyself." You need to assess your skill set, personality characteristics, and the investment opportunities that are available to you.

You are either a businessperson with the necessary skills to survive and thrive in real estate, or you are not. If you're not yet ready, don't lose heart. Provided you're willing to make the investment of time and energy, you can acquire the knowledge and experience needed to build that successful career.

This book will help you get started on the right foot. First, consider these questions:

- Do you have the ability to say "no" and mean it?
- Can you handle different personalities?
- Are you capable of controlling your expenditures?
- Is the up-and-down life of an entrepreneur right for you? Your family?
- Are you willing to stay on top of changing economic developments?
- Can you be realistic and honest with yourself?
- Do you trust your own instincts?

Surprisingly, your answer to the last question is perhaps the most important factor in determining whether you have the necessary skills and abilities to succeed in real estate. An instinct for real estate is an internal capacity and one a smart property manager will develop. If you can't trust yourself, it's unlikely that you'll be successful trusting or earning the trust of others.

The Right Personality

Property management requires a tremendous set of people skills for long-term success. Do you have the personality for owning or managing property? You have probably seen a movie or two that portrayed

> You need to assess the investment opportunities that are available to you.

an evil landlord who bullied all the tenants, ignored their needs, flaunted the law, and generally got away with every dirty deed. It's not like that in the real world. People have rights, and these days people are aware of those rights.

A good property manager has to be adept at handling all kinds of different and volatile personalities. It's just part of the job. Sometimes you have to change your own personality from one door to the next. You might have to be the "good cop" at Apartment A and then switch over to the "bad cop" at Apartment B. You can't take anything for granted when it comes to dealing with people. They will continually astound you.

A property manager has to look at things with a mature attitude. He (or she) must be emotionally removed from the professional duties of the job. You must develop a thick skin. It's important that you become once removed from the people you have to deal with. If you can't get over this hurdle, you'll find that the chief reason for selling your property isn't to make a profit but to get the heck out of property management.

Evaluate Your Business Skills

Moving into any business activity unprepared is dangerous to your financial well-being as well as to your mental health and family life. Real estate is full of wonderful opportunities. It's a great way to build wealth and security. However, if you don't know how to play the game, there are just as many opportunities for disaster.

Developing Your Skill Set

If you do not know what skills you need, you will need to do some research. Obviously, you'll need a good understanding of basic business. That begins with the fundamental law of all business: Your income should exceed your losses. In other words, make more than you spend. That's obvious advice, but you'd be surprised at how many otherwise smart people get so wrapped up in property management that they forget to apply it.

Family and Personal Life

How your career in real estate affects your family and personal life depends on you. The key to balancing a successful business and family life is to never forget that you're running a business. Yes, you may be providing a roof over someone's head, an opportunity for a business to grow, a retirement nest egg for yourself or some "nice little old lady" investor, but you have to put the "warm fuzzies" aside when it comes to managing the business.

You'll also need to know what kind of rental applications and disclosures you are required to use for tenants in residential property. It's against federal law to discriminate, as defined in the Civil Rights Act of 1964. If you demonstrate that you have problems with certain kinds of people, the law could make certain kinds of problems for you. You'll also need to know the local and state requirements in this area. Your research will involve a lot more than checking out locations.

Furthermore, you'll need to find a good accountant, lawyer, and banker. Get to know the real estate brokers in the area. Participate in community and real estate industry programs geared toward new property owners. There are more resources, many of them free or at affordable prices, than you can probably imagine right now.

In addition to the classroom-style lectures, you can gather up a wealth of printed material on everything from sound business practices to local rules and regulations. Books, brochures, fact sheets, and all kinds of handouts can provide all kinds of essential information.

Go Back to School

One of the best ways to acquire hands-on experience in property management before you make the full commitment is to attend classes that your local board of Realtors sponsors. You'll find them well worthwhile for many reasons. They're great sources of information and are usually taught by licensed real-estate professionals who know the "book learning" and the "real world," as well as the differences between the two, particularly in your local area.

One of the real benefits of these classes is the opportunity for cross talk with your peers. Many of these folks are in your position, just learning the ropes, but others might be old hands brushing up on their facts and figures or getting a look at a new business arena.

Never be afraid to ask questions at these classes. The only dumb question is the one that's not asked, and that's especially true in property management. Another benefit you'll reap will be the "dumb" questions other participants will ask. You'll be surprised at how much valuable information comes out of those question-and-answer sessions—you'll frequently hear people exclaim, "I never even thought of that!" Learning even a small bit of information can often be worth thousands of dollars or even more once you get into business.

Adopt a Business Attitude

Success demands that you act and react as a businessman or businesswoman. That often requires you to act in ways that might seem offensive to friends and relatives who see you in action. That's okay. You're not dealing with friends and relatives but with people you depend on to do a day's work for a day's pay. Your tenants depend on those folks too, but you're the one who'll get all the grief if the job's not done right and on time. You must be willing to be firm and conduct yourself in a businesslike manner.

Adopting this attitude doesn't for a second mean that you have to become angry, mean-spirited, or gruff with people. It just means you have to treat business people as business people. They expect it and respond to it. And with most people you'll find there's plenty of room for common courtesy once the business relationship is established. State your needs plainly and honestly. Your objective for the given task is efficiency, thoroughness, and thoughtfulness in owning and managing your own property.

People Skills

Property management involves many things: location, market trends, real-estate taxes, "crunching numbers," projected rents versus actual income, maintenance and repair, depreciation, and many other physical and financial concerns. But the most important aspect in any building or real-estate transaction is the ability to deal with people. If you don't learn how to handle them, they will surely learn how to handle you. The better you are at dealing with people, the better the deal will be for all concerned.

How Well Do You Deal with People?

The answer to that question will give you a pretty good view of how you'll likely deal with people in the real-estate business. Remember, the stress of the job doesn't come from the task at hand but from dealing with other people. The crack in the bathtub isn't the real problem. The real problem is the guy threatening to sue if the entire tub isn't replaced before breakfast. The problem is your plumber,

Always Be Prepared

Realize now that you will at some time have to face challenges and crises that you do not necessarily know how to deal with. You'll find unexpected opportunities. You'll enjoy a sense of freedom unknown to many people in today's business world. Despite all the challenges that may arise, you will be in a position to call your own shots, be your own boss, and control your own destiny. Although this book does not have all the answers, it will offer you a lot of assistance along the way. More important, it can help you be really prepared to face and overcome the problems you will likely face and to help you excel in your new career.

who decided to take a week off to go hunting in Colorado without telling any of his customers. The problem is the new kid at the supply store who doesn't know where the tub-and-tile section is located. People looking over your shoulder, second-guessing your judgment, and expressing unrealistic expectations are your real problems.

There are many personality challenges out there, and this book will come back to some potential problems. For now, it may be sufficient to note that it's important to curtail as many of these types of problems as soon as they arise. For example, when it comes to dealing with workmen, it's important, and sometimes critical, that they actually do the work they're paid for. You might be surprised at how many "professionals" don't hold to this theory.

Pay such suppliers only after they've completed the task you've hired them to do. Always pay after the work is done. Period. No argument. Case closed. (As an alternative, you can go out there and learn this lesson the hard way. Don't say you weren't warned.) Your supplier may appear to be the nicest, most honest, most decent person in the world, but appearances can be painfully deceiving.

Maintenance and Repair Skills

If you are buying your first building and you don't have experience in maintenance, try to buy a building that is in good condition and doesn't require a lot of repair. If you lack the time and opportunity to invest daily, a rehab may not allow you to enjoy your first endeavor.

Just think about the large number of areas where something can crack, break, leak, peel, rot, or go bad. Are you qualified to work on air conditioning, boilers, furnaces, interior and exterior walls, plumbing, electrical wiring, interior and exterior lighting, roofing and gutters, sidewalks and grounds, windows, stairways, elevators, parking lots and curbs, swimming pools, and a lot more?

If you're not qualified, you could easily create more maintenance and repair troubles than you had before you started out fixing them. It's best to find a reliable individual or company to handle those chores. Remember that your tenants will consider this person as a representative of your company. Make certain that the maintenance person knows this and will act accordingly. In addition to being qualified in maintenance, your employee should be courteous, neat, and clean. He or she should be concerned with taking care of tenant problems and should always behave in a dignified manner.

If you do pay a workman in advance, prepare to invest a lot of time on the telephone listening to a lot of excuses, some of them heartrending. You'll be amazed at how many kids with broken arms or impending surgeries one plumber or painter can have.

Also, plan on hearing a lot of "He'll call you right back" messages and the "beep-beep-beep" of the answer machine. Painters, carpenters, plumbers, electricians, contractors, and a lot of other people are great at making promises. Some actually keep them. Find those folks and stick with them, but do your finding without paying up front.

Learn the Art of Listening

People buy. People rent. People sell. They sign mortgages, dodge bill collectors, won't answer your calls, and surprise you in the most delightful ways. They create your problems, and they create your opportunities. They may come from different social, religious, or ethnic backgrounds than you, and they may have different biases and ways of thinking. And you have to be able to deal with them all.

One of the best traits to develop (or enhance, if you already have it) is your ability to listen. There's a significant difference between *hearing* and *listening*. When you really listen, you understand the problem, situation, or opportunity that's being presented. Listening means understanding, even if you disagree with the premise of the conversation. When you can really listen, you can be honest and fair because you can work on the heart of the situation, not what you "think you might have heard, maybe." The ability to listen will allow you to realize that many of the obstacles thrown in your pathway to success aren't as big or as challenging as they may originally have seemed. Many of them will prove not to be obstacles at all. Listening is one of the greatest skills a property manager can have, and it can lead to real achievement.

> When you can really listen, you can be honest and fair because you can work on the heart of the situation.

Define Your Market

Every city is one large neighborhood, which may be subdivided into a number of smaller neighborhoods. Within the neighborhoods are distinctive areas, sections, and streets. In some cases you will find considerable variation in property and property values within a single neighborhood. In fact, even a single street may have good blocks and bad blocks. A street that is full of lovely, well-maintained houses where people take pride in home ownership may be located a block away from a neighborhood that looks like the remains of a bad economic depression or even a war zone in some third-world country. It happens. The important thing to remember is that good and bad deals can be found in both areas.

Even a high-rise apartment building can be considered a small subneighborhood. Just because the property rises vertically instead of horizontally doesn't mean the folks within can't be a community. Many neighborhoods or streets organize regular block parties. That's where everybody gets together for an afternoon or evening of fun, food, and friendship. That's about the smallest region that you can define as a real-estate market.

Shopping for an Opportunity

Whether a market is good or bad *for you* depends upon many factors. For example, a young female entrepreneur down South found herself in a remarkably bad housing market. The bottom had fallen through the basement and was digging its way down to China. Many good homes were selling for as little as 20 percent of their old value. Small homes in poorer neighborhoods were going for $5,000 or less. This was a horrible market, and it remained bottomed out for years. The economy gradually forced banks and insurance companies to take back all kinds of real-estate properties, but they didn't really want these properties, and the lending institutions were trying to unload as many as possible as quickly as possible to get the drain off their books.

The situation was unfortunate for a lot of people, but this young woman said, "Aha! There's money to be made here." Fortunately, she had the capital, knew what she was doing, and wasn't afraid to invest. She knew she could afford to wait for better times, so she started buying up some of those low-end houses. As the economy began to improve, she was able to offer those homes at

> Whether a market is good or bad *for you* depends upon many factors.

higher and higher prices and to make a substantial profit on her investments. The lesson here is this: A "bad" market for most folks turned out to be a great one for her.

Study Your Chosen Neighborhoods

Each block or subdivision or rural route has its own personality. That's a universal fact. For example, the north-south and east-west streets of Chicago provide a definitive grid for the entire city. Blocks are easily identified by their geographic location.

Chicago is an amazingly diverse city; each city block may also be identified by its personality. Wave after wave of immigrants arrived there over many generations, and each group tended to settle in its own neighborhood. Even today, you can find four- to eight-block areas that are identified as Polish, African-American, Italian, Chinese, Jewish, Korean, Yugoslavian, Spanish, Irish, Czechoslovakian, or Indian neighborhoods. Many more people continue to pour into the city, and each group adds its own assets to the economic and cultural heritage of the city. Each group tends to form a distinctive neighborhood. Other cities are much the same.

When considering going into real estate, do not attempt to study, analyze, and evaluate an entire city. The task is just too daunting for most owners and managers. Even large companies with a staff of research personnel are cautious about taking on such a task. Choose a neighborhood, a street, or even a block. Study it. Take your time. Get all the information you can. Really concentrate and focus your efforts. In a surprisingly brief amount of time, you will be able to realistically evaluate property, select the kinds of properties you want, reject what you do not need, learn the rules and regulations that apply to that particular area of the city or community, and give yourself the opportunity to get to know the people, community groups, and city personnel you will be working with.

Do You Have What It Takes?

Only you can provide the answer. By now you should have a pretty good inclination, one way or another. Just in case you still have a few

Invest a Year in Research

Good research takes time and effort. Conducted properly and in sufficient depth, it will be one of your most valuable assets. As a rule of thumb, you should plan on spending about a year on research before you purchase your first property. The more information you gather up front, the fewer unpleasant surprises or unexpected events you'll encounter down the road. It's far easier to alter your course or even bail out while you're still conducting your research than after you've jumped in with both feet. It's easy to land in economic quicksand. Remember: Research is cheap, and mistakes are costly—in fact, they could bring about the end of your real-estate ventures.

questions, here are a few more thoughts on the pros and cons, myths and misconceptions, and the decision on making your move or giving it a pass.

The Entrepreneurial Spirit

A landlord needs some of the entrepreneurial spirit. Don't panic. We all have some somewhere. Didn't you have to "sell" yourself to your current spouse? Didn't you have to "make a case" to get your current job, promotion, or pay raise? Don't you have to present your side on issues at church, your civic club, or with your neighbor next door? Basically, that's what the entrepreneurial spirit is all about. It's found in anyone who believes enough in something that he or she is willing to initiate a change to make it happen. An increase in your income should serve as good motivation for you to mobilize your entrepreneurial spirit.

Many people believe a typical landlord (as if such a person ever existed) is market-driven. He or she picks up on what the market-place wants or needs and goes about supplying that product or service. People in property management are certainly aware of the market, but they're not in retail. Instead of waiting to respond to the market, they want to lead it. Often they will get there well ahead of people in retail businesses.

For example, a landlord may buy a building in what many people think is a poor risk area, turn it around, and make it into a great place to live—and his financial success. Other landlords will follow the lead and create more successes. Only then will you see the market-driven retail operations move in. By then, the real-estate leaders have already moved on to newer, better opportunities.

Are people in real estate addicted to risk? Not really. The free-wheeling "let's blow it all on one chance" landlords make for a good story, but they aren't realistic businesspeople. Yes, risks do exist and risk-taking is involved in the process of managing real estate, but the successful people in this business keep it to a moderate level. If they're addicted to anything, it's not risk but the challenge of making things happen.

It's Not an Inherited Trait

You don't need to come from a wealthy family in order to become a landlord. Successful landlords come from all walks of life. Those without inherited wealth scrimp, save, and plan until they earn that wealth. They have two significant advantages over most people born with wealth and over most people in general, really. They can visualize the future, and they have the get-up-and-go attitude to make that vision a reality. They have a innate sense of what needs to be done and how to go about doing it.

Successful landlords aren't infallible. Mistakes are common in any business, especially in one based on the intangible future. But successful people learn from their mistakes. They pick themselves up, dust themselves off, and say, "Well, I won't do that again." Then they get moving. Most of the time, they're "moving on up."

People in this business tend to be visionaries. Some appear to be downright psychic. They look at a home, a building, a block, or some other piece of property, and they see the potentials. Then they set out to make the potential happen. People might look at an old, decrepit building and see an abandoned machine shop, a ruin, or financial disaster in the making. However, a real-estate professional will see this site as a potential—an upscale apartment complex or an office building. He or she will see a challenge, an opportunity, and money in the bank.

Don't Get Intimidated

It's easy to be intimidated by something you don't fully understand. That's doubly true for the real-estate industry. Suddenly you're in a quagmire of local, state, and federal laws and regulations. You're handling all types of personalities. And you're having to find, hire, and build relationships with a wide variety of suppliers, all of whom know more about their business than you. Here are two important bits of advice:

1. Learn what you need to learn before you make a decision.
2. Don't try to bluff your way through a situation.

Your first real-estate transaction will be very important to you. For many folks, it remains the most significant of their career simply because it's the deal that got their career on the happy path to success in real estate. Keep in mind that it's not really as complicated as you might think. Very soon, you will become more comfortable with the process.

> Your first real estate transaction will be very important to you.

For more information on this topic, visit our Web site at www.businesstown.com

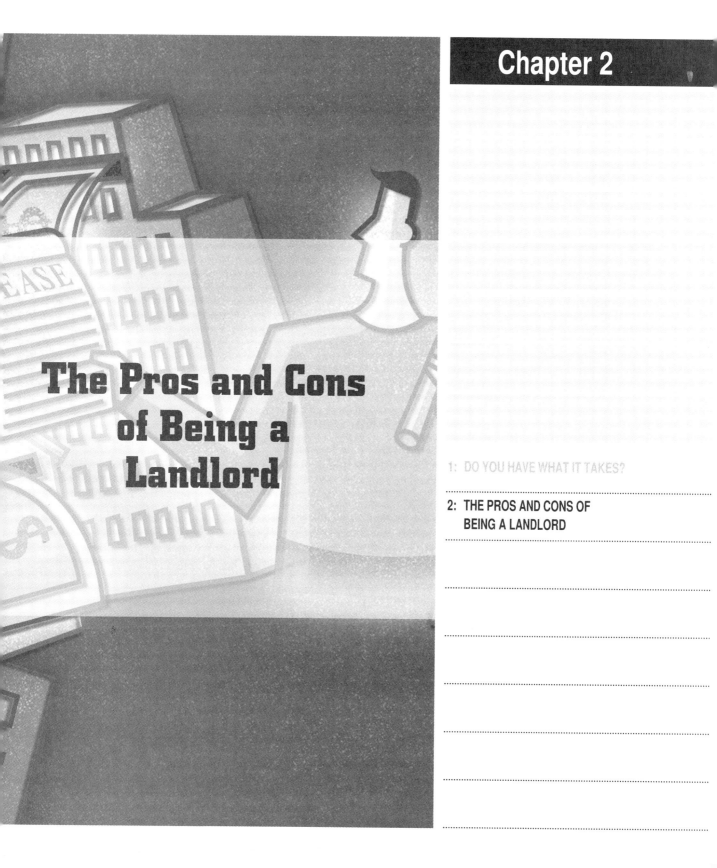

The Pros and Cons of Being a Landlord

Punch Your Own Clock

Most people go to work and come home at the same time every day. After eight hours of hard work (or, sometimes, of hardly working), they "punch out" and head home or to the corner bar, where they complain about the job, the boss, and the company. Some people find comfort and security in that unpleasantness. But other people seek alternative options.

Regular office hours may be a blessing or a curse, depending upon the job holder's perspective. People in real estate don't have nine-to-five jobs. The perspective of the property manager is, "Who cares, I set my own hours." That is true—to a very large extent.

t is an unalterable law of nature that everything that goes up must come down. The theory of gravity applies to economics and management, too. As with any occupation, you will experience the ups and downs, the good and the bad of property management. For every check that arrives on time, there is also a leaky faucet at 3:00 A.M. For every terrific investment, there is a layoff down at the plant. For every nice tenant in a business suit, there is a Beelzebub in a bathrobe.

The overall approach of this book is positive. Being a landlord and managing property is an exciting, challenging, and financially and emotionally rewarding undertaking. But there is no need to sugarcoat the difficulties that come with this profession. Do the pros outweigh the cons? That is for you to say. Here is the information you'll need to make up your mind.

Pro: It's Not a Nine-to-Five Job

Take a mid-morning or mid-afternoon trip to your local health club during the week. You'll see a lot of businessmen and businesswomen working up a sweat. Why aren't these folks at the office? Head out to the golf course on a Wednesday afternoon, and notice the number of people swinging, putting, slicing, and throwing their Number Three irons into the duck pond. Don't these people have day jobs? The next time you're riding around town, take a look at how many tennis courts, riding stables, and marinas are busy during normal business hours. What is going on here?

Many of the people who support those clubs and organizations aren't the sons and daughters of America's elite. They are hardworking folks, and you'd be surprised how many of them are working hard in real estate. The cash flow from their properties supports their leisurely lifestyle. And that's one of the real benefits of being a landlord. You have the ability to put some real style into your life.

Your Own Schedule

Sometimes the manager's schedule is subject to some unforeseen event, but floods, fires, earthquakes, and errant asteroids are really quite rare. You'd be surprised at how many landlords manage to get through their entire careers without being hit by a comet. Those rare exceptions aside, as a landlord you can set your own schedule day in and day out. If you have unoccupied rooms, offices, or dwellings, you can show prospective renters or buyers the properties at your leisure. It isn't as if you're a salesperson in an automobile dealership drumming your fingers on the latest brochure, desperately hoping for a prospect to walk in the door.

You're not tied down to your investment (unless, for some reason, you choose that path). You can sink a twenty-foot putt, grab your cellular phone, call Mr. or Mrs. Jones, and set up an appointment to tour your property whenever it is convenient . . . for you. Why spend your time staring out the showroom window when you can be breathing the cool clean air on the ninth hole?

Remember, with rare exceptions, landlords just don't run into crisis situations. The "emergency" of a flooding kitchen that a rather paranoid tenant might complain about will more than likely turn out to be nothing more than a leaky faucet. A few questions over the

Know Your Suppliers' Hours

Imagine this scenario. A tenant has just left, and a prospective new tenant is coming by for a tour first thing in the morning. You're working on the apartment at night, making sure the tenant left it in good condition and that there are no last-minute problems that could interfere with the tour. Of course there are last-minute problems. Let's say you discover a long crack in the wall. It's nothing serious, but it's in an obvious spot and will surely be noticed.

No problem. You don't need your maintenance man to slap on a little lightweight spackling and a bit of paint. It's no big hassle. So, you're off to your friendly neighborhood spackling store. You might be late for supper, but you'll have the wall fixed, and the paint will be dry by tour time. Fifteen minutes later you're standing outside the store looking back and forth between your watch, which reads 8:04 P.M., and the sign in the window, which reads: "We close at 5:00 P.M."

The way around this little problem, which could turn into a major hassle, is to keep a record of the store hours of all your suppliers. Just keep a small notebook with the stores, their phone numbers and hours, and alternate suppliers.

telephone can reveal the true nature of any so-called crisis; a leaky faucet can wait until you can get your repairman out there the next day. Most things that can be painted, plastered, or pounded with a hammer can wait until tomorrow. And your tenants can survive until then, too.

See and Be Seen

Although landlords do have the authority over their working hours, it does not mean they don't work at all. Set up a schedule for visiting each of your properties. In the event that you just can't do this—if, for example, you are an absentee landlord—establish a routine for your maintenance man. Tenants need a sense of stability. They like to know someone is taking care of things, even when there's really nothing to take care of at the moment. They're always thinking, "You know, Marge, that pipe just might burst any time now." Regardless of whether the problem is real, just knowing that the owner or maintenance man is around eliminates a lot of tenant worry. And if they're not worried, they're not going to worry you.

Being seen is important, but it is also important for the owner/manager to see. "Management by walking around" is a long-established and well-proven method of conducting business. This is especially true in real estate. It is important for the manager to actually see what's going on at his or her properties. Nothing can replace "eye-balling" the situation. As an owner, you will see things from an entirely different perspective than anyone else. For example, a minor "touch-up" job that your maintenance man might legitimately be planning to postpone for a week or so might suddenly become a real priority for you because of the prospective tenant coming by for a look within the hour.

Tenants like the feel of a set rhythm. It builds confidence and a certain level of comfort. Try to be at one property on Monday, another on Tuesday and another on Wednesday. That will leave Thursday and Friday for other matters or for returning to a particular property to handle a specific problem or opportunity. Of course, you'll create your own schedule according to your own properties and availability.

Absentee Landlords

The ideal situation for absentee landlords is to own multiple properties and employ someone who is good and whom you trust to handle the day-to-day management. That puts you back on the golf course, tennis court, boat, horse, or back-road adventure.

With such an arrangement, rent checks come in regularly to a post office box or your office. You can handle all the paperwork yourself, or you can hire a secretary. Property management isn't a retail operation. You don't have to come in on a daily basis to oversee your employees, check on the inventory, or smile at the customers. This really is one of the great benefits of property management.

Con: It's Not a Nine-to-Five Job

Unless there's a fire, flood, or earthquake, you can pretty much put off any so-called emergency until later. Be warned, however, that sometimes the dam does break and the flood waters do come rushing in. Here's a true story to illustrate what could happen.

Property ownership and management can allow you to work only half a day; however, as Mark Weiss discovered when he purchased a building that was built in the 1800s, "half a day" sometimes means twelve hours a day. The property was a stately gray stone structure in the Lincoln Park/DePaul area of Chicago, an upscale community where rents are high. The building had been completely renovated and redecorated, and Mark considered this property the "crown jewel" of all his real estate acquisitions. It was a good building, in a good neighborhood, bringing in good money.

One night the jewel sprung a leak. The tenant of a garden apartment called his office, complaining that a waterfall was cascading throughout his kitchen. When the tenant leased a garden apartment, he hadn't counted on irrigation being part of the deal. To make things worse, all this water was coming from a heating vent.

In his fifteen years in property management, Mark had never heard of or seen anything quite like it. The tenant even took photographs to back up his claim. The waterfall didn't appear every day or even at regular times. It seemed to have a will of its own, and it seemed to be focused on making the tenant's life miserable. Of course, the tenant passed along that misery to the landlord.

Maintenance men were promptly and regularly consulted. At first it appeared that the problem was due to a tenant upstairs who didn't pull a shower curtain tight. That situation was addressed, but it didn't stop the flood. Perhaps a toilet was overflowing, but that idea didn't make sense. In fact, none of the proposed solutions made any sense. One day, a registered letter from the tenant arrived. A solution to the problem would have to be found and found fast, or the property would soon be a vacant water park.

A property manager sometimes has to follow his or her own "gut" instincts. After multiple consultations with plumbers and maintenance men, multiple visits, and multiple cases of analysis, Mark

> A property manager sometimes has to follow his or her own "gut" instincts.

listened to his own common sense. The maintenance men were summoned to cut a hole in the wall of the unit above the garden apartment. A problem with the bathtub overflow valve was quickly discovered. The overflow valve is the drain right below the faucet on the tub. As the name indicates, its purpose is to keep the water from overflowing. In this apartment, a piece of eroded rubber allowed this water to fall on the sides of the drain, which caused it to flow right down to the apartment below.

A two-dollar adapter solved the problem. This was an unusual case, but before he managed to figure it out and fix it, the mysterious waterfall disrupted the owner's routine repeatedly for nearly a year.

In the Event of an Emergency

However, real problems do happen—and when they do, they can distract you from other important business and play havoc with the most carefully contrived schedule. Here's another interesting case

Set Priorities

Time is money. Your time has value, and you should invest it in actions or pursuits that bring you a return. That's not as easy as it sounds, especially when a tenant is screaming over the telephone about something that needs maintenance or repairs. There goes the golf game, the evening with the spouse, the kid's piano recital, or that afternoon with a good book. Maybe the day or evening is ruined, and maybe it's not.

Is the problem a legitimate emergency, such as a burst water pipe, or is it a simple problem that can wait? Don't turn a deaf ear to the screaming. Instead, turn down the volume and evaluate the situation. Serious problems require serious and often very rapid solutions. It's just good business to take care of your tenant's emergency—you maintain good relations with your tenant, and you prevent your property from incurring major damage.

The key is to set priorities in advance. Give serious thought to all the different things that can go wrong, and have your answer prepared in advance. If a small crack in the wall just needs spackling, you can afford to wait till the store opens in the morning. If water is coming out of the walls or ceiling, get on the phone to your plumber. In either case, take the time to explain to your tenant what you're planning to do to correct the situation, and provide a reasonable timeline for doing it.

that illustrates how tenants can confuse an orderly schedule. A landlord rented out his apartment in a multitenant building to three young women. One day, someone left a pot boiling on the stove. Not only did this tenant leave the apartment with the pot still boiling, when she returned she went straight to the couch for a nap. At some point during her nap, the pot's contents underwent a metamorphosis and became thick black smoke. Assisted by a fire alarm, smoke detectors, and a number of concerned neighbors pounding on the door, the young woman finally awoke.

Landlords do not like to hear about fire and smoke in their properties, and they are even less happy if they are not informed of the fire and smoke immediately. The metamorphosis had occurred around 7:00 P.M. on a Monday. The landlord didn't get his call until Tuesday afternoon. And the call had to come from other tenants who had a more responsible attitude.

Perhaps their hearts were in the right places, but the three young women caused a lot of trouble by their delay. They said they were too embarrassed by the event to call and "ruin" the landlord's evening. Perhaps, but one is tempted to think the landlord's feelings weren't their first priority. The landlord realized from their description that the fire had not been catastrophic. The tenants had already begun cleaning up.

The landlord dropped everything, grabbed his camera, and rushed to the property. He needed photographs for insurance purposes, and it was urgent that he get to the apartment before the "helpful" tenants cleaned up the mess or even made it worse.

His day had not included provision for such a massive disruption in his schedule. Handling the situation so preoccupied his time that he missed an important meeting the next morning with a government official, a meeting that had been scheduled weeks in advance. Although the situation didn't turn into a crisis, it did mangle several days of a carefully worked-out business schedule before the owner was able to get back on track. Much of this could have been avoided if the tenants had just exercised common sense and common courtesy and called right away.

You never know when you may be called out at a moment's notice. Often the "simple" little detail you have to handle can turn

> You never know when you may be called out at a moment's notice.

into a monster of a problem right before your eyes. The problem with the garden apartment boiled down to a little piece of eroded rubber. However, the effort to find that problem took nearly a year of valuable time, lots of extra money, and a toll on the patience of the landlord and tenants. If you're the landlord, you have the responsibility of taking care of your tenants. When that means dropping whatever you're doing to handle a crisis, then you have to drop it and get moving.

Often your schedule will be dictated by the schedule of someone else. For example, you can certainly schedule your time to show an empty apartment according to your convenience, but if there's a tenant still living there, you will have to comply with the tenant's schedule. He or she (and the apartment) might only be available for showing before work hours or in the evenings after work. Keep in mind that local tenant rights ordinances may require a forty-eight-hour notice to existing tenants before the property owner is allowed the right to enter the apartment. In a way, you can still be tied to the dictates of an eight-hour day. Of course, you can always wait till the apartment is empty to show it, but you can't make money from an empty apartment in the meantime. That's part of the flexibility allowed by property management.

Even though they can really louse up your schedule, you want tenants to call about their problems. You may not want them calling you, but you do want them to at least notify your maintenance and repair people. A tenant who calls about a tiny leak under the sink will be saving you from a major expenditure compared to the tenant who doesn't call and allows the slow drip to warp and rot out the wood and even the flooring under that sink. It's those "little" problems left unattended that really foul up your schedule.

Pro: Virtually Anyone Can Succeed

There are no educational requirements for becoming a property manager. All you need is property and the drive to manage it. If you're interested in becoming more educated in the field—which is a very good idea—there are plenty of opportunities. Colleges, trade schools, and trade associations offer basic courses and even specialized

---

Ways of Communication

It's a good idea to have an unlisted phone number. You do not want to receive calls at all hours about leaky faucets, loose tiles, or funny smells coming from the apartment next door. That doesn't mean you leave your tenants out on a limb or eating dinner under an umbrella. Leave an office number where you have voice mail or an answering service.

Also, leave the pager number of your maintenance man. He should be the first contact in the event of a problem anyway. Most often he'll be able to take care of the situation without disturbing your golf, dinner, or sleep. The tenants will also appreciate being able to speak directly and quickly to the person who is responsible for fixing the problem. Make sure your maintenance man has your unlisted number, however, just in case the floodwaters really are rising.

learning. However, what you need more is the drive to learn more. Without that, nothing else can happen.

One of the best aspects of this field is that anyone can play on it. When you meet property owners, you'll encounter professors, blue-collar workers, men, women, young people and old, folks with roots dating back to Plymouth Rock, and folks just off the boat. Some of them wear coats and ties and drive expensive cars. Others wear jeans and work shirts and drive secondhand trucks. The difference between those folks and everybody else isn't what's on their backs but what is in their hearts. Everybody wants a piece of the American dream; these folks simply made the effort to begin earning their share.

Anybody who wants to do it can do it. That's a fact. The wealth of this world is in real estate, and anybody can own real estate. You can build up a real-estate empire. You can acquire wealth. You can earn security and personal satisfaction. There are many routes to success in America these days, but property management is one of the shortest, most direct, and even the most fun to take.

Con: The Learning Curve

Every human activity on the face of the earth, except breathing and the like, requires some education. A learning curve is a natural part of any process. Do not be intimidated by the learning curve of property management. Don't let this necessary transition period slow you down or prevent you from following your heart into the industry.

Everyone's learning curve will be different and will involve different people, places, things, and events. Yours will be unique. If there is one cardinal rule to follow it is to stay alert and on the lookout for any and all opportunities.

As an example, consider the landlord who did not buy rehab property or buildings with less than six units who was presented with one of those learning opportunities. This was a "teardown" building if there ever was one, a frame unit with tarpaper siding. It was in serious need of rehabilitation. Additionally, it could only be converted into four apartments. But the neighborhood was upscale

> The wealth of this world is in real estate, and anybody can own real estate.

with homes averaging (today) $800,000–$1,000,000. There was real potential. There was also a learning curve.

The landlord paid $208,000 for the building and renovated the property. That's when the learning curve kicked in. The building was in Chicago, and the city had the property listed as a three-unit structure. The owner floundered around for a while until he learned that he needed a special-use letter from the local alderman. This would allow him to complete the project legally as a four-unit, residential building. Riding that learning curve also meant he paid more than he should have for the upgrade. This is what he called his "tuition." Later he sold the 4 units for more than $800,000 in the aggregate, making the entire process well worth the time, energy, money, and learning experience. Despite the learning curve, he made good money.

Again, the point is to always be on the lookout for opportunity. Had the owner stuck to his rules of not buying rehab or less than six-unit properties, he'd have missed out on a real plum of a deal. He'd also have missed out on all that valuable learning, which turned out to be information he used again and again throughout his career. Look at it this way. You'll have to experience the pains and pangs of learning at some time in any career. Why not go ahead with confidence in yourself and your abilities and get through the process as quickly as possible? Use the gray matter between your ears to learn. There's always something new in real estate, and that means there's always new opportunities.

> There is something really exciting about owning real estate.

Pro: Unlimited Potential for Success

There is something really exciting about owning real estate. You can't imagine the thrill of driving by various buildings and pointing them out as your property to friends and family. The phrase "that's mine" carries the pride of ownership, the satisfaction of having made a sound business decision, and the knowledge of doing a job successfully. Knowing that you'll pick up a nice check at the end of the month helps, too.

You'll be collecting rent and having your tenants pay for the mortgage on that same property at the same time. In most markets you'll experience the benefits of market appreciation. There are always exceptions, of course. Towns where the economy is based on a single industry can experience cyclical periods that dramatically affect the prices one can charge for property or rent. Employment, or the lack of it, is always a strong factor in real estate.

As a rule, you'll find that most homes or investment properties sell for higher prices each time they're sold. You can always hear tales of people "going bust" in real estate, and it does happen, but it's a rule of life that bad news always gets more "press" than good news. The number of people who have made it big in real estate—really big—far outnumbers those who have gone bust. Real estate tends to grow at an annual rate of 4 percent. That's a national average and will be skewed by local markets, but the figure is a good one to use as a rule of thumb.

Seek Win/Win Opportunities

Property is value-driven, and most buyers are driven by value as well. When the economy is hot and money is flowing, people often overpay for property. If they haven't made a profit when the economy takes a downturn, they can be caught in a financial vise. Real estate that cannot support itself becomes a drain: Most people can't continue funding negative cash flow investments. The owner gets in a position where he or she or could lose the property to creditors.

There is a phrase used down South for people who load up their dinner plates with more food than they can eat. "His eyes overloaded his stomach," they say. The same thing can happen to property buyers. Their dreams of financial wealth can blind them to the reality of a situation. As the owner gets older, or as business interests change, he or she will have a need for liquidity and will be looking for a deal.

Look for such a win/win situation. It's okay to pay a little more for property, provided you're getting just what you want.

Look for such a win/win situation.

Look Beyond the First Deal

Opportunities are everywhere. If you miss out on one, another might be just around the corner. For example, there is the buyer who had a building under contract, only to be informed by the seller that the city only recognized the building as a two-unit structure. The buyer had based all his plans on having three units. Some cities require a zoning certification to verify the number of units prior to obtaining transfer stamps. This requirement is meant to keep the legal amount of units appropriate to zoning requirements. The reduction from three to two units also reduced the value of the property to the new buyer.

This buyer ended up killing the deal. The unexpected restrictions made the matter far less attractive. As he walked away, he walked into another deal just two blocks away. He purchased exactly what he was seeking for $70,000 less than the original price of the first building. As an additional bonus, the property was in better physical condition and required significantly less in initial capital infusion. If he hadn't killed the first deal, he'd never have found the better one just down the street. The rule is simple: Every time you think you're missing an opportunity, you'll find something to replace it. Often the replacement is a better deal anyway.

> The opportunities in major markets are incredible. If you live in San Francisco, Los Angeles, Chicago, Atlanta, Phoenix, New York, or any other big city, you will find an amazing variety of property to buy.

The opportunities in major markets are incredible. If you live in San Francisco, Los Angeles, Chicago, Atlanta, Phoenix, New York, or any other big city, you will find an amazing variety of property to buy. Many of the people in those cities will find themselves needing liquidity. If you're keeping an eye out for opportunity, you'll be able to find it. This can happen on a daily basis in major markets. Win/win deals are everywhere if you're willing to look for them.

Con: Unlimited Potential for Disaster

Big fish eat little fish. Fishermen catch and eat big fish. Fishermen invest in buildings and get skinned. We're always reading about some major real-estate project going belly up. Bankruptcy notices are all over the financial or business pages, sometimes on the front pages. These are large projects and a lot of people have usually invested a lot of money. When a lot of people are involved in big projects, they make their money on fees and charges, not off the investment. That's something to consider when involved in a project. How are your associates making their money? What is their risk compared to yours? Inspect the property. Inspect your partners. Inspect the deal.

Haste Makes Wasteland

If the deal is a good one, then it's worth enough time to really investigate it. Time is one of the best investments you'll ever make in any transaction. Haste, on the other hand, can create so many problems and can tax your mental energy to such a level that it is wise to avoid it. It's not the way to make money, build a career, or enjoy your life.

If you want to avoid personal disaster, follow these rules:

- Don't buy property if something doesn't feel right. Trust your instincts. You'll know when it's right and when it's wrong.
- Don't buy if the salesperson is too pushy. Why is he or she in such a hurry?
- Don't buy if the property needs too much work. Look around some more. There's probably a better deal just around the corner.
- Make sure your partners are comfortable with the deal. That applies whether they are business associates, friends, or relatives. This is business. Treat it so.
- Don't make unrealistic income projections.
- Know your equity partner(s). They can bring disaster to the sweetest of deals. Unrealistic expectations, dissatisfaction with the way you're managing the property, or an entire host of other concerns can preoccupy you to the point where you become distracted from your real work at the property. Sometimes the partner just isn't worth the hassle.

Whenever possible, use your own money and avoid partners altogether. That way, you can afford to listen to that quiet but important voice whispering in the back of your head. Listening to that one voice, the one you're familiar with, is far better than listening to a half-panicked, half-baked partner with grandiose ideas, unrealistic demands, or the latest reason why "you're just not pulling your weight."

> Don't buy property if it doesn't feel right.

Keep these guidelines in mind. Keep your own counsel. And keep your mind focused. You really shouldn't have any unconquerable problems, but always be sure to do your homework, watch the people involved with you in the project, and always, always go with your instinct.

> Always go with your instinct.

A Property Manager's Pop Quiz

If you're considering a career in property management, take the following quiz. It might clear the air for you. Remember, this isn't a pass/fail exam. All the answers are correct.

Y N

☐ ☐ 1. Do you have the motivation, the "fire in the gut" to get involved property management?

☐ ☐ 2. Do you have the courage, the perseverance, and the patience to "ride the tiger" to success?

☐ ☐ 3. Are you psychologically suited to handle risk taking, even on a moderate level?

☐ ☐ 4. Do you have the high level of intelligence needed to excel at this profession?

☐ ☐ 5. Do you have the energy to see your projects through to completion?

☐ ☐ 6. As a child, were you a leader and an organizer? Did other kids follow your lead?

☐ ☐ 7. Have your education and experience prepared you to wear a lot of different professional "hats"?

☐ ☐ 8. Can you be objective about yourself, your properties, and your prospects?

☐ ☐ 9. Do you have the knowledge and experience you will need?

☐ ☐ 10. If necessary, can you acquire additional skills?

☐ ☐ 11. Do you want personal and financial independence?

Again, there are no winners and losers. If, after you've answered these questions, you determined that a life in real estate isn't for you, fine. You've just saved yourself a lot of wasted time, money, and heartache. If you have the drive and the courage to look at yourself that honestly, you'll surely succeed in any field you choose. For the rest of you, those who have just had your appetite whetted for success as a landlord, let's start building that career right now. You can move on to Part II, "What You Need to Know to Get Started."

For Further Information

For further information about property management, you may wish to contact any or all of the following organizations:

Building Owners and Managers Association
1221 Massachusetts Ave. NW, Suite 35
Washington, D.C. 20005
(202) 638-2929

Community Association Institute
1423 Powhattan St., Suite 7
Alexandria, VA 22314
(703) 548-8600

Institute for Real Estate Management
430 N. Michigan Ave.
Chicago, IL 60611
(312) 661-1930

National Apartment Association
1101 14th St., NW, Suite 804
Washington, D.C. 20005
(202) 842-4050

For more information on this topic, visit our Web site at www.businesstown.com

PART II

What You Need to Know to Get Started

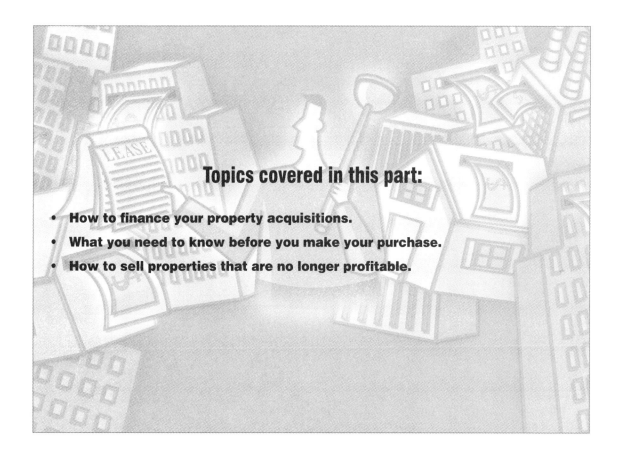

Topics covered in this part:

- **How to finance your property acquisitions.**
- **What you need to know before you make your purchase.**
- **How to sell properties that are no longer profitable.**

Your Financial Options

Now that you have decided that property management is right for you, the first step is to acquire some properties to manage. But before you can sign the papers and become the proud owner of a piece of property, whether it is an office building, a two-family house, or even a parking lot, you need to consider how you will pay for it. Sure, you could have inherited millions of dollars from your great aunt, but chances are good that you need to find other, more practical ways of financing your new undertaking. Let's consider the financial investment side of property management.

Making Your Investment

Real estate provides a pretty stable environment for investment. It's true that property can gain or lose value, but the process isn't quite the roller-coaster ride you would probably experience with the stock market. You just don't find property values dropping (or skyrocketing) in a matter of moments, a common occurrence with stocks. While there are exceptions, buildings tend to hold their value over time and to hold that value well.

Avoid Overpaying

The most important thing about buying property is to avoid paying too much for it. Too many people start out on the road to ruin by making this basic mistake. To safeguard against overpaying, you need to do your homework; you can't allow the emotion of the moment to overrule your good judgment.

Again, invest the time to investigate your purchase. Ask around. Get several opinions. Explore the market thoroughly. As excited as you may be to get started, making a serious effort to gather information is never a waste of time. Chances are you'll find the right property at the right price. It can be frightfully easy to pay an inflated price, especially when you're feeling that charge of excitement about ownership. On the other hand, if you're too pessimistic or intimidated by the prospect of owning property, you could just as easily pass up a great deal. Information keeps you on track.

Real-Estate Profits

People buy property for cash flow, appreciation, or both. Cash flow (that is, income) is what everyone in real estate wants. Basically, your cash flow is what's left over at the end of the month after you've paid your mortgage and other expenses. If there's no income left over, there's some kind of dam blocking the flow (such as low rents, high expenses, sloppy bookkeeping, etc.). You'll need to clear the blockage as quickly as possible to get that income flowing again.

This cash flow can in some cases just be enough to cover payments on the property by itself. That's still a great position because your property isn't costing you anything during the time you own it. In that same time frame it is also appreciating in value. You are therefore gaining capital. You may buy for $100,000, earn nothing at the end of the year, and yet in five years that property may be worth $125,000. That means you have an additional $25,000 to invest when you sell the property. You can buy something else with those profits, perhaps something that will generate cash flow.

Buy for Long-Term Gain

While this book is being written, Mark will probably purchase three to six buildings. That's a bit out of the ordinary, but he's having a good year and he's been exercising that good eye for bargains. He's sold some property and is exercising his right to buy more property by deferring his capital gain taxes under IRS Rule 1031. (You'll learn more on that later in the book—for now, just remember the rule and the fact that it allows you to sell property and reinvest the proceeds in replacement property without any taxable gain to be paid until the final property is sold.)

Basically, opportunity has knocked on Mark's door. He is in buying mode even though he knows he'll take a minor hit in the cash flow department. Careful planning and a well-executed buying strategy will provide ample cover for the short term. More important, his appreciated resale value by the closing date when he sells these properties will have increased exponentially. Every once in a while you come across a legitimate opportunity to make a killing very quickly. A lot of the time, however, such opportunities don't really pan out in your favor. It's a wise player who plays the real-estate game over time for long-term success.

Leveraging to Buy Property

Money borrowed from the bank to finish your transaction is what makes the real-estate world turn. That's how people leverage and buy property. This is an important rule of thumb in the real-estate business.

For example, let's suppose you want to buy a building priced at $250,000 (or any price, for that matter). How many of us have a quarter million dollars lying around for such an investment? That's why somebody way back when invented bankers. They have the money. To get your hands on it, you'll have to jump through a few hoops. Before a bank loans you the money to buy your property, the loan committee will require you to provide 20 percent of that amount. In layman's terms, to get cash you have to put up cash. In this case, 20 percent of $250,000 is $50,000.

Without that equity, the bank just won't let you borrow the $200,000 balance of the purchase price. So, what's the bottom line here? You have to have money to make money. You've heard of the business world's version of the "golden rule," haven't you? *He who has the gold, rules.* The lender, in this case the bank, has the money so that institution gets to set the rules for the transaction. Banks are businesses. Just like you, they are in business to make money. If you want this partner in your real-estate business—and you do—then you must realize that they will want to see real cash in the deal: *your* real cash.

> Money borrowed from the bank to finish your transaction is what makes the real-estate world turn.

Ten Tips: Working with Lenders

Here is what you need to know about working with lenders. (For a more detailed discussion of banking and finance issues, see Chapter 23.)

1. **Start local before going global.** Sure, we're in the era of global markets, but banks and lending institutions are for the most part grounded locally. That's especially true for getting real-estate loans. Wherever you are, you have access to a number of local or regional banks. Start your search there. Mark even advises starting with the bank that is closest to

the property you wish to buy and, if things don't work out to your satisfaction, moving outward from there.

2. **Have your paperwork in order.** Lending institutions are sticklers for detail. Consult your accountant and/or financial advisor before you even think about walking into the bank. Find out exactly what type of documents you'll need and how detailed they'll need to be. One of the worst things you can say in an interview with a lender is, "I'll have to get back with you on that."

3. **Rehearse your presentation.** The tourist asked the local New Yorker, "How do you get to Carnegie Hall?" The local responded, "Practice, man. Practice." That's an old joke, but there's wisdom in it. Practice your presentation with your spouse, a friend, or your financial advisors. Become so familiar with the materials and likely questions that you can roll the information off your tongue like a professional actor. Remember, however, that your presentation will not be a speech. You'll be interrupted and asked questions throughout. Practice so that you will be comfortable with the process, but don't turn your presentation into a memorized monologue.

4. **Be confident.** This is where your practice sessions really pay off. Lenders respond well to a confident applicant. Nervousness is like a contagious disease, and bankers are very susceptible to it. You should have satisfactory answers to all questions, but if one throws you off, don't try to bluff your way out. They'll catch you and all your credibility will disappear down the waste chute. Also, don't confuse confidence with arrogance.

5. **Avoid back-slapping.** Certainly, you should be friendly, but don't try to "buddy up" to your banker while asking for money. They've seen all the tricks and know all the games. Be cordial, be yourself, be professional, and remember that even if you are best friends, business is business.

6. **Dress the part.** Even if you're applying for a loan to purchase swamp land and your daily work garb consists of khakis and mud boots, wear business attire to meet your

> Don't turn your presentation into a memorized monologue.

lender. Remember, you're entering their world and you must play by their rules.

7. **Control your emotions during the presentation.** Show your enthusiasm, but keep the adjectives under control and your voice down to conversational decibels. Don't allow your presentation to slip into melodrama or a comedy routine. Again, business is business. If your deal appears to be a money-maker, they'll be interested. That's what they're there for in the first place.

8. **Answer every question immediately and with a short, direct response.** If your answer requires elaboration, provide it after your short response. It's very easy to confuse or lose the attention of the lender if you provide supporting data before they know what it is that you are supporting.

9. **Stop when your presentation is over.** Don't continue talking when you have nothing more to say. Many a salesperson has closed a sale only to lose it by continuing to sell a sold customer. It is definitely possible to do the same thing with a lender.

10. **Follow up.** Don't call every day and nag your loan officer, but do make a phone call to thank him or her for listening to your presentation. State that you are very interested in hearing the bank's response, but don't push for an answer. It'll come in the bank's own sweet time. Also, if the answer isn't the one you want, call back or go by for a visit and discuss the problems. You could gain a lot of insight that will make your next presentation a better one.

> Follow up. Make a phone call to thank him or her for listening to your presentation.

Read the Writing

Sometimes investors develop bad memories, which can create really bad experiences for you. You can put an end to a lot of problems by referring the one with the faulty memory to a written version of your agreement. Having things set up in writing also takes a lot of personality conflict out of the situation because the matter being discussed or questioned is all laid out in black-and-white documentation.

This, too, is important: Read these documents carefully, preferably with your real-estate lawyer. A lot of people don't like to muddle through such documents. They take the lazy way out, giving the paper a glazed-over look, and they sign their lives away. Don't join that club. Go over every document page by page, paragraph by paragraph, line by line, and word by word. This is your investment, and it is your obligation to understand your rights and responsibilities.

It is also important that you understand the nature of the business and the terms used in that business when working with a mortgage company. This is not the time to nod sagely and fake your way through a technical conversation. If you don't understand a clause, a phrase, or even a single word, look it up or ask for clarification.

Read your documents. If you don't know facts like your interest rate, whether it's fixed or adjustable, when it's due, your legal liabilities, or any number of other equally important details, you could easily lose that property to the company that loaned you the money to buy it.

Business Deductions

Did you know that if your primary business, as defined by the Internal Revenue Service, is real estate, then you can deduct real-estate losses from your personal income? This benefit is the direct result of the Revenue Reconciliation Act of 1993, which covers RREAs (rental real estate activities).

If you qualify, your RREAs are not subject to limitation under the passive loss rules of the IRS. Of course, you have to meet certain criteria. Your real-estate business can't be a sideline or part-time affair. The law requires that you be materially involved in real estate.

Your real-estate commissions, wages, interest, and dividends are subject to income taxation. That's obvious, but full-time real-estate professionals can deduct their real-estate losses at the end of the year. In other words, if the accounting from your property shows a loss due to expenses added to depreciation, you can deduct that paper loss from your professional income. Real estate is the only profession that allows that deduction to pass through.

Please keep in mind that tax laws are changing all the time. Always consult your accountant before filing to make sure you're up to date on the latest changes.

Everybody Needs a Partner

The key word here is "partner." In real estate, you can't do the dance alone. Bankers aren't going to enter a transaction in which they have all the risk. It just won't happen. Partnership means each party shares some of the financial load. When everybody shares the burden and works together, you create one of those win/win situations. The bank makes money. The property owner makes money. Then they work together on a new investment—everybody is happy. For more details on investment groups, go on to the next chapter.

> Bankers aren't going to enter a transaction in which they have all the risk.

For more information on this topic, visit our Web site at www.businesstown.com

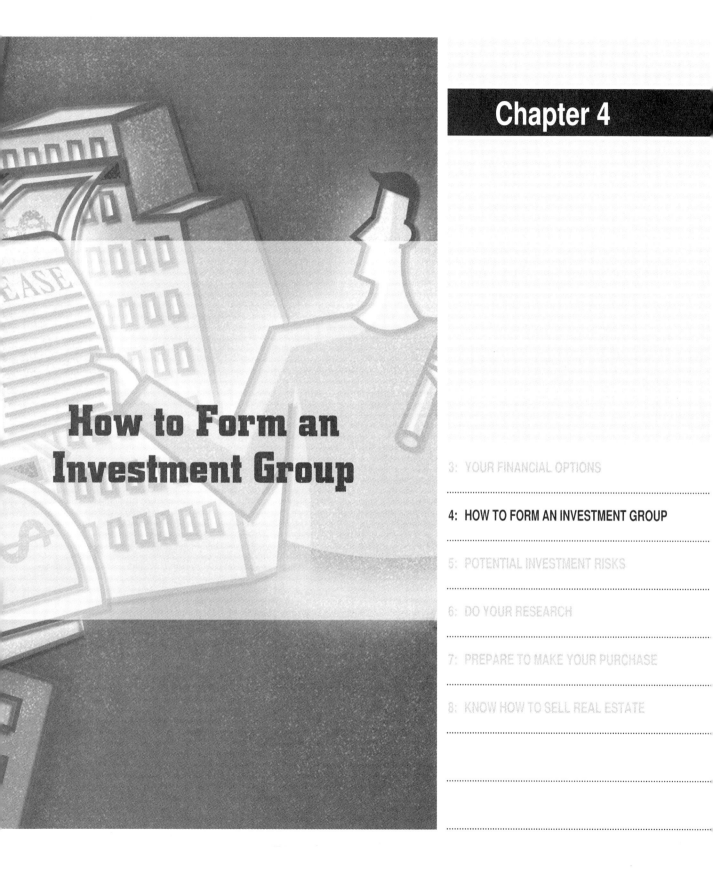

How to Form an Investment Group

Investments require money. Well, as the kids say, "Duh!" What if you don't have enough money and don't qualify for bank loans? Frequently, individuals see a great investment, but they lack the resources to make the purchase, to get the project rolling, and to keep maintaining it. That's why investment groups are so popular. It's the modern-day equivalent of an old-fashioned barn raising. A group of people gets together, pools their individual resources, and creates something none of them could do on their own.

A group, any group, must have a leader or a manager.

Establish Management Responsibilities

Getting involved with a group of investors will probably allow you to make more money than you would on your own. Sounds great, right? It can be. A group, any group, must have a leader or a manager. The manager must have authority to act in the name and for the good of the group without undue interference from the group. That's a much easier goal to set than it is to accomplish. Once people put their money in the pot, they generally want a hand in stirring things up. Good investors aren't necessarily good managers, and unwarranted interference can ruin even the best of investments.

The manager of an investment group is central to the success of that group. He or she must be knowledgeable, committed to the project, and trustworthy. Other (bonus) attributes that will come in handy are a nice smile, a strong handshake, and a twinkle in the eye, but those first three attributes are essential.

Consider Individual Personality Needs

When working with your group, remember that everything is in the eye of the beholder and that you have a lot of beholders. One investor may always focus on the downside of any investment. Another member may only see the bright and rosy future of any project. There's a positive and a negative side to every investment, so neither one is 100 percent right or 100 percent wrong. Handled properly, their input is valuable information and advice.

A group may have one goal, but it is made up of many personalities. Some members of your team will be shy or quiet. They may prefer to remain in the background. Some of them might even communicate more by memo than by direct input. Others will speak out at any opportunity and may try to dominate the group. Different personality traits can lead to friction. A certain amount of friction is okay, even desirable. That's how new ideas come out. The important thing is to never let disagreements cause permanent damage to the group or its goals.

The Downside of Sharing a Load

One of the hardest tasks for a partner in an investment group is sharing profits with someone who does not carry his or her own weight. That can be aggravating, unpleasant, and downright painful. People like to shoot off their mouths, but too often they turn into silent partners when it's time to do the real work.

Research your prospective partners before you sign any papers and long before you get too deeply involved in planning and organizing. There's often a lot of politics involved in an investment group. Opinions vary, and people can become so committed to them that they'll lose sight of the long-term goal just to prove themselves right in a short-term argument. Partners can be high-maintenance. Do you have the time, energy, and desire to handle all those ongoing tensions?

Many property managers prefer to work on their own rather than to get involved with the hassles of partnerships. They prefer smaller, more manageable properties that an individual can buy, manage, and eventually sell at a profit. If they spend many sleepless nights over their investments, those nights are at least devoted to the property, its maintenance, and profitability. They're not wasted on worry over a partner's hurt feelings or how to guard against the latest crazy scheme to "make a killing" in the market.

Some partners like to keep the lines of communication open. That's not a bad idea in and of itself. The problems start when one or more of your partners starts calling at 3:00 A.M. with the latest brainstorm, fear of imminent failure, or reason for you to do something you know to be irresponsible. A lot of property managers prefer to answer to only one boss—themselves. They may not have the largest real-estate company in their town, but they have the peace of mind that comes from calling their own shots, taking their own risks, and making their own fortunes.

Keep It in Perspective

Remember, an investment group is simply a real-estate partnership. It's not a loose association. It's not a New Age commune. It's not group therapy. As they say in the Texas oil patch, it's "bidness." Once you have decided to acquire a property, a series of agreements must be made, agreed to, signed, and honored. Someone must be put in charge. Percentages of ownership must be clearly delineated. The rights and restrictions of partners must be stated. The services of a real-estate attorney are essential in drafting this document. Everybody's needs must be met, or satisfactory compromises must be achieved. Any matter left unattended will come back in the form of an explosive land mine sometime during the project.

Defining a Partnership

Despite the ease with which you can form a partnership, your agreements must still be within the law. Two acts govern partnership law: the Uniform Partnership Act (UPA) of 1914 and the Revised Uniform Partnership Act (RUPA) of 1994. Check with your attorney before forming a partnership because other changes could be in the wind.

The UPA defines a partnership as an "association of two or more persons to carry on as co-owners of a business for profit." RUPA expanded the definition, but it has not been adopted by all states. Let's break down the definition.

The term "association" refers to a voluntary agreement to share profits and liabilities. A "person" may represent people, partnerships, and even corporations who may be participating in the partnership. The phrase "co-owners of a business" alludes to the control of an activity that is deemed a legitimate business, such as a trade, occupation, or profession. The "for profit" element simply defines the reason you're forming the association in the first place and that you're operating under commercial law.

Know Your Partners

Forming a partnership, any type of partnership, is something like entering a marriage. It's not for everybody. As Mae West once said, "Marriage is a great institution, but I'm not ready for an institution yet." There are upsides and downsides to every partnership. The smart property manager invests the time to really know his or her partners before deciding to "get hitched" or go on alone and continue the single life.

If you decide that partnering up will work for you, make sure you get to know your partners—before they become your partners. One investor new to the real-estate market was a bit timid and decided to "partner up" with a lawyer and a lender to acquire and develop a certain property. He lacked the wherewithal to pull off the deal on his own, and a partnership seemed like a good way to make things happen.

Sure enough, lots of things happened, but not the way the timid newcomer expected. During the initial meeting he discovered that the attorney wanted excessive fees for his work. The lender had equally big dollar signs in his eyes. He wanted additional points and fees for his work. He also wanted to include dilution of partnership interest if and when a payment was made late. That meant that if any of the other partners were late by even a moment he would receive additional ownership in the investment. The young property manager began to feel an unpleasant churning in his stomach, which is Nature's way of saying, "Are you *sure* you know what you're doing?"

Luck was with him, and a confrontation was avoided. The lawyer backed out of the deal. Negotiations continued with the lender and a fifty-fifty split arrangement was agreed upon. Both partners stuck to the business plan and carried equal weight throughout the length of the project. Sometimes when one negative influence drops out, positive attitudes can begin to flourish.

It's Always a "Handshake" Deal

Set the rules and regulations of any partnership clearly and up front. Everyone should fully understand them before signing the agreement. If you don't understand a clause, a condition, or a regulation at the signing, you will probably get a rather painful and perhaps costly lesson later on. No matter how much your attorney reassures you that the partnership agreement is "ironclad," it's not. You can always find yourself in court fighting a dispute with one or more of your partners. There's never a guarantee of victory, and anybody can sue anybody else over anything. Some people initiate lawsuits knowing they'll lose. Their goal could be revenge, to hassle the other partner(s), or to create so much trouble that the partnership will dissolve or sell out. When one partner was confronted about not living up to his part of a contract, he responded, "Contracts were made to be broken." This is the attitude some people maintain. Most people will have a track record of business behavior. Make calls. Ask around. Protect yourself.

The reasons are really irrelevant. The main thing is that you're unnecessarily paying a small fortune to your lawyer and wasting time before a judge when you should be taking care of your tenants and your property. Regardless of that small fortune or your belief in the rightness of your cause, you can still end up stuck (or punched, or gouged) with the short end of the stick. You can never know how any given judge will rule.

Regardless of the paperwork, every deal is only as good as the word of the partners involved. Every agreement is only as good as the handshake binding it. That's why it's essential that you know, really know, all your partners.

Your Partnership Options

The form your group decides to take depends upon the needs of the group. You have a lot of choices, including the following:

- Unincorporated partnerships
- Partnerships
- Limited partnerships
- Limited liability limited partnerships (LLLPs)
- Limited liability partnerships (LLCs)

Use Written Agreements

A real estate trust acts as a separate entity from the property ownership, where you are the beneficiary. You and your partners will surely want to operate using one of these business vehicles. Your partnership agreement should clearly spell out the roles of all the partners. It should note all the rights and obligations and also the structure you will use to manage the property. If you're just getting started in real estate, you can't yet imagine how important it is to put things into writing. Ideally, you will follow the advice here, and you won't have to learn this lesson the hard way.

Before making their decision, everyone in the group should explore every option and every possibility before proceeding, and every member should consult his or her lawyer. Furthermore, the group as a unit should consult the lawyer they have all selected to handle the formation.

Unincorporated Partnerships

Forming a simple partnership is, well, simple. Joe and Marie can simply agree to co-own a property. There's no requirement to formalize the agreement. Documents and filing with the state are most likely unnecessary. You don't even have to shake hands. Double-check your state regulations, though, just to be sure. It may be possible legally to be in or to form a partnership without even realizing that you have done so.

Unless you make other arrangements, each partner has equal responsibilities, equal authority to act for the partnership, and equal liability. Check very carefully the status of a partnership in your state. In some, it may not be considered a "person" under the law and cannot be sued. In such a case, lawsuits will be filed against the individual partners. In other states, a partnership may be able to be sued.

Remember, a partnership is also a contract. If a partner leaves for whatever reason (death or disability, for example), the partnership may cease to exist. That doesn't automatically mean that the business being conducted by that partnership ceases. Advance planning for these types of situations may eliminate confusion, disruption of the business, and losses incurred at such a time. Forming and operating a partnership is remarkably simple, but complications can and often do arise. Consultation with an experienced attorney is essential.

> A partnership is also a contract.

Limited Partnerships

A limited partnership combines some of the features of an unincorporated partnership with some of more formalized ways of business. A limited partnership includes limited partners and general partners. The general partner or partners have the authority to run the day-to-day operations of the business. The limited partners are passive; once they have brought in their investment, all they can do is offer advice and counsel. They acquire the benefits of partnership taxation, ownership of the property, and a share in the profits, but without liability for the debts of the organization.

Before the creation of the limited liability corporation, the limited partnership was the only means to get this combination of investor benefits, and it is still a very popular form of conducting business. In addition to the aforementioned benefits, limited partnerships offer simplicity and ease of forming and operating the organization. There is a considerable amount of law behind this type of partnership simply because it has been around for a while. If you form a limited partnership, you will be required to file documents with your secretary of state.

Limited Liability Corporations

You've certainly noticed those three little letters that sometimes follow a company name–LLC. That means the company is a limited liability corporation. This type of organization clearly states the legal liabilities and obligations of all partners in the transaction.

The LLC is designed to limit the liability of the members of the corporation resulting from lawsuits related to anything that may occur on the property or to something related to that property. If someone slips, falls, and has an injury, that person has the right to sue the LLC for damages. Because the individual members of the LLC cannot be sued, you and your personal estate are protected. Without that protection, it is possible that you could be completely wiped out in a lawsuit. Remember, in the event of any serious problem with your property, you do not want legal ramifications to affect you personally.

In an LLC, most of the partners are passive. That is, they invest their money, risk only that amount of money, and have no direct say in the day-to-day management of the investment. This is a relatively new form of business; it only won approval from the IRS in 1988. All states now have their own LLC statutes in place.

In an LLC, it is the general partner's responsibility is to control the transactions and make all the decisions on managing the

Limited Liability Limited Partnerships

The LLLP is available in some states and it has a number of similarities to the limited partnership. However, in an LLLP, the general partners are also granted some limited liability. Obviously, this is an attractive inducement to the general partner. Again, papers must be filed with the secretary of state, so it is a much more formal organization than a partnership. As with the limited partnership, the state may require that you designate your group as an "LLLP" or some similar designation as part of your name.

An LLC Is
Not an LLLP

Before the introduction of the LLC in the late 1980s, the only business association offering similar benefits was the limited partnership. It offered numerous benefits: ownership, some control over the business, the tax benefits of a partnership, no personal liability for the obligations of the business, a long track record in various courts (so that its ramifications were well known), and a clear distinction between the general and the limited partners. The limited partnership is still used throughout the country, and, for the above reasons, is very popular.

The LLC is considered a better choice in many cases because the partners can exercise a degree of control without putting their own personal finances at risk over the debts incurred by the business. There is much better protection in this area under an LLC than under a limited partnership.

investment. Although the limited partners shouldn't be shut out–their input should be welcome, or at least tolerated–the actual responsibility for the project remains in the hands of the general partner. The general partner is morally and legally bound to report to the limited partners on the progress, problems, and obligations of the investment.

The benefits of an LLC are impressive. A general partner manages day-to-day operations, yet the other partners can exert a certain amount of control. The business remains flexible. Limited partners earn the tax advantage of partnership, but they are not personally liable for the debts and obligations of the partnership. It's quite attractive for many people entering real estate in groups.

LLCs exist in all the fifty states. Compared to the amount of paperwork involved in forming a traditional corporation, the LLC is quite simple to set in motion. In fact, a single individual may act as an LLC.

You are required to file appropriate organizational forms with the state. Forms and requirements vary, but generally you'll have to list the following:

- The name of the company.
- The fact that it is to operate as a limited liability corporation.
- Address of the principle place of business or its registered office.
- Name/address of the organization's registered agent.

Some states distinguish between an LLC that is managed by its members, which is similar to a partnership, and an LLC that has one member who acts as manager on behalf of the group. It's important to determine the rules, regulations, opportunities, and limits that apply in your state. For example, some states prohibit a member from acting as an agent of the business simply because he or she is a member.

Generally (depending on the state) consent of all the members is required before a transfer can take place. Check with your state to see if your membership agreement can modify this requirement. Another area to check in your own state are the limits on dissolution of the organization. Does the business cease to exist if a member leaves the group? Or can it continue with a simple vote to continue by the remaining member(s)?

Individual Property and Partnerships

By definition, a partnership is a very loose arrangement between individuals. It is therefore most important that you and your partners define rights, responsibilities, and limits up front. Make sure everyone is on the same page. For example, who owns property purchased during the life of the association? If a partner buys property on his or her own, can that be considered the property of the group? How much individual control does a single partner have over group property? What is the procedure for buying and selling property? Who has the authority to make final decisions?

This is why it's so crucial to check with your attorney to determine which rules apply to your situation in your state. Rules and regulations vary, but generally property clearly purchased by and for the partnership is considered property of that partnership and not the individuals within it. Still, the waters can get quite muddied. For example, if individual partners have a track record of paying off individual debts with partnership funds, exactly who owns what can be quite confusing.

There are other concerns that could affect the definition of ownership. How the property is listed on the group's books, how the property is put to use, the manner in which it is depreciated for tax purposes, and who has actual possession could have a dramatic impact on who owns what.

Generally property clearly purchased by and for the partnership is considered property of that partnership and not the individuals within it.

For more information on this topic, visit our Web site at www.businesstown.com

Potential Investment Risks

Chapter 5

L oss is always a possibility in any real-estate transaction. That's just a cold, hard fact of doing business. You're reading this book to become a smart property manager, and one of the traits of a smart manager is to minimize the risk of loss. What could you lose in real estate? Lots. Even though this chapter looks at the possible downside of being a landlord, it isn't meant to be a "downer." It's possible to examine the subject of loss realistically, in order to get a better idea of what you're about to get into.

Remember, property management is an exciting and rewarding business. It has proven to be the way to wealth for many people, as long as they know how to avoid some of the roadblocks along the way. So what are the financial risks of property management?

Losing Your Investment

This brings us back to the basic question. Can you lose your investment? Yes, it's a possibility, but unless you decide to default on your payments to the lender, it is very unlikely that you'll lose your investment. Losing your investment isn't easy. It's something you have to work at, and most folks prefer to pour all that energy into success.

If you've followed the financial news during the last two decades, you've seen property prices continually rising. That's pretty much a rule across the board. Of course, there are exceptions. For example, if the major employer in a one-industry town goes out of business or moves, the economy takes a real hit and property drops, but that's not always the case. If you invested the time to investigate your purchase and made a good buying decision, you can still make up for your investment. Even in difficult times, the owner can get back what he or she paid. And that's not the bottom line, either. The property should have been generating income all the time you owned it. As an owner, you should have been enjoying a comfortable cash flow and perhaps some appreciation in the value of the property all along.

Losing Family and Friends

Now that you're feeling a bit better about the risks of financial loss, it's only fair to give you another warning. There is the possibility that

---

Financial Management Rate of Return

The average rate of return on a piece of real estate is 4 percent a year. That basically describes capital appreciation but not the cash flow. Combining cash flow and capital appreciation figures gives you something called the financial management rate of return (FMRR), a method of measuring investment performance.

The FMRR is a variation on the internal rate-of-return method. The calculation involves two after-tax reinvestment rates: a liquid rate obtainable for liquid deposits, and an average rate earned from a typical investment measured over time. To make the calculation, negative cash flow is discounted to a current value at the first rate. Cash coming in is compounded to the investment resale date at the second rate. The financial management rate of return, then, is the rate equal to the present value of the negative cash flow compared to the future value of the cash coming in.

you could lose more than just your investment—you could lose family or friends.

It happens. And, sadly, it happens all the time. Many wonderful relationships have been ruined when friends and family members decide to become business partners. There can be a real temptation to break the common-sense rules of good business because people think that they are different, that their bonds with family and friends are stronger, and that they could withstand business tensions. That may or may not be the case, but do you really want to find out the hard way?

Too often people try to get into real estate without investing their own cash and by borrowing from friends or family. That's generally a bad idea. As a rule of thumb, all partners should share equal risk in the transaction. For example, if the property costs $100,000, then each partner should carry an equal load—ten people at $10,000 each, four people at $25,000 each, or whatever sum is appropriate for the number of investors. That way, everyone has the same amount invested in the deal. No one should feel slighted or that they are carrying too much of the load. Such feelings can ruin a business opportunity and, worse, they can ruin relationships. Everybody in the deal should be at equal risk.

"Family" Business Is Business

This isn't to say that you should never invest with family and friends, only that you should be extremely careful about such investments. The point is to know your investors. Cousin Bob may be a great guy around the Thanksgiving dinner table, but he could be a disaster in handling tenant relations. Cousin Betty may have a great business mindset, but she might also be a frightened investor who'll drive you and the other partners crazy with her fears. It's important to ask yourself just how well you know Bob and Betty as potential business partners. If you don't conduct this essential business research, come next November you could be the turkey that's been picked clean.

How to Make It Work

Family and friends can be wonderful business partners, but people have to work at partnership. Here are four key elements to making

> Everybody in the deal should be at equal risk.

Build Reserves

Always raise 110 percent of the money you need to buy the property. You'll need those reserves. Going into a business or a project under-capitalized is one of the biggest and most common mistakes in American business. There's just no way anyone can accurately forecast what expensive surprises await in the future. For example, you will continue to have the same expenses even if tenants vacate your property. Another problem that can arise is an increase in your taxes.

You and your investors will need those reserves to cover the lost income. Raise the money long before you need it, and bank it. Collect the interest, and make sure the capital will be available when and if you need it. If you're not prepared, repairs, maintenance, vacancies, and unexpected expenses can turn a "damn good investment" into a "damn shame."

the deal work. First, really get to know your partners as partners. You may have grown up with Bob and Betty, but that doesn't mean you have a clue as to how they'll conduct themselves in business. Make it your business to find out before you sign any dotted lines. How will they conduct themselves with tenants, the loan committee, or your suppliers? Can they handle the stress of broken water pipes or a downturn in the economy? Will they agree to let the property manager really manage the property?

Second, put the deal in writing. You're involved in a business transaction. Regardless of personal relationships, the matter has to be "all business." Someone has to take responsibility for creating and maintaining a businesslike environment. If that task falls to you, so be it. Perhaps everybody will understand the need, but don't count on it. The investment in time you make up front will pay big dividends down the road. Here are a few considerations:

- How much operating expenses will be needed?
- Will capital improvements be needed?
- How much will those improvements cost?
- Can they be staggered over time, or will you and your partners have to cover all the expense at once?

Third, create a realistic timetable for when you think you'll want to sell the property. How long do you want to hold on to the property? Does everybody understand, and are all partners in agreement? Is everyone aware of how and when the money from the sale will be distributed? Is everyone satisfied with the structure of the agreements?

Fourth, spell out the rules for input from your partners. Some may want nothing to do with day-to-day management. Others may want to be actively involved. Neither option is necessarily good or bad. It's just important that everyone understand who does what. As a general rule, property should be managed by someone who knows what he or she is doing. The important thing is that everyone realize who has the real say-so.

Rules in Your Favor

You'll need professional guidance in very technical areas. You may acquire legal liabilities from the previous owner. Your tenants have specific rights with respect to interest on security deposits, for example.

Every community is different. You'll need to play by the rules that are in place in each one. In Illinois, as well as in other states, you will be required to get a department of revenue letter (IDOR). This means that the seller of the property does not owe the state any sales tax or revenue from income. In the state of Illinois this gets passed on to the real estate. Without an IDOR, you could have the liability and have to pay revenue to the state from the private property's owners operating a business unrelated to the specific real estate. In other words, you could end up paying for someone else's carelessness. You certainly don't want that liability.

This isn't just a matter of technicality. Mark estimates that getting the IDOR prior to closing has saved him more than $100,000 in fees he would otherwise have been required to pay the state on behalf of a prior owner's negligence.

> Your tenants have specific rights with respect to interest on security deposits.

Get Insured

Common sense should tell you to avoid any legal liabilities in anything you do, and insurance is one of the best forms of protection available. You would purchase automobile insurance to protect yourself in the event of a crash or an accident. You would buy homeowners' insurance to be prepared for a fire, hail damage, someone slipping and falling, or for many other sound reasons. The thinking is the same in real estate. Protecting yourself, your partners, and your company is a primary responsibility. Do not take this task lightly.

Insurance is a necessity. Your lender will require you to have insurance to protect the investment. Fires, hail, tripping and slipping, and other dangers are very real. Without protection, you and your investors could easily lose the entire property—and more.

Additionally, if your property generates income, you will certainly want business interruption insurance. If the building is damaged for whatever reason—such as a fire or water damage from a burst water pipe—you could lose all your income while the structure is being repaired. Business interruption insurance protects you against loss of rents. The insurance company will provide for the rents you did not and could not collect during the period that the property was uninhabitable (and unprofitable). This type of insurance is particularly appropriate for properties carrying a large amount of debt combined with a slim margin of profit. It's also appropriate for managers who have a large number of long-term leases that may have been negotiated at very favorable rates—again, with a slim profit margin. Business interruption insurance should also cover additional related costs, such as temporary housing for tenants while the property undergoes renovation.

Purchase Insurance

Even if you have accumulated enough wealth to purchase a piece of property without getting a mortgage, you will still want insurance to protect your investment. Recently, Mark received a call from someone who wanted to sell some property. The woman wanted him to look at some acreage in a very well developed southwest suburb of Chicago. That raw land would be available in this region of Chicago seemed odd, but he agreed to take a look.

During the call, he asked a number of questions, including where the utilities approached her property. She paused and said, "Just a minute. Let me look out the window of the bus." He was a bit startled by her response and asked for clarification. The woman said, "One of the reasons we need to sell this property is because our home burned down two years ago. We didn't have insurance and so my mother and I have been living in a school bus." Think about that. These folks owned valuable property in a very affluent part of town, yet they were living in a school bus. It happens.

These were well-off, educated people who should have known better than to live without proper insurance. Rebuilding a home after a disaster is an expensive proposition, and most people just don't have the ready cash to even begin that process. Insurance is essential. The money someone thinks he or she is "saving" by not getting insurance is a case of "penny wise and pound foolish." It's just not worth the risk.

Insure for Full Recovery

When getting insurance, especially if you're buying property for the first time, cover all your bases. Invest time with your accountant and lawyer. Make sure the insurance covers the cost of repair or replacement of your property. The replacement cost of a building will certainly be more than the value of the property. For example, if your building was constructed in the 1920s, do you really think you can buy replacement lumber (paint, brick, copper, and other materials) at 1920s prices? Again, the risk just isn't worth it.

Don't make the mistake of thinking you're fully covered with actual cash value (ACV) insurance. That might cover the cost of repairs to a building, but certainly not the cost of actually replacing it. In most cases, only portions of the building, not the entire unit, are damaged. Property damage could be minimal or disastrous. The key point to remember is how much will be required to get you and your investors completely back up to speed.

There are many other types of insurance that could be beneficial to your operations. Among those you should definitely consider are the following: liability, fire, flood (consider the waterbed, too), earthquake, vandalism, contents, boiler/furnace, machinery, mortgage, title, fidelity, worker's compensation, automobile, and an umbrella policy.

Avoiding Legal Liabilities

In addition to insurance, you'll need professional guidance in very technical areas. For instance, you may acquire legal liabilities from the previous owner if the tenants have specific rights with respect to interest on security deposits and perorations.

Every community is different and you'll need to play by local rules. In Illinois, as already noted, the buyer is required to provide proof that the seller does not owe certain debts.

> There are many other types of insurance that could be beneficial to your operations.

Markets Change Quickly

When markets are good, every investor is a genius. If you are interested in property management for the long term, you will eventually experience both the ups and downs of the marketplace. When the market begins to slack, don't panic. It's not all that bad; as previously noted, real estate doesn't experience the boom and bust roller-coaster rides of the stock market. That said, it is a fact that real-estate markets change. Let's look at a few famous markets.

- The Gay Nineties, the 1890s period during Theodore Roosevelt's administration, was a time period marked by a recession.
- A few decades later, America experienced the Roaring Twenties. People made vast fortunes, and the country seemed to be in the midst of a never-ending party.
- In 1929, the stock market crashed, and the world entered the Great Depression.
- The "baby boomer" generation was born during the post–World War II boom but had to live through a recession in the 1970s.
- In recent decades, booming wealth creation was matched by a savings-and-loan scandal that rocked the financial world.
- At the turn of the twenty-first century, the country was excited by the dot-coms, until their bubble burst.

As you can see, the market is cyclical, dipping down and the surging up again. So what's ahead? More change. Booms are followed by busts, which are then followed by booms. No one can really predict the future, but savvy investors would be wise to be heavy in cash during the years 2009–2012. A good guess would be that the nation will be experiencing another period of recession.

Again, the bottom line is that things change. Anyone wanting to succeed in real estate had better plan for changes in the long run. And today, markets are changing more and faster than ever before. These changes aren't necessarily to be feared, but it's a good idea to be prepared for them. Lots of people prosper during changing times, even during the times of difficulty.

More Control, Less Frenzy

Compared to the stock market, real estate is a much less frenzied way to earn a good living or to build wealth. One of the real

> Anyone wanting to succeed in real estate had better plan for changes in the long run.

benefits is that the real-estate market just doesn't change all that quickly. The investor has much more control over his or her property and investments as well as more time to think and plan. XYZ Corporation stock may drop ten points in an hour on the big board and cause thousands of investors angst, heartache, and financial grief. Buildings, raw land, dwellings, and other properties just don't plummet like that.

The careful investor who does his or her homework can often see trends coming long before they arrive. Let's say you have a rental building and you've been increasing your rents 5 or 6 percent a year for some time. Then XYZ Corporation announces it's downsizing the workforce. Some of those workers live in the building, and you're naturally concerned about a downsizing of your investment.

You have options. You could hold off on the next rent increase until the economy bounces back. This isn't a bad idea. Maintenance, repair, and other costs associated with resident turnover can be rather extensive. You can avoid many of those extra costs by keeping your tenants. Holding down or forgoing a rent increase also helps build and maintain a good tenant/manager relationship.

If you think about the situation with a long-term perspective, forgoing a rent increase shouldn't be a major problem. You're just holding on to a good investment when things are slow. When the economy picks back up, so will your rent increases. A fast-buck mentality will not work to your advantage, but careful planning, taking care of good tenants, and keeping a long-term perspective will. Many people start buying real estate in their twenties. Then they enter their thirties, forties, fifties, and beyond. Gradually, that property becomes a valuable, mature investment in an expanding portfolio. With continual study and evaluation of your market, you can take full advantage of one of the primary benefits of real estate–stability.

Real Estate Is Job-Driven

When the economy changes, people generally start losing their jobs. The logic is inevitable. When companies cut back, they require less office space, less warehousing, and fewer workers. When people are laid off, they often have a difficult time paying their rent because a lot of folks are living from paycheck to paycheck. When that money stops, everything else stops too—including your rental payments. That's true for all real estate, but it's especially true for residential markets. It doesn't really matter whether the interest rates drop to zero. People who aren't working and who aren't making any money can't invest in real estate, regardless of the rates.

Regulations Can Lower Profits

In case you haven't already figured this out, governments just love to govern. The men and women who get elected and appointed seem to be filled with a burning desire to legislate public rights, tenant rights, property owner rights, and lots of other rights. They always seem to cost landlords a great deal of their hard-earned money. When cities or counties need more money, the folks in charge take aim for the landlord's profit center by raising taxes, an action that directly impacts the landlord's cash flow.

In addition to taxes, government regulations may require annual, presale, pest, and other miscellaneous inspections, as well as the installation of smoke alarms, sprinklers, and handicapped access ramps, among other things, on your property.

It's all part of the game that costs you money. Here's a particularly odious example. The city of Chicago requires building owners to register their buildings every year. This is an old regulation going back some time. You'd think that once a building was registered, the city fathers would realize it is where it should be and that it hasn't sneaked off to some new neighborhood. But no, every year the building has to be registered again—just to keep the landlord paying the registration fee to the city.

Here's another example. Each year, Chicago property owners can count on receiving expensive violations relating to trash pickup. This regular event occurs during the first and second quarter of the year when snow really piles up in the Windy City. Heavy snow, combined with the occasional long weekend, means that a lot of trash doesn't get picked up. In many cases it can't be picked up until the snow is cleared out of the way. Some genius downtown saw this as a great way to squeeze a few more dollars from the city's landlords.

The city sends out private inspectors to photograph trash that has collected and has not been picked up, and an automatic $100 fine is issued. Then the landlord has to go to an administrative hearing. No judge is present. No lawyers are involved. The hearing is run by an administrative hearings officer who automatically issues a $300 fine. Property owners in Chicago just have to treat this event as part of the cost of doing business.

Every town and every government is different, and you will discover all kinds of different rules and regulations coming your way. It's costly, time-consuming, and it takes valuable dollars out of the private economy and puts them in government coffers. Mark Twain once said that there are only two constants—death and taxes. Perhaps there is a third. Government regulators will always increase regulations, which will always lower your profits.

> Every year the building has to be registered again—just to keep the landlord paying the registration fee to the city.

"Out of the Blue" Concerns

Sometimes lightning strikes out of the blue, and there's just no way to prepare for it—except to realize that, like change, it is inevitable. As the saying goes, you have to expect the unexpected. It is better to be reactive than proactive for the simple reason that no one can possibly prepare for all that might happen. It's better to wait and let it happen (whatever "it" might be), and then react accordingly.

In some cases there's just no way to handle a situation as well as you'd like. For example, let's say it is late afternoon, on Thanksgiving eve, and a tenant calls to say the oven isn't working. He or she has a ton of food ready to cook for the big family get-together and the day's ruined and . . . well, you get the picture.

What can you possibly do? It's a holiday evening. Your mainte-nance man is out with his family. The electrician is away in Wisconsin visiting his aunt. And you don't know how to repair an oven. The best you can possibly offer is to get a repairman out there first thing Friday morning. If that's all you can do, then that's all you can do. Do your best to take care of your tenant, listen to their complaints with some empathy, and then move on to do the best you can.

When you open your eyes every morning, you have no idea what the day can bring. That's really one of the joys of this line of work. Of course, you'll experience a bad day now and then. Something will always come in out of the blue, but those days are surprisingly few and far between. Your best defense is to maintain a positive attitude and rise to every challenge.

> Your best defense is to maintain a positive attitude and rise to every challenge.

For more information on this topic, visit our Web site at www.businesstown.com

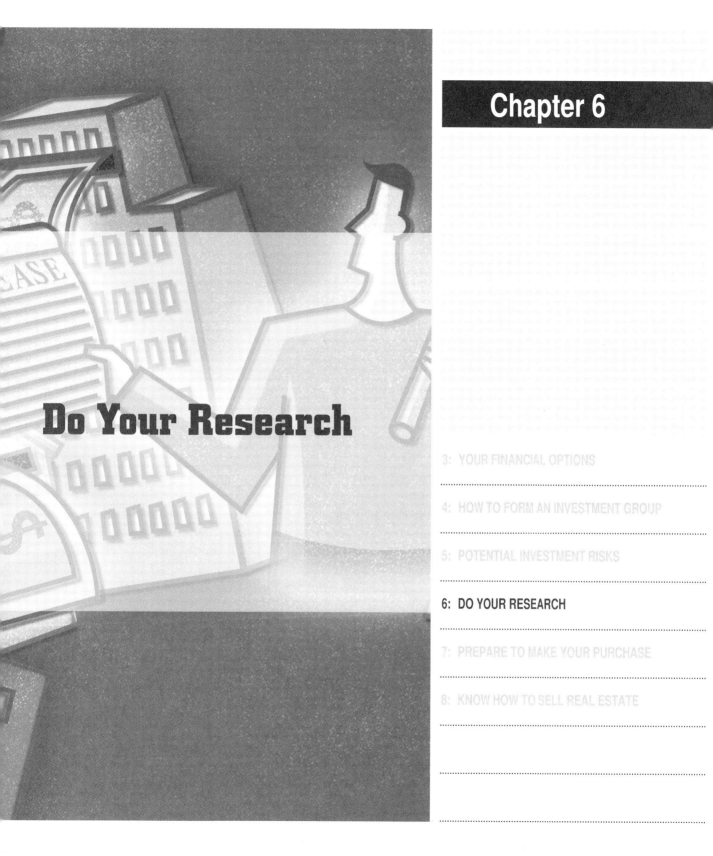

Chapter 6

Do Your Research

The quest for *good* property is an ongoing process. Once you're in the business, you'll need to develop an eye for opportunity. Consider yourself on a twenty-four-hour, seven-day-a-week reconnaissance mission. You're always on the lookout for solid investments to rescue from the hands of sellers who'll let them go to just about anyone with ready cash. Find the property that looks and feels right, one about which you know in your heart that you're the best person in the world to buy and manage, and then acquire it.

The Right Property

As mentioned earlier, looking for the right property is a long-term commitment. If you're just starting out, plan on investing a year of your life before you make your first purchase. Yes, yes, yes, you're chomping at the bit to get the race started, but remember the story of the tortoise and the hare. A fast start doesn't guarantee success. If you're a newcomer, you want to be extremely careful with your first effort. Too many careers, fortunes, and happy lives have been ruined by first-time property managers who leapt before they looked.

Really, that first year is where the fun begins. Don't look upon that time period as drudgery or something you have to plod through. Enjoy the experience and the learning curve. Take your time and do all the assigned homework. Get a feel for your market. Make friends and contacts and start developing that eye for a good bargain. This one-year course of study and preparation will be one of the best career investments you'll ever make.

Once started, you'll find it impossible to keep from evaluating properties up, down, sideways, backwards, and forwards, inside and out. Don't worry about developing a case of burnout, either. Every day brings something new. It's almost like studying a new subject every time you go out because you're always seeing something you've never seen before. And a moment will come when you'll discover you have developed the skill, experience, and knowledge to say, "That's the one!"

Opportunity Is Everywhere

Burling Street is in Chicago. At one time it was lined with small, single family dwellings. Back in the 1890s, they sold for about

> A fast start doesn't guarantee success.

$2,000–5,000 each. Those were 1890s dollars, a tidy sum. A hundred years later, a lot of folks looked at those buildings and mumbled, "Tear them down." Fortunately, a few real-estate professionals with that eye for the elusive good deal had a vision of homes selling for $1,000,000–$4,000,000. The land had greater value! Now large homes abound on double lots!

That's the magic of real estate. Opportunity is everywhere for those people who invest the time to look for it. Today's big cities have more investment property than you can imagine. Most people look at an area and see what exists at that moment. Real-estate professionals look at the same street, block, or neighborhood and see much more:

- Single-family dwellings
- Duplexes
- Apartments
- Condominiums
- Land to be developed
- Mixed-use buildings
- Shopping centers
- Retail stores
- Warehousing space
- Parking lots
- Amusement parks
- Golf courses
- Resorts
- Industrial property
- Commercial property

> Today's big cities have more investment property than you can imagine.

Most of all, they see opportunity. The list can go on and on, limited only by your imagination.

Find a Good Fit

It is important that you feel good about the property you're considering. A good deal for some might be a not-so-good deal for others. Suppose you have the desire, experience, and education to run a top-flight miniature golf course. That's your goal, and you have found the perfect bit of raw land to develop. It's available, priced right, and you can get started right away. That's great unless your "deal" is in northern Maine. Few families will try to enjoy a round of putt-putt under several feet of fresh snow. Your earning season will be rather limited. How about looking down in Florida, near Phoenix, or around Southern California?

Use the Forty-Minute Rule

Your property should be within a forty-minutes ride of your home or office. Problems grow at exponential rates with distance. For example, suppose a tenant calls with a complaint about not having any hot water. If you are a short drive or even a short walk away, it's really no problem to invest a few minutes to light a pilot on a hot-water heater. If, on the other hand, you or your maintenance man has to drive two hours there and back, you've wasted half a day or more—and wasted time cuts deep into your profitability. The closer you are to your property, the better.

Realize that you are now becoming an entrepreneur. You're a businessperson. One of your key business decisions is finding a good property that's a close fit close by. That's why it's so important to invest that year in studying your market. At some point during those months, you will inevitably find a property that fits you like a glove.

Match your goals to your abilities, resources, and environment. If recreation isn't your interest, you might want to consider apartments. People always need a place to live. You have many more options in many more parts of the country because having a roof over one's head takes precedence over sinking a putt under the purple windmill.

Cities are broken down by socioeconomic conditions. You'll find upscale, middle-class, blue-collar, and poverty-ridden areas. Within those neighborhoods and communities, there are many different kinds of housing. Even if you narrow it down to apartment housing, there are still many variations. Some cities experience a flurry of conversions in which apartments become condos to be rented at high rates. Some apartments, which at first glance appear to be poor bargains, may be rent-subsidized under various government programs. These may actually mean reliable rent payments despite the economic condition of the surrounding neighborhood. The point is that there are many opportunities. Find the ones that will make a good fit.

Start Looking Now

There's no time like the present to get started looking around for potential purchases. Start investing your evenings and weekends, and take tours of open houses in your targeted neighborhoods. Most of your time will be focused on residential property. Open houses are usually limited to homes, condos, and town homes. Looking at commercial or industrial property usually involves setting up appointments with the real-estate broker or the owner.

The Mechanics of the Process

The mechanics of the process are really quite simple. There are five basic steps to getting started:

1. Get your Sunday newspaper.
2. Open it to the real-estate section.
3. Start reading and circling interesting properties.

4. Begin calling the listing brokers or the "by-owner" ads.
5. Be prepared to ask proper questions.

It's that simple, but that doesn't mean it's all that easy to do it right. It's very difficult to sound experienced when you're just starting out, but by following this list you'll be headed in the right direction. You'll pick up the experience you need as you go along.

Don't let the jargon throw you either. If you hear an unfamiliar term, look it up in the glossary (in the back of the book), and memorize it for future use. In no time at all you'll be sounding (and acting) like a real-estate pro. After you're comfortable, you can go it on your own with complete confidence.

Apply the Inverse Theory

Taking one year to do your property research will allow you to apply the inverse theory. Here is how it works. Look at every property seriously, and start disqualifying the ones that don't fit. Start rejecting the real estate that just doesn't work for you. Here's a tip: The first rejection will be the hardest. You'll have a natural tendency to take that leap without looking. Resist, and move on to examine other locations.

If the property, the deal, or any particular detail just doesn't feel right, give it a pass. Trust your instincts. If it feels bad, it probably is bad, at least for you. It's a lot like buying a new pair of shoes. If they don't fit well, don't buy them. Even when the salesperson tells you, "Oh, they'll break in and feel great," listen to your toes. Remember, there's opportunity everywhere. Move on and find the one that's just right.

Listen to People Who Know

Here's a true story of someone who failed to heed this advice. A computer consultant was trying to get involved in property management. He approached a friend who was knowledgeable and experienced in the business of real estate. His friend told him about a great deal, a starter two-flat in a northern suburb of Chicago. It was in a good location and could be picked up at a good price. The friend

Obstacles to Inspection

When you visit a property, try to look at everything, although sometimes this is just impossible. For example, at the time of writing this book, Mark is in the process of purchasing a building that was constructed in the 1920s. This building consists of four apartments in a "hot" rental area.

This opportunity is presenting some interesting obstacles. Since the 1930s, members of one family have lived in one of the apartments and have been using the other three for storage. As you can imagine, over the years the amount of stuff stored there has increased, filling up rooms and hallways. When Mark arrived for an inspection of the property, he found it almost impossible to conduct a thorough walk-through in, around, over, and under all that accumulated family stuff.

Storage items can hide a lot of problems with a building. When just starting out, it's a good idea to get experienced help with your initial inspections.

knew the consultant could manage the property for a few years and then sell it for a nice profit.

The consultant and his wife had not invested that year in research. They had failed to develop an eye for opportunity, and they just didn't like the location or the program suggested by their friend in real estate. Instead, they acquired a property in Springfield, Illinois. Why? Because the consultant's sister really wanted to get into property management.

Springfield was three hours from the consultant's home, but he saw a "good deal." He and his wife could own the property without having to manage it. Unfortunately, things didn't quite work out the way he planned. Remember the section on being wary of doing business with friends and family? This fellow learned that lesson the hard way. His sister soon discovered she really didn't care for property management, so the property didn't get managed: Tenant complaints were ignored, repairs weren't made, and a nightmare developed. City inspections revealed a number of additional problems, which required immediate care. The consultant was disgusted. He began to hate the property and his need to constantly pour more money into it. The distance only made things worse.

He didn't listen to those who knew. He overpaid for a problem building in an inactive rental market. He relied on a family member without making sure that she was really reliable. When last heard from, the consultant was living in Southern California, avoiding his sister, and facing default on his loan. Had he purchased the property originally recommended, he could be living in one of those units today, have a paying tenant in the other, and be in a position to sell the property for a nice profit. Someone else took that original advice, and for that person, this is exactly what happened.

> Apply your knowledge and intellectual powers to evaluate the properties, your ability to make sound judgments, and even your instincts.

Get All the Information

Researching property, weeding out the poor choices, and homing in on the good ones isn't as difficult a chore as you might think. Certainly you'll have to apply your knowledge and intellectual powers to evaluate the properties, your ability to make sound judgments, and even your instincts. But a lot of what you have to do is basic labor that requires little more than your willingness to work at gathering data. Your choices of what to research fall into six basic categories:

- Raw land. You can buy the land and just sit on it to allow for appreciation over time. A tract of land worth $50,000 today could easily be worth $75,000 in a few years.
- Raw land for development. You could purchase your land and sell or lease it to someone else for further development.
- Raw land you'll purchase, lease, or lease/purchase to develop on your own.
- An existing property that you'll rent.
- An existing property that you'll rehab or renovate for sale or rent.

That being said, how do you find that ideal property? Here are a few tips.

1. Read the ads. Your local newspaper is a source of available properties. As your knowledge of the community expands, you'll be able to weed out the less desirable properties quickly and easily, even from the sparse details in a tiny ad. Although you'll probably develop other sources throughout your career, never neglect this basic resource.
2. Keep your eye out for "For Sale" signs. Look for them wherever you go. A lot of signs go up before the ads for those properties hit the papers. If you drive the same route all the time, start taking new roads. Take a different path every day or every time you head out. Bring your notepad and pencil, and take notes along the way.
3. Contact brokers, agents, and other real-estate professionals on a regular basis. Put your network to work. Get those feelers out there and provide the same service for others in your network.
4. Call on professionals in businesses related to real estate. You can find rich sources of property information in bankers, lawyers, accountants, financial advisors, property managers, appraisers, mortgage lenders, and consultants. Again, use

> Contact brokers, agents, and other real-estate professionals on a regular basis.

your network. The investment of a phone call, a cup of coffee, or a lunch now and then can yield incredible amounts of valuable information.

5. Call on your friends, relatives, and associates in the community. Never neglect this vast storehouse of information. You know people in all segments of society living in different parts of your community. They're an excellent source of current real-estate information, like this: "Come to think about it, my neighbor said something about selling that lakefront property of his." A few words in the right place can steer you in the right direction.

6. Check out real-estate auctions in your area. Not only can you find good deals, you can use the opportunity to expand your network of real-estate sources.

7. Find the foreclosures. Read your local newspapers, business journals, and notices provided by local, state, and federal government agencies. Banks and other lending institutions are also good sources for information on foreclosures.

8. Call people out of the blue. If you see a piece of property that draws your interest, give the owner a call. You never know when your interest in buying might match or even create an interest in selling. Additionally, even if the owner isn't interested in selling, he or she still might know of someone nearby who could be.

9. Get connected with professional real-estate institutions. You will find them an invaluable source of information. (Some of the more prominent organizations are discussed in Appendix A.)

Again, carefully examine all aspects of every deal and every property before you make a purchase or enter into a lease agreement. Be sure to involve your network of friends, advisors, and professional consultants, too. Here are the most relevant areas to pay attention to:

- **Use.** Is it adaptable to your residential, commercial, or industrial needs?
- **Future use.** Are there serious plans on anyone's drawing board that could affect your intentions? What are they, and

> If you see a piece of property that draws your interest, give the owner a call.

what are your options? Are there plans to move in a hog-rendering plant upwind of your proposed residential development?

- **Population.** Is it growing, dwindling, or projected to remain stable? Which is best for your proposed use?
- **Potential for disaster.** Is the property located in an active flood plain, in a "tornado alley," near a receding shore line, or in an earthquake zone?
- **Zoning.** In which zone is the property located now? Are there plans for zoning changes? Can you get the zoning changes you want?
- **Traffic patterns.** Are they sufficient? Are improvements on the drawing board? Will those improvements help or hinder your operations? How long would construction tie up your business?

Look Out When Looking

The old adage that you can't tell a book by its cover applies to real estate. Naturally, you'll take a close look at the exterior of the building, but there are a lot more areas to examine before you examine a contract.

Check the weather. Is the area prone to excessive rain, wind, or other weather factors that could affect the value of the property? Look at the land on and around the property and even throughout the neighborhood to see if there is any erosion. Notice whether any areas are subject to too much or too little sunlight.

Examine the soil and what's beneath that soil. Is the topsoil thin and likely to blow away with the next windstorm, or is it deep and secure? Check the appropriate government agencies to determine if there are any hazardous wastes buried on the property. Include the right to inspect for such dangers within your contract. Then see that a professional makes a thorough examination. In some parts of the country where heavy manufacturing or mineral extraction has been going on for decades, people haven't the slightest idea of what's just beneath their feet.

Make sure the property complies with existing zoning ordinances, that it will stay in compliance through projected changes, or that you can bring it into compliance. Double-check the entire property for any deterioration, such as water stains on the walls, roof damage, cracks in the exterior, and so on. Have a qualified engineer thoroughly examine the property to report any existent or potential problems. After you get the engineer's list, get estimates on how much you'll have to pay to bring those items up to standard. Will the time and money invested pay off within your timeframe?

- **Utilities.** Are they in place? Will you have to pay extra to get them in?
- **Schools.** Are there schools nearby? People are more likely to move to a neighborhood with a good school. Also, some cities restrict the types of businesses that can be located within a certain distance of schools.
- **Recreation.** Are these needs met by your desired neighborhood or area? If not, what is the likelihood that they can be provided?
- **Safety.** Are police, fire, and other services available?
- **Sanitation.** What are the provisions for sewerage and trash disposal?
- **Parking.** Are your needs met by the location, or will you have to make additional and costly arrangements, like valet parking, for example?
- **Public transportation.** Is it necessary? If so, is it available?

The value of the answers to these questions depends upon your plans for the property. The point is to conduct a very thorough research before you start making those plans.

A Residential Inspection

Before you buy residential property, have it inspected by qualified people to find any defects and potential problems. But there are a number of things you, even without professional training, can do on your own.

You need to begin asking questions even before you get to the site of the property. For instance, find out the complete address of the property. When inquiring about an apartment building, always ask the number of units the building contains. Different owners, brokers, and companies have differing ideas about how they describe property. The "great little opportunity" you think is a duplex may in fact be a seven-story apartment building. Be sure to ask about the unit mix. Are there studio apartments? One bedroom? Two bedrooms? How many rooms in each apartment?

Ask how the apartments break out. Do the two-bedroom apartments have a dining room, a kitchen, and a sunroom? Are there two

> When inquiring about an apartment building, always ask the number of units the building contains.

baths, one-and-a-half baths, or just one bath? Is that one-bedroom apartment simply a single room with a kitchen/living room combination? Residential housing comes in many sizes and shapes. Find out what you're about to step into before you take that first step.

Start with the Basement

When you do get to the property, begin your inspection at the bottom and work your way up. In the basement, look for any obvious defects: inward bulging of walls, cracks or crumbling mortar, fresh patches, high-water marks, signs of leaking or seepage, a damp odor, a hidden sump pump, or mildew. Each of these items are clear signs of past or ongoing water damage. If you see any of these signs, take an second and very careful look at all possible sources of leaking or leaching water or fluid.

The problem could have resulted from a flood, especially if the dwelling is in a flood plain. If you've lived very long in the area, you'll probably remember any significant floods in recent years, or you can check with the local newspaper. That will give you an idea of how long the problem may have gone unattended.

Leaks from faulty pipes or equipment could also be the cause. Look for corrosion on basement pipes. If any is present, determine the cause and the severity of the damage. See if there's been any leakage and subsequent damage to other areas as a result. Hot water pipes should be made of copper. It's the safest and most reliable material. Cold water pipes should be made of either copper or plastic. The use of other materials could lead to problems you don't want to face. Insulated pipes are a plus. If they're not insulated, you might have to cover that expense out of your own pocket.

Look for signs of termites or rotting. Probe with your pocketknife. If the knife goes in the wood easily, that's a sure sign of rot. Learn to distinguish between ants and termites. Ants have pinched abdomens (like those of wasps) and their antenna bend at right angles. Termites have straight antennae and two pairs of wings of equal length. Knowing the difference between the two species could mean the difference between calling a pest control company or hiring a team of carpenters to rebuild the floor, roof, and walls.

> When you do get to the property, begin your inspection at the bottom and work your way up.

Examine the joists. These are the parallel boards holding up the planks of a floor or the panels of a roof. If any are propped up, find out why. Is there too much weight on them? Has one or more cracked or broken? What was the cause of the break? How long has the situation gone unattended, and is there any additional damage?

Check the fuse box. An average eight- to twelve-room house will need sixteen to twenty circuits. If the property is not wired correctly, you'll need to make the appropriate changes. Otherwise you could be setting yourself up for electrical or fire damage if there's an overload. Look for damage from sparking or from an electrically caused blaze in and around the fuse box and its wiring.

Walk Through the House

Check for warped doors, doors that won't close easily or at all, loose doorknobs, creaking floors or stairs, loose tiles, poor plumbing and any resultant water damage, and too many electrical cords plugged into a single outlet. These can be clear signals of sloppy maintenance or even negligence on the part of the owner and/or tenants. You don't want to be responsible for someone else's lack of responsibility.

Make sure the closets and storage areas are large enough for your needs. If not, see if there is room enough to make enlargements or if there are areas you can adapt for these purposes.

An electrical water heater should hold sixty gallons. A gas unit should have a thirty to forty gallon capacity. Anything less can mean not enough hot water for the tenants, which could put the new landlord (you) in hot water.

Look for any cracks or repairs in the walls, which may indicate a problem with the structure. Patches may indicate water leakage. Again, consider the use of a professional who knows how to spot these problems, someone who can give you a straight answer about the nature, seriousness, and possible costs of making repairs.

Also step up into the attic. Look for any watermarks on the underside of the roof, which are signs of leakage. If you see anything suspicious, follow the trail of water to see if there's been additional damage to other areas, such as the attic flooring or wiring.

> You don't want to be responsible for someone else's lack of responsibility.

Head Outside

Examine the exterior for any sagging, which could mean that load-bearing elements aren't bearing their load very well. Too much weight could send the roof or a wall crashing in on your new tenant. Also look for poor alignment of the walls, missing mortar, broken bricks, extra-wide mortar joints, or cracked walls. These signs could indicate a need for basic maintenance or something more serious, such as a poor foundation or shifting soils that may have caused the house to settle unequally. Sure, you could realign the settling, but you don't want to be the one to cover the expenses.

Touch the walls. Peeling wooden walls may indicate an unacceptably high moisture content. If the windowsills are freshly painted but the rest of the wall isn't, someone may be trying to cover up a rotting sill. Again, these are good places for a judicious use of your pocket knife. If it slips into the wood with little or no resistance, you might have a problem on your hands. Aluminum siding is a positive. The material holds up, holds paint well, and is a good insulator. Many upkeep problems can be minimized with good quality siding.

Break out the step ladder and climb up to the roof. Look for such potential problems as broken, missing, or patched shingles; tar paper bubbles; poor repair work; and leaks or breaks in the gutters. These could be signs of poor original workmanship, material, or maintenance, or it may be damage caused by harsh weather conditions. Also, check metal sheathing around the chimney and ventilators—it should be watertight and made of nonrusting material.

Because so many serious problems can literally be dumped into a house because of a faulty roof, you'd best examine this area carefully, or hire an expert for an appraisal.

A Leaky Roof

A leaky roof is a major problem itself, but the leaks can lead to more problems down below. Water damage can easily ruin the structure of a building requiring major replacement, repair, or reconstruction. Leaks can also ruin the furniture, belongings, and attitudes of your tenants. If you are serious about purchasing the property, make sure to get the roof checked out by a qualified inspector. Otherwise, you could find even more leaks in your monthly bank account.

Responsibility for the Utilities

When you are considering property, be sure to ask who pays for utilities. This is an important factor for your profit-and-loss columns. If the building (you) pays for these bills, you will have a higher overhead.

Paying for Heat

If the tenant pays the heating bill, the expenses to the owner are significantly lower. In "four-season" areas, it's a good idea to have the tenants pay for their own heat. Certainly, you will have to offer a lower rent charge, but this strategy allows you to eliminate the monthly heating charges that will have to be subtracted from your profit anyway.

Also, determine what type of heat is installed in the property: forced-air gas heat, radiant heat, electric heat, hot-water baseboard heat, or even the old-fashioned Franklin Stove. Again, know what you're getting into so you don't get in over your head.

> Determine what type of heat is installed in the property.

Why Do Landlords Pay for Water?

A landlord may have four tenants, twenty tenants, or over a hundred of them in a single building. Regardless of the number of units, the water utility company will have only one meter for that building. They won't put in four, or twenty, or a hundred meters. As far as the water company is concerned, it's just too complex a process. This is why the landlords find it simpler, easier, and less time-consuming to absorb the cost of the water utilities rather than try to figure out a way to have each unit pay for their share of the water supply.

Trash Removal

Does the city pay for trash removal, or is that the landlord's responsibility? You may have to contact your local department of sanitation for a clear answer. Different cities have different policies and procedures. For example, property owners in Chicago face a special situation. If you have a building in which tenants paid for their heat prior to July, 2000, the city will pick up the trash for that building. In general, the city always collects trash for buildings with four units or less, and for larger buildings with tenant heat. What is the situation in your area?

Potential Profits

How much income will the property you are looking at generate? This is a very easy question to answer. If the owner or broker holds back this information, take the hint. Something's wrong, and it's time to move on to another building. As a rule of thumb, if you're not getting accurate answers to your questions on any subject, you really don't want to get involved with that property, the manager, the broker, or the owner. It's probably just not worth the effort.

As a customer, it is your duty and your right to ask questions. It is the seller's duty to provide complete and honest answers. Many brokers and agents will refuse to represent a property if the owner holds back this data. They realize that without complete information, they can't accurately and honestly evaluate the property. Be certain to get a "rent roll." The document lists every unit, the length of each lease, and exactly how much the owner is making from each unit.

Real-Estate Taxes

Taxes are a sure thing, and if you're not careful, they can mean the sure death of a sweet deal. Often, paying real-estate taxes forms the largest expense in property ownership. These taxes are based on the assessed value of your property. If property X is valued at Y, then the tax is Z.

Some cites restrict the increase in real-estate taxes over a certain amount until the property is resold. For example, if California raises its taxes, your taxes will not increase over the term of your ownership of the California property being taxed. That's because California will make up the difference: The state (or another appropriate governing body) will, upon the sale of the property, significantly raise the taxes.

Don't buy any piece of property without getting this little matter of taxes cleared up. Experience has shown that property taxes on some buildings can increase by as much as 300 percent. In these situations, the owner had better be prepared to come up with the additional funds or to dip into the reserves to cover the difference. All this must be factored into your overall business plan. You can still make money on a building, even when your real-estate tax situation changes. Millions of acres, square feet, and bricks and mortar are sold for tens and hundreds of millions of dollars every year in the United States. Just be sure you are aware of your tax liabilities so that you will be buying and managing at a profit.

Status of Current Leases

Leases are an important part of property management, and every city has its own set of rules and regulations. Violate them at your own peril. Residential leases are the most heavily regulated, and a tenants' bill of rights is usually involved. Business people operate on an entirely different plateau, and therefore you rarely find a tenants' bill of rights associated with commercial properties.

When you are beginning to review the income and expense information, request a basic copy of the standard lease used throughout the building. Some landlords choose to avoid month-to-month leases. For many, this is a sound business practice. Because you will be required to honor the city's tenants' bill of rights or ordinances, you will need to know all about these before you make your investment.

Prepare to Make Your Purchase

Whether you realize it or not, you are already starting to evaluate property. Your interest in property management and your reading of this book has put you in a natural frame of mind to look at property and "wonder if." You're probably already looking in the Sunday real-estate section and playing the same game. You might even be driving around looking at properties, going to open houses, and checking out the forty-minute rule. That's good. It's all part of that first year of education.

Everybody who gets into real estate does it for one of two reasons: either cash flow or capital appreciation (and occasionally both). Make sure you have decided which is your primary motivation. If you have partners, make doubly sure you are all on the same page. If some want cash flow and others want appreciation, you will have conflict, and conflict cannot help your bottom line. Once you've decided your motivation, it's time to decide your course. It's time to evaluate buildings. Here's how you go about it.

> Everybody who gets into real estate does it for one of two reasons: either cash flow or capital appreciation (and occasionally both).

Visualize the Future

When looking at any property, keep an eye on the future. Where will this property be in ten or twenty years? Where is the neighborhood and even the city headed? Don't be fooled by first impressions. Listen to this story of a young investor who headed out to make his fortune, a brand-new copy of *How to Invest in Real Estate with No Money Down—No Kidding, Pal* in hand. He was young and inexperienced enough to believe the title of the book. Figuring to make it big, he thought he'd start out big. He made an appointment to visit a 300-unit apartment building. For a first-timer, that's thinking really big.

The first thing he noticed was the location of the building. It was in a seedy part of town. Had he done his homework, he'd have known this before making the first call. The broker was a seasoned veteran who could tell right off the bat that his prospect was wet behind the ears. That how-to book had not prepared the prospective buyer for important details like what to look for in a building, how to ask questions, or any other information that might have been useful to his current situation.

He looked around and discovered cockroaches scurrying across the floor. The vermin, the poor location of the building, and his own lack of experience sent him running out the door. This was a negative experience, but that's not the point of the story. Never let immediate or shallow first impressions rush you into a decision. Why? That property the young man dashed away from became an affluent area within a decade. He could have done quite well had he done a bit more homework and had the vision to see the future.

Ramifications of Inaction

Things can go the other direction too. The owner of a twenty-four-unit apartment building passed on the opportunity to purchase a vacant lot next to his building. It seems the lot was really run down and infested with rats, field mice, and all kinds of unpleasant creatures. Someone else bought the lot, and all those nasty critters were soon displaced by new construction. Would you care to hazard a guess as to where they sought sanctuary? They all headed to that nice, upscale building right next door. The property owner then had to take care of a new and unplanned expense—insect, rodent, and creepy-crawly extermination, which nearly exterminated his profit margin. Again, the point is basic. Always look to the future regardless of how bright and shiny or dark, dank, and dingy it may appear.

Working with a Buyer's Agent

Find a real estate agent with whom you are comfortable and work with him or her in an exclusive buyer agreement. That way your agent can work in your best interests. It is far better to have a single, dedicated person working for you than a poorly-motivated group, no matter how many are in it or how prestigious the name on the door.

Sometimes you have an opportunity to purchase property before it goes on the market. This can make for one of the best deals around. For one thing, the lack of competition can provide real motivation for the seller to move things along. That's where building and participating in your business community is important. Someone about to advertise a property will often call a few trusted people in

Seek out the Best

To find a good agent, try asking friends and acquaintances for references. Look around. Visit a lot of offices, and meet a lot of agents and brokers. Buying property is serious business. You want to be represented by experienced professionals. Be wary of walking into a real-estate office and "signing up" with the agent on duty. In a real-estate office, responsibilities are assigned by rotation. On any given day you could meet the best, the worst, or the most mediocre. There's just too much at risk to play that game. Just visiting with an agent or conducting an interview doesn't commit you to a business relationship.

the industry first. "If you're still interested in a duplex (or shopping center, land, retail space, and so on), I might have something for you." Working with someone who is really working with you provides a real edge in the marketplace. Here are a number of good tips for working with real estate agents:

1. Be honest about your finances. Agents want to make things happen for you. That's how they earn their commissions. You'll be in a far better position if your agent is working on ways around your financial obstacles from the start, than if he or she has to start scrambling later in the process. If you have a bad credit report or some other problem, lay it on the table right away. In most cases, it's better if you can approach an agent with your financing in hand. That way the agent can begin doing what you came to him or her for in the first place—finding you a property to buy.

2. Understand the roles. You'll actually be working with two different persons—a salesperson and a broker. Occasionally they are one and the same. A broker is a person or company licensed by your state to buy and sell property, and only brokers can legally enter a real estate contract. Most brokers have a staff of salespeople working for them. These people may be working full-time or part-time; they are most commonly referred to as agents. Even though they cannot enter into a contract, they can be very helpful and should do a lot of the "leg work" for you.

3. Use your agent's MLS books. MLS stands for multilisting service; it is a group of brokers who have agreed to share information about their properties with each other. The properties are listed in books, which allow buyers to examine many houses from many brokers. Commissions are split between the listing broker and the agent who makes the sale. Your agent's books will save you hours, if not days, of property research. Your agent can also show you pricing for comparable properties in the area, which can save you from paying over the market value.

4. Allow your agent to screen your selections. Agents know the neighborhoods, property values, and trends in the market.

> Be honest about your finances.

That knowledge can save you an amazing amount of looking-around time. Tell your agent what you want and how much you can afford, and let him or her do all the "weeding out" for you. Help your agent during the process. After looking at each selection, express what you liked or didn't like about it.

5. Ask for community and neighborhood news. It's part of an agent's job to know what's happening in the area. Also, many community organizations leave their flyers and brochures at real-estate offices. Get all that apply to your selected area and study them carefully. Then ask more in-depth questions the next time you meet with your agent. This information is also a great resource of contacts for people who want to get involved in their new neighborhood.

6. Let your agent smooth out the bumps in the road. Buying a property can be a nerve-wracking experience, especially for someone new to the business. Your agent will have been through the process numerous times and should know all the ropes. Don't be shy about asking for reassurance. It won't be the first time he or she has heard the request. Let your agent put all that experience at your service.

7. Use your agent as a resource for other goods and services. Agents are a great source for finding legal services, home maintenance and repair experts, gardeners, swimming pool construction companies, suppliers of all types of home and garden equipment and materials, insurance agents, mortgage brokers, and so on.

8. Be loyal. Once you have done your research and made sure you have chosen the right agent working in the right company, work exclusively with that agent. (The exception would be if you're looking at properties in more than one area.) Let your agent do the legwork for you, and never try to go behind his or her back. It's just not worth it. You expect and deserve loyalty from your agent. Loyalty is a peculiar trait. To receive it, you have to give it away.

9. Do not sign a contract with a broker. Most agents or brokers represent the seller. They're paid their commission from the money paid for the property. A buyer's broker is an entirely different matter. You, the buyer, will be paying a fee for the

> Use your agent as a resource for other goods and services.

agent's services. Fees can vary from community to community. If for some reason you must sign a contract, put severe limits on its duration. Thirty days is acceptable; do not sign for longer than two months. Speaking of fees, pay for the agent's services only after those services have been performed.

Elements of a Contract

A contract is an agreement among competent parties to do or to refrain from doing certain things that are under consideration between the two parties. For example, buyer Smith contracts with seller Jones to purchase his property for a specific amount of money. Jones may be required by the contract to certain specifications, such as repairing a leaky roof or fixing a broken water line. The contract is put into writing and signed by all parties. For a real-estate contract to be valid, it must contain the following elements:

> A contract is an agreement among competent parties to do or to refrain from doing certain things that are under consideration between the two parties.

The offer. The seller cannot agree to a price and terms until they are presented by the prospective buyer. This is usually a very simple statement of how much the buyer is willing to pay for the property. It will probably be stated in a numbered subsection of the document and will read something like the following: "The purchase price is TWO HUNDRED THOUSAND DOLLARS AND NO CENTS ($200,000.00) payable as follows . . ." The "as follows" would state whether the amount is to be paid in one or multiple installments and the amount of those installments.

Acceptance. There can't be an agreement between two or more individuals or organizations until all parties accept the terms of that agreement. Signing on the dotted line signals that agreement.

Competent parties. All parties signing the document must be legally competent to do so. For example, a mentally incompetent person cannot sign the contract. However, a legally authorized representative may be able to sign contracts for such a person.

Consideration. This is anything of value that is offered to encourage someone to enter into a contract. Consideration can be money, but it can also be virtually anything else. Land, buildings, valuables such as jewelry or stamp collections, even personal services provided to the other party may be used as consideration. This is where your thinking and negotiating skills really come into play. If you lack money to close the deal, think about something else the other party wants or needs. If you can supply it, that might just be the impetus needed to get things back on track.

Legal purpose. Obviously, the transaction should be conducted in the furtherance of legitimate business or personal activities. Buying a building to set up an illegal drug manufacturing lab or to fence stolen goods isn't a legal purpose.

Written documentation. That's the contract and any supporting documentation you may need to consummate the deal. Always operate under the assumption that if it isn't written down, it isn't real. Too many "solid" or "handshake" deals have been smashed to bits because one of the parties received a better offer at the last minute.

A description of the property. This is a legal description, not a general one. "Old man Jamison's place out on Route Five" won't do. The description will read something like this:

> The South Half of the Southeast quarter of Section Four (4); the Northwest quarter of the Southwest Quarter of Section Three (3); the South Half of the Southwest quarter of Section Four (4); the North half of Section Twelve (12) . . . all in Township Thirty (30) North, of Range Eight (8) West 5th P.M. in Iowa containing 40 acres, more or less. Including all appurtenant easements inuring to the benefit of the above land as the dominant tenement and subject to all easements to which the above land is the servient tenement.

That's a lot of verbiage, but it's necessary to make absolutely sure that what's being sold is exactly what's being bought.

Signatures of the principals (or their attorneys-in-fact). Again, the contract isn't real until all parties sign the document in the proper spaces.

If you lack money to close the deal, think about something else the other party wants or needs.

Other items in the contract might include a prorated payment of taxes on the property, earnest money, provision for title insurance, language that the property is free and clear of all encumbrances not noted within the contract, any affidavits to be furnished by the seller, the right to inspect the property for hazardous waste or related concerns, and any other matter deemed appropriate by the parties involved.

How to Negotiate

Don't be intimidated by the thought of negotiating for property. Once you develop the skill, it's a lot of fun. The first important step is to tie up the property with a contract. Every contract should include two key clauses. You should have sufficient time to inspect the property, and you should also get a second period of time for approval of the contract by your attorney.

There Is No "Right" Price

Buying and selling real estate isn't like retail. You don't, and you shouldn't, walk into the real estate "store," look down the shelves, select your product, and pay the cashier the amount on the sticker. Real estate isn't really like buying a car either. Certainly, you negotiate with your car salesperson, but the car you buy in California is identical to the model on sale in Connecticut. *No two buildings are ever alike.*

Not only is every building unique in reality, they are also considered unique in law. That's why there's a contractual term called "specific performance." It is used when a seller denies a contract after acceptance. It is an enforceable clause that you will find in most real-estate contracts. It obligates the seller to deliver the contracted property because of its uniqueness.

Once you enter the real-estate profession, you enter the age-old world of barter. You give me this for that. Learn this early: Money isn't everything. Many times you can reduce your cash outlay by bartering something you have for something the seller wants—so make sure you know what "they" really want. There are many motivations other than money, and you can often negotiate a more favorable deal if you keep this point in mind.

Again, different governments have different rules and regulations. For example, the State of Illinois requires that attorneys read and review contracts. In California, title companies handle closings; attorneys rarely get involved.

You must obtain disclosure reports on the property. This is a requirement everywhere. Disclosure reports list items that may or may not affect your maintenance and repair requirements to the property being purchased.

Hire an Inspector

You want to make doubly sure that the great deal you just concluded really is a great deal and that it requires the services of a professional inspector. You don't want a deal-breaker who will notice every tiny flaw and imperfection. You don't want to use the inspection report to browbeat the seller into a better deal, either. It's just important to get an honest and objective opinion of the condition of the property. This is standard operating procedure.

Meet the inspector ahead of time to discuss fees, which usually run in the $200–$300 range. Think of these fees as an insurance payment, money well spent even if you don't buy the property. A couple of hundred dollars invested up front can save you thousands or tens of thousands of dollars down the road.

Continue this process throughout your career, even after you become really knowledgeable about the business, because even experienced pros can make mistakes. Remember the old saying, "A lawyer who hires himself has a fool for a client." A few years ago, Mark bought a really nice house without really looking at it. Later he discovered that the property was electrically heated, the most expensive way to heat a building. His heating bills ran to over $1,000 per month, a figure not included in his original estimates. Later, he converted the property to more efficient gas heat, but at a cost of several thousand dollars.

You'll only know what you're really buying after a complete inspection. It's one way of learning whether you need to renegotiate the purchase price.

The Rule of Thumb for Pricing

The rule of thumb is that there is no rule of thumb. Every property is different, and common sense can be a great help in pricing. If a property is being offered at a reasonable $400,000, common sense tells you not to offer an unreasonable $200,000. There are some people who believe in starting the negotiations by offering half of the stated purchase price. That's someone trying to play the win/lose game. You shouldn't try to conduct your business that way.

Some folks begin by offering 10 to 15 percent below the stated price. That's okay, but don't consider the figure a rule of thumb applicable in all situations. *Make a respectable offer that makes good economic sense for all parties.* Generally, you'll receive a counteroffer. That's all part of the negotiating process. If a counteroffer doesn't come in, there's nothing to stop you from going back with a different offer yourself.

Financing Options

Once the property has been inspected, a contract price is agreed upon, and your attorney has given a green light to the project, it's time for the next step. You need to come up with the money.

If you think you can buy property with no money down, it's time to readjust your thinking. Realistically, you will be required by the lender to provide 20–25 percent of the purchase price as a down payment. If the property is residential, and you plan on living in it, financing may be available in the 5–10 percent range. Seller financing is sometimes available, too.

If you look at the statistics from 1940 to the present, you will find that, with the exception of the years 1978–1983, interest rates have always been in the 7–10 percent range. If you figure out the cost of money, that's not a bad range. Better than that, for most of those years the rates remained at the bottom of that range.

Owner financing can look very attractive, especially when interest rates are high or you can't borrow money from traditional sources. But using the seller as your bank can be an invitation to trouble. If you miss a payment, the seller can foreclose, and some of them just can't wait to do just that. Dealing with people instead of institutions means you have to work with the whims of an individual's personality. Often those whims can be unpleasant.

Owner financing can make for a long interruption in your plans. For example, a building can have been sold many times. All those ownership claims and obligations must be cleared up before you can legally make the purchase. Getting the paperwork and clear title can be a lot more tedious from individuals compared to the full staff and computerized operations of a lending institution.

Check out the Sunday newspaper's real-estate section for the current residential interest rates. If you want rates on commercial property, just call a local lending institution and ask. Also get the down payment or equity payment. A lot of the information you need is readily available and easy to acquire.

It's always a good idea to shop around for the lowest rates and the best deal, but in general you will find most lending institutions offer pretty much the same deal. They'll require you to put down

Lending Is Local

The first time Mark approached a bank about getting a mortgage, the vice president of lending asked him about the location of the property. Mark pointed out the window to the nearby building he wanted to purchase. The banker smiled and said, "If I can see the building from here, I'll lend on it."

Your chances of getting financing are generally much better with local institutions. *Go to the lending institution nearest the property you want first.* Many local banks have an obligation to invest in their communities under the Community Reinvestment Act. CRA lending is a win/win situation. The buyer gets his or her financing, and the bank meets its obligation to the government.

20–25 percent of the purchase price and will offer whatever the current rate may be.

Beware of Prepayment Penalties

Banks earn money from the interest charged on the amount of your loan. When you pay off the loan before it is due, they lose that interest. Therefore, the lending institution charges a penalty for early payment. Before signing any agreement, consult with your attorney, a banker you trust, or your real-estate broker or agent. Get the facts and know the penalties.

"Never put all your eggs in one basket" is a good rule, especially when dealing with lending institutions. Still, you have to start with one egg. Find a good bank and banker and establish a solid relationship. Stay with that institution for your first transactions. Only then should you start expanding to other institutions and then

Put Funds in Escrow

Escrow is an agreement between two or more parties that certain monies, legal instruments, or property be placed with a third party for safekeeping while a property transaction is taking place. The funds remain in escrow until the successful conclusion of a specified act or condition, such as closing of a sale. For example, the deed and earnest money in a real-estate transaction could be placed in escrow until a specified clause in the contract is enacted. The escrowed funds are generally placed in the hands of an escrow agent, someone who is engaged in the business of receiving escrows for deposit or delivery. Escrow accounts are sometimes referred to as "trust accounts" (the meaning is the same).

This is how the concept of escrow works. The buyer places his or her funds with the escrow agent. At the same time, the seller places the deed in possession of the same agent. Once all the appropriate conditions are met, the agent transfers the money to the seller and the deed to the new owner. Often the title company involved is chosen to act as the escrow agent.

As a landlord, you should consider keeping a separate savings account for your refundable deposits as an escrow account. The deposits, although in your possession, are still the property of your tenants. Having a separate account will assure you that the funds will be available when it's time for their return.

> Good real-estate transactions build in an appropriate amount of time for proper research and verification.

still concentrate on building and maintaining firm relationships with all your lenders.

The Worst Kind of Financing

The worst kind of financing is the kind that's "too good to be true." Owner financing usually falls into this category. So does borrowing from friends and family.

Listen to that little voice inside your head. Trust your own instincts. Don't violate your conscience. Good real-estate transactions build in an appropriate amount of time for proper research and verification. If that time isn't part of the deal, there's a reason, and you probably won't like it. Unfortunately, you won't know until it's too late. Like the basketball coach says, "Wait for the good shots." Take your time. Invest your time. And make your fortune.

For more information on this topic, visit our Web site at www.businesstown.com

Chapter 8

Know How to Sell Real Estate

n old Hungarian proverb states, "A bashful beggar has an empty purse." Developing the art of selling is an essential element in your development as a real-estate professional. Of course, to succeed you must have creativity, education, experience, and ambition. But without the ability to sell your properties, your ideas, and—most importantly—yourself, you cannot reach the heights that would otherwise be open to you. Boxer/entrepreneur George Foreman recognized this fact when he said, "I learned something very early in life. If you sell, you'll never starve. In any other profession, you can find yourself out on the street saying, 'They don't want me anymore.' But if you can sell, you will never go hungry."

The Selling Process

In most cases, the process of selling property is basic:

- The buyer takes a look and learns what's really for sale.
- A contract is drawn up, amended, and agreed upon.
- A down payment is made, usually to be increased to 10 percent of the purchase price.
- Attorneys review the agreements.
- Inspections take place.
- Financing is arranged.
- A closing date is set, usually 45, 60, or 75 days after the contract is signed.
- The property officially changes hands and everyone walks away a winner.

Years ago, Mark knew a real-estate broker who tried everything other than the conventional, tried-and-proven way to earn a living. He would try to buy with no money down. He tried dealing with people who wanted to buy property, but who just didn't have the money to do so. He wasted tremendous amounts of time trying to create transactions that experienced people in the business knew would never work.

One morning he and Mark had breakfast together and the poor man poured out his troubles. Mark wrote something on the back of a business card and handed it over. He said, "Every time you have someone call you about acquiring one of your properties, pull out this card and read that person these seven words." The back of the card read: "Give me a contract and a check."

The man actually turned around his business using this simple technique. Regardless of your customer's excitement or his or her promises, either you have a contract and a check, or you have nothing at all.

Master the art of sales and not only will you avoid hunger, you'll feast on the profits of your own success. If you're new to sales, this chapter includes a few tips on the art. First, let's take a close look at the practical side of selling real estate.

The Mechanics of the Process

Selling real estate begins with one simple act: marketing. When you determine that the time is right to sell your property, you have to get that information out to the marketplace. Buyers can't buy until they know you're selling. Always remember, this is a competitive business, and you can't afford the luxury of sitting on your property and waiting for the offers to come in. Basically, you have to go out there and get them. If you don't make the effort, other, more aggressive real-estate professionals certainly will.

> Buyers can't buy until they know you're selling.

Tools of the Trade

You have numerous marketing tools at your disposal. The effectiveness of any given one will vary according to many factors: availability in your market, the audience of advertising media, your marketing budget, the local economy, and your competition. You can choose from the following marketing tools:

- Signs on the property.
- Newspaper ads.
- Radio and television ads.
- Other print advertising.
- Direct mail.
- A local real-estate broker.
- An MLS (Multiple Listing Service) listing.
- Your own "golden voice."

Stake out Your Signs

Advertising and public relations are covered in greater detail in Chapter 24, but it wouldn't hurt to stress one very important item here. Whether your property is residential or commercial, signs on location are extremely important. Some owners of apartment buildings or properties are reluctant to put up signs. They fear the tenants will get nervous. Those on a month-to-month lease might decide to pick up and go early, leaving the landlord without that rental income. Some are concerned that their tenants will become resentful and might decide to take out that hostility on the owner. Others fear the tenants might even cause a problem or two.

There are plusses and minuses to any decision. Basically, if you don't put out a sign, you deprive yourself of your best marketing tool. That sign represents a one-time, inexpensive marketing effort that will work for you twenty-four hours a day, seven days a week. No other advertising vehicle can make that claim. Remember, just as you're out there all the time looking for properties, so are other real-estate people. Some of those people live right in the neighborhood, and they may start your phone ringing even before you can begin other marketing efforts.

> If you don't put out a sign, you deprive yourself of your best marketing tool.

Your Marketing Plan

To achieve your ultimate goal, getting the highest possible price for your property, it is important to create an aggressive marketing plan. Don't be intimidated if you've never developed a marketing plan. Selling a property isn't the same as selling Ford, Chevrolet, or Nissan to international markets. You don't need a 300-page document full of demographics, psychographics, marketing jargon, charts, and graphs. All you have to do is answer a few basic questions.

1. What do I have to sell?
2. Who can afford to buy it?
3. Where are those people?
4. How can I reach them with my message?
5. How much can I afford to invest in marketing, and what are the best tools of the trade to use?
6. What is my schedule to implement this program?

Please learn this early. It is important to constantly evaluate the effectiveness of your marketing tools. Which tools performed well, and which performed poorly? Did the sign bring in more calls than the newspaper ad? Did you get a better response from the Realtor community or the open house? It's important to evaluate marketing efforts over time. Study which ads work in which medium and why. Get the big picture of what works best for you and then apply what you have learned.

Why "Fizzbo" Fizzes

Often a property owner believes he or she will make more money by eliminating the services of a real-estate professional. That's where all of those "For Sale by Owner" signs come from. In the industry they are referred to as FSBOs (pronounced "fizzbos"). This book recommends that you always work with the best professionals in the business. That applies to your doctor, your financial advisor, your plumber, and it should certainly apply when it comes to selling real estate.

The reason that some sellers take the "fizzbo" route is simple: They hope to make more money on their own. That can happen, but it is an extremely rare event. Here's an interesting fact. When real-estate brokers see a FSBO sign, they immediately start calling the number on the sign to offer their services. The owner, who probably said he didn't want to deal with Realtors, still finds himself dealing with them. Why? If "fizzbo" works so well, those agents wouldn't waste their time on useless calls, would they? They call because they know sooner or later, "fizzbo" will fizzle out and the owner will realize his or her need for professional help.

The problem with FSBO efforts is basic. The owner lacks the skills to effectively sell a property and the in-depth knowledge of the market necessary to get the best price in the shortest amount of time. Wouldn't you agree those are two mighty big obstacles?

Real-estate professionals earn their commissions by getting you the best price in the shortest possible time. This isn't to say that if you feel confident in your abilities you shouldn't give it a try. As noted, sometimes it works. But talk to any Realtor, and they will tell you of numerous clients who have come to them after an unsuccessful attempt at FSBO. Better yet, look for FSBO signs in your community. When a Realtor's logo finally appears on them, drop in and ask why the owner made the change.

FSBO Is Not Necessarily Cost-Effective

Someone going the "fizzbo" route usually neglects to calculate just how much going it alone costs in real time and real dollars. For example, calculate how much your time is worth per hour. Now, supposing you're going FSBO. How many hours will you have to invest having signs printed, putting them up, writing and placing advertisements, periodically changing those ads, writing and printing brochures, answering telephone inquiries, conducting walk-throughs, negotiating, filling out documents, and writing and haggling over a contract? Then factor in the hours wasted just waiting on those phone calls that never come or the no-shows for your walk-throughs. Suddenly that real-estate commission you're trying to save doesn't seem so outrageous after all.

Hire an Attorney

Part of the mechanics of selling is having your attorney, the one who helped you make the purchase, help you review the contracts when you're ready to sell. The best way to sell property is "as is." Once you get the money and the purchaser has inspected the property and taken possession, you have no further responsibility in the transaction. "I owned it. You bought it. I'm outta here."

In most states you will be required to provide a disclosure form, which may deal with such matters as the physical condition of the property and environmental concerns. For example, it's only fair to let the buyer know the property has a leaky roof or a basement that tends to flood, or if it is located over an abandoned nuclear waste dump. A buyer has a clear right to be informed of any substantial condition that could have a detrimental effect upon the property being purchased. The seller has a legal obligation to disclose such matters. Of course, laws, regulations, and limitations can vary depending upon your area, but it's a good idea to forgo any thoughts of letting a condition "slip by" and to disclose any questionable areas. Failure to do so could come back to haunt you later on.

And speaking of haunting, you may be obligated to inform a potential buyer of any ghosts, ghostly activities, poltergeists, or other psychic phenomena relating to the property. Don't laugh. Whether or not you believe in ghosts, in some communities you are legally required to inform the buyer that the local Casper might show up and say "boo."

Never try to hide a problem. It's illegal, it's wrong, and it will irreparably tarnish your professional reputation. It's far better to disclose any problems up front and show that they were repaired, and that the value of the property has therefore been enhanced. There's always some young lawyer out there looking to make a reputation by suing the pants off some "unscrupulous landlord." This can happen even if you've been frank, open, and honest with the buyer, so why take additional risks by hiding the truth? Besides, anyone who knowingly fails to disclose a material defect *is* unscrupulous and deserves to meet that young lawyer.

> In most states you will be required to provide a disclosure form, which may deal with such matters as the physical condition of the property and environmental concerns.

Find a Real-Estate Lawyer

Make sure the lawyer who handles your real estate is an attorney trained in real-estate law. You'll probably never know what little traps are waiting to spring at you in your state, county, or municipality's set of rules and regulations. For instance, there is a little-known law in Illinois that affects anyone buying property. If the prior owner owes the state any taxes, even if there's no lien on the property being sold, the Illinois Department of Revenue can get a lien on the property. This can happen even after the property has been transferred to a second owner. You still may be responsible for paying taxes owed by the previous owner even if those taxes are due from another business or his or her own income tax. A smart property manager always gets an Illinois Department of Revenue Letter (IDOR) to avoid this problem. It's saved people thousands and tens of thousands of dollars in paying taxes for other people.

What little nightmares are waiting in your community? Local laws vary from state to state and community to community. Whatever you think you might save in legal fees could be eaten up in liability costs down the road. It's far wiser to invest money up front than to unnecessarily pay penalties later on. For more details on how to hire a real-estate lawyer, refer to Chapter 16. To examine some legal issues that you might encounter in the real-estate industry, also make sure to read Chapter 21.

> Local laws vary from state to state and community to community.

Kick out the Tire Kicker

You find "tire kickers" in every business. They are the fellows with "new car fever" who go around to all the dealerships kicking the tires but never actually buying anything. Tire kickers exist in real estate too. These people will devour your time and sap your energy and for no good purpose at all. It's one thing to wear yourself out in pitching, negotiating, and concluding a good deal, but it's another thing altogether to exhaust yourself only to see your so-called prospect walk away. You have to develop an eye to determine a genuine prospect from a tire kicker.

Developing that eye takes experience, but there is a technique that provides a short cut, and it is a technique you will find useful as long as you are in the business. If you want to determine a customer's real intentions, *ask for a contract and a check*. If the customer offers anything else, you know you've got a tire kicker on your hands. Be polite and professional—someday that person may actually be a legitimate customer and there's no need to burn bridges. In the meantime, however, concentrate your efforts on real prospects. Just as you need to be a confident seller, you need to have a confident buyer, not someone out just to kick a few tires.

Be Wary of Holding Out

Many prospective buyers will in fact follow through and make you an offer for your property. If the offer's a good one, take it. Although you might be tempted to wait for ever-bigger offers, think of what you are losing while your property remains unsold—time, Realtor and attorney fees, and cash, which could be earning interest for you.

As this book is being written, Mark is in the process of closing a sales transaction for the bankruptcy court representing what's commonly known as a debtor in possession. In a nutshell, a husband and wife made some bad business decisions and were forced to declare bankruptcy.

This couple owned a home in a prominent area of Chicago's southwest suburbs, an area where home prices average between one and three million dollars. Their home was valued at $1.3 million, listed with a local Realtor at $2.1 million, and was later reduced to $1.8 million. No one made a serious offer on such an overpriced property. Perhaps the couple was holding out for that pie-in-the-sky price in the hopes of getting some extra money to pay off additional creditors. Anyway, they continued to hold out.

Mark was brought in. He conducted a thorough comparable cost analysis and recommended listing the home at $1.3 million, a reasonable and profitable figure. The couple insisted on a $1.5 million price. As soon as the new listing was posted, a Realtor called up with an offer of $1.1 million. It turns out that the offer was from a

> If the offer's a good one, take it. Although you might be tempted to wait for ever-bigger offers, think of what you are losing while your property remains unsold.

buyer who had made a previous offer when the home was at a higher price. What happened?

Previously, the buyer offered $1.75 million for the property, but then discovered some problems with the sewer system and lowered the offer to $1.5 million. Considering the problem with the sewer system, that wasn't an unreasonable change. The couple still turned it down. All of this took place some six to nine months before Mark was called in.

The property was eventually sold for $1.3 million. The moral of the story is obvious. This couple holding out for a higher price had an offer at one time for $1.5 million, but eventually ended up settling on $1.3 million. Not only did they lose the $200,000, they could have used that money to pay off debts that continued to accumulate while the property remained unsold. Holding out also cost them additional attorneys fees and other related costs. Like one of those old Wild West highway stickups, they were robbed. Only in this case the victims were also the perpetrators of their own misfortune.

Don't let this story happen to you. Every seller believes he or she could have gotten more, and every buyer thinks he or she could have acquired the property for less. That's fine, but there is no point thinking too much about it. Whatever the amount you think you lost won't mean much in terms of the rest of your life. Think about making a lot of good profit over the long run, rather than making a killing on one deal. Be a good seller and move on to the next deal that will make you good money.

Tax Considerations

Remember, governments love to govern, and every once in a while they manage to get things right. That's even true of the U.S. government. Owning real estate is the only way the federal bureaucracy allows you to defer capital gains. A capital gain is the gain on a capital asset. For example, if Jill purchases land for $10,000 as an investment and then later sells it to Joe for $15,000, she's made a $5,000 profit. This profit is reported as a long-term capital gain on her income taxes. As a landlord and property manager, you are a

> Whatever the amount you think you lost won't mean much in terms of the rest of your life.

member of an exclusive club and can benefit from a wonderful piece of legislation.

Welcome to 1031 Exchange

That's not an address in New Orleans. It's an opportunity, and it refers to Section 1031 of the Internal Revenue Code. Basically, here's how it works. When you sell a property, instead of paying taxes on your profit, you place it in the care of a third party while you find a replacement property to buy. You then buy the replacement property without ever having to pay taxes on the profit from the original sale. Let's break it down.

The process is really quite simple. Once you sell your property, you pay off your expenses, including your mortgage, title costs, attorney's fees, brokerage fees, and other expenses. Then, instead of taking your profits, you place them in an account with a registered exchange company, often a local title company or bank (they're not hard to find). All the proceeds are held in escrow. You can't get at them as long as you're buying property under 1031.

You then have forty-five days from the date of closing to find a replacement property. This is another reason why it's good to be looking for opportunities all the time. In many cases you could already have your replacement property selected. You can have up to three potential replacement properties, but you must close on one of them within the next six months.

Some people wait until the last moment or have trouble finding appropriate replacement property. During the past few years, companies have emerged to fill that need. The way this works is quite simple too. Knowing that you are going to sell property A, you start looking for replacement properties. You find properties A, B, and C, which meet all your needs, and you select property C. The problem is, you haven't sold A, so you don't have the money to buy C. Someone else could slip in and "steal" your property.

Instead of losing out on C, you contact a replacement property exchange corporation, which will buy it for you. They will hold the title, essentially placing it in inventory until you have the available funds to buy it yourself. Each replacement exchange corporation

> Once you sell your property, you pay off your expenses, including your mortgage, title costs, attorney's fees, brokerage fees, and other expenses.

operates under its own rules and regulations. Each charges its own fees and has its own requirements for equity commitments. Sure, the service is costly, but if you consider what you will be saving by not paying capital gains taxes, you'll be delighted to write that check. To find one of these organizations, just ask your local title company.

The Art of Sales

Everybody is a salesperson. Even if you don't make a living in sales, you still have to sell. You have to sell your boss on the benefits of giving you that raise, promotion, or new challenge. You have to sell your church, civic club, or neighborhood group on your brilliant idea to help the community. You have to sell your spouse on vacationing out west or back east instead of going down south this year.

People sell a lot more than they think, so they should get good at it. Selling is an important part of the real-estate professional's life, and it's not limited to when he or she is selling property. As a landlord, you have to sell a prospective tenant that your apartment is superior to the half-dozen others in the neighborhood. You have to sell the city council on not raising property taxes (again!) on your type of property. You have to sell your maintenance man on giving up the day off you promised when that meteor breaks through the earth's atmosphere and plummets down to land on your roof. Sales and selling are now part of your life, and it's your responsibility to learn how to do it right.

Getting Started

Just in case someone walks in your door within the next fifteen minutes or so and asks you to sell some property, here are a few basic selling techniques you might find useful:

Ask questions. One of the greatest mistakes salespeople make is to start selling before they discover what the customer wants to buy. You may need to "push" your apartment building, but if the buyer is seeking a place to locate a small printing company, you're missing a very important boat.

> **Get Involved in Real-Estate Politics**
>
> This is largely due to the efforts, time, and money of the national real-estate community. One politically active element of the real-estate community is the Realtors Political Action Committee (RPAC).
>
> RPAC is "in the trenches" every day fighting to help maintain the rights of landlords, property managers, and other real-estate professionals throughout the country. Consider making a donation or, better still, regular donations to this invaluable organization. You will see a real return of your money over the long term through additional tax breaks and other important benefits.

Questioning is an art in itself. It's shouldn't be a high-speed interrogation, but a pleasant drawing out, a process by which you discover your customer's real needs. Often, the customer's real intent isn't clear right away. Only careful questioning can shed light on the potential buyer's real needs and the motivation behind them.

Listen. Really listen, not just nodding your head up and down with a big smile on your face. People will provide you with amazing, valuable information—if you will only let them—so after you ask your questions, listen to the responses. The days of the fast-talking, high-pressure salesperson are long gone. The occasional ones you run into these days are merely kept around for comic relief.

Establish and build rapport. You may not become best buddies with someone, but you can become a trustworthy person to someone in a remarkably short period of time. Empathy is important. Show that you are actually hearing what they are saying. Prove that you sincerely believe it's your job to help solve their problem—because it is.

Qualify. Make sure the person you are selling to can really buy. Qualify every step of the sales process from the first hello right up until someone signs on the dotted line. Take that fellow looking for a location for a print shop. Suppose he's someone the owner is sending around town to gather information on various locations. He can't say "yes" to your sales presentation because he doesn't have the authority. That's valuable information; knowing that, you can accomplish two things. One, you can avoid wasting time making a presentation to someone who can't buy. Two, you can start finding ways to meet the owner so you can show him or her why yours is the best location in town for a print shop.

Make your presentation. Explain why your location is the best choice according to the specific needs of the prospective buyer. It's already wired for heavy equipment, so there's no extra cost rewiring for those printing presses. The neighborhood is loaded with small businesses, so there's a good customer base waiting to be served. The location is near the

Make sure the person you are selling to can really buy.

interstate, so the delivery trucks have immediate access to a large area and can make excellent time.

Handle objections. They always come up, but many of them aren't really objections at all. A simple "I'll address that a bit later in my presentation if you don't mind" will eliminate a lot of them. Handling objections is an important skill. Never lie, distort, or "tap dance" around a serious question. You can put something in the best possible light, but don't cover it up. Once you get the hang of it, you'll discover that most so-called objections are really just requests for additional information.

Close the sale. Ask for the contract and the check. Get serious and get down to business. A lot of people fear closing, but there's really nothing to it, provided you've properly handled all the preceding steps. In many cases the parties slide right into a close without any effort at all. It can be just that easy and just that natural.

Stay in touch. You're always on the lookout for new opportunities. The people you sell, the people from whom you buy, and the people you meet in the normal course of the day can be your eyes and ears. A network can cover a lot of ground a lot faster than an individual.

> A network can cover a lot of ground faster than an individual.

One last bit of advice on sales: Many people are needlessly intimidated by the selling process. If you're in that category, consider a statement made by F. W. Woolworth, who quipped: "I am the world's worst salesman; therefore, I must make it easy for people to buy." Surely, you can do that, can't you?

For more information on this topic, visit our Web site at www.businesstown.com

PART III

The Ins and Outs of Managing Property

Topics covered in this part:

- **What are your real-estate options?**
- **How to be aware of special opportunities that may come your way.**
- **What you need to know to have a good relationship with your tenants.**

Chapter 9

Managing Residential Property

P eople need a place to live. No matter in what part of the world, no matter what the conditions, no matter what shape the economy may be in, everybody needs a home. Economies go boom and bust and boom again. People move from high-income homes to hovels and back. One thing remains constant, however: the search for a roof and indoor plumbing. Real estate is a noble profession, one that provides a basic human need.

Start Small

Because people are always in need of a place to live, there is always a need for residential property. Even in the worst economic downturn, people will be searching for single or multifamily dwellings. Not only do you have the privilege of helping them, you get to make money while doing it.

For most folks starting out in the business, the acquisition of a single-family dwelling is the first step. Single-family dwellings can come in the form of a traditional house, a condominium apartment, or a town house. A single-family dwelling is probably the most affordable investment for most first-timers.

It's also the most manageable property, especially for people who have little or no experience in property management. One stopped-up toilet in the little house down the street is a lot easier to handle than a gushing flood from the third floor. A small start also gives you a chance to learn how to deal with people one-on-one rather than one-on-thirty. It's a good way to develop the people skills you need to succeed in property management.

If you invest in a single-family dwelling, you have to know that the biggest financial risk involved in this undertaking is having the property become vacant. Although the rent checks will stop coming, you still have to pay for all the expenses of owning the property. Somebody has to pay the mortgage and the taxes and the upkeep. Pipes burst, concrete cracks, boards warp, and the weather causes damage even when there are no tenants around. Can you carry the financial responsibility if and when your tenant moves out? If so, for how long? All of this should be factored into your business plan.

> If you invest in a single-family dwelling, you have to know that the biggest financial risk involved in this undertaking is having the property become vacant.

The strain of a lost tenant isn't as great with a multifamily unit. Rents can be structured so that one or more cover the expenses of maintaining the building, while others can be considered profit. That way, if someone moves out, you're at least making your monthly expenses and not going into the hole. Ideally, you'll work into a situation where even if you lose several tenants, your basic expenses will still be covered by rent payments from the others.

The Ups and Downs of Residential Ownership

On the positive side, owning and renting a single-family dwelling can earn you a lot of money. Your rent payments should not only pay your costs of ownership and upkeep but should also provide cash flow along the way. How significant the cash flow is depends on many factors, such as competition and demand of the local real-estate market.

However, your profit won't be as high as it would be if you were to purchase and rent out an apartment complex. With a single-family dwelling, you can't spread your costs over multiple tenants (and rent payments) the way you can as the owner of an apartment building.

The key to success is a very careful, honest evaluation of the risks versus the rewards. Will the rents cover your mortgage payments, maintenance-repair personnel, equipment and supplies for upkeep, taxes, permits, and so on? Examine the rent control situation (described in the following section), and look into your zoning ordinances. For example, find out if it's possible to make improvements on the dwelling that would allow you to increase the amount of rent.

> Find out if it's possible to make improvements on the dwelling that would allow you to increase the amount of rent.

Rent Control

Rent control is a perfect example of the law of unintended consequences in action. Rent control is a law governing the rate that may be charged for space, such as an apartment. Cities in New York, California, New Jersey, and Maryland as well as Washington, D.C.,

Regulating Residential Property

Residential property owners are governed by numerous laws and ordinances that don't apply to industrial and commercial landlords. The rights of an individual or family to the quiet enjoyment of a home are respected coast-to-coast. Provided there is balance and both landlord and renter are equally protected, this is a good situation. However, sometimes the scales are tipped, usually in favor of the tenants.

have adopted this policy. This type of regulation sounds good in principle. The cap on rent assures renters a "fair shake" while at the same time assuring landlords of a steady income. In practice, however, rent control hasn't worked out as well as expected.

Rent control began after World War II as an effort to put a stop to rapidly inflating rents. However, rent control has led to one serious problem–deferred maintenance. Landlords put off, or completely neglect, necessary maintenance for the simple reason that they cannot afford the expense. Maintenance and repair cost more than the rents provide. In the end, landlords suffer because their revenues are low and tenants suffer leaky roofs, stopped-up pipes, poor heating, and weakening infrastructures.

For proof all you need to do is compare residential rental property in New York against similar property in Chicago where there is no rent control. In Manhattan many older buildings show undeniable signs of deferred maintenance. These buildings, and many like them in other rent-controlled communities, will continue to deteriorate due to lack of care, maintenance, and repair. Deferred maintenance is not unheard of in Chicago, but it is the exception and not the rule. Landlords can afford to keep their residential buildings in good shape because, well, they can afford it. The income from rent allows them to keep their properties in good repair.

Become thoroughly familiar with your community's position on rent control. You certainly may be much better off owning residential property in an area without rent control than an area with it, especially if you really want to take good care of your tenants and make a profit as well.

Lease Compliance

Laws and tenant bills of rights have been created to protect both sides of the equation but especially the tenants. This need not be a win/lose situation for the landlord. Your leases must be in full compliance with all applicable laws, rules, and regulations. For example, a landlord must pay interest on a security deposit. Now, you can write a clause into your lease clearly stating you don't have to pay this interest, *but that clause would be illegal even if the tenant willingly signed it.* The laws just don't work that way and you'd be putting yourself at risk of heavy penalties. The law takes a dim view of playing fast and loose with the rules.

Become thoroughly familiar with all the applicable local, state, and federal laws, and stay current on them. You'll avoid a lot of potential problems by knowing your obligations and fulfilling them as required. Your leases should be reviewed by an attorney who is competent in the arena of real estate and who knows the laws applicable to your specific community. Make doubly certain that you are in full compliance with all codes, that you do not discriminate, and that you fully inform all tenants of their rights. Again, happy tenants cause far fewer problems. Helping protect tenant rights is one sure way of keeping your tenants happy.

Explain Your Lease

Tenants have rights even if they are unaware of them and even if they don't give a darn about them. For example, if your property was painted before 1978, you have to inform your tenant of the possibility that lead-based paint may have been used. Because lead paint has been tied to some health-related concerns, especially with children, there are special rules and regulations that apply to such properties. These regulations vary from state to state and from community to community; it is your responsibility to know and live by the ones applicable to your properties.

> It is unlikely that many tenants actually read and fully understand the leases they sign.

Sometimes you even have to take responsibility for people who are too lazy to accept it for themselves. It is unlikely that many tenants actually read and fully understand the leases they sign. It is important that you as the landlord invest the time to go over the lease completely. Make sure they understand the document they are signing.

Most of us take it for granted that when someone signs a document, he or she intends to live up to their word. It doesn't always work out that way. Things change. Times change. People change. Cover the lease in detail. For example, be sure to explain the penalty for late payment of rent. Make sure they understand. The

Beware the
Tenant-Handyman

It's just not a good idea to leave
maintenance and repair to a tenant, even if he or she is a true
handyman. Now and then you
may come across a truly responsible person with handyman
abilities, but that's rare. Entrust
them with those responsibilities
only if you know them as completely trustworthy individuals
who have established a good
track record with you. Even
then, you'd better double-check
their work.

person who says "I don't know" or "I just never read the lease"
will cause more problems than you can possibly imagine. It's human
nature to be in a hurry and to avoid looking at the fine print. Do
yourself a real favor and make it your responsibility to make sure
that your tenants understand their obligations. Above or below the
signature line, include a phrase that states something along the
lines of "I, the undersigned, have read and understood the terms
of this lease agreement."

Evaluate Your Maintenance Skills

No matter how thorough your inspections and no matter how carefully you pick, probe, and ponder over the property you're about to
buy, you will miss something. It's inevitable, and that's not necessarily
due to a lack of diligence on your part or that of your inspectors.
Things break, crack, bend, wear out, drop down, and spring a leak all
the time. It's likely that some of that will occur between the time your
inspections are complete and the time you sign on the dotted line.

Grin and bear it, and get to work. Even if your property is in
excellent shape, wear and tear is inevitable and you will sooner or
later be faced with maintenance and repair. That's one of the reasons
many new landlords sell their property so quickly after making the
purchase. They simply misjudged the amount of time and money
involved in keeping tenants happy by keeping the building in good
shape. Instead of sitting back and counting the money, they find
themselves dealing with stopped-up toilets, pilot lights that won't
light, and roofs that are suddenly gone with the wind.

Even if you are a real handyman, you'll still be challenged. Your
property will require constant maintenance and repair. That's just the
nature of the beast. And keeping tenants happy all the time, and at
all hours of the day and night, is not exactly the same as happily
"puttering" about your own house.

Solve Problems Before They Occur

One of the best ways to handle maintenance and repair problems is to "head them off at the pass." Take care of situations before they develop into problems. Finding and replacing an inexpensive part can save a small fortune compared to the damage caused when that part caves in, wears out, breaks down, or blows up. Preventative maintenance is the key.

For example, when you acquire a building, immediately conduct a thorough sewer-line cleanup. Don't even think, don't evaluate the situation, don't procrastinate, just do it. One big problem that frequently comes up (literally!) happens when basements flood after or even during a big rain because the pipes start backing up through the drains. There's just no way of knowing when or how often the previous landlord cleared out the sewage line. Some landlords are quite conscientious, and others aren't. Assume the worst and act accordingly.

Schedule Regular Maintenance

Hardware-store people notice a run on air filters every time the country goes from daylight savings to standard time. There's nothing magic in the air. Somehow, it has become a universal date for landlords to replace their air filters. The stores also notice a run on replacement batteries for smoke alarms. What's going on here?

The landlords are just using a memory device. They replace air filters and batteries on that date because it's easy to remember. The chore becomes an automatic preventative maintenance ritual.

Your lease agreement may require your tenant to replace filters and batteries. Fine, but don't count on it. Tenants forget, or they're too cheap, or they just don't care. You shouldn't count on them to handle even the most basic responsibilities in this area. That's no criticism of any tenant or group of tenants, it's just human nature.

Furthermore, many tenant's rights ordinances around the country put the responsibility of maintenance and repair squarely on the back of the landlord. Just to be safe, when you set your watch back, set out for your building to change those batteries and filters.

There are many simple things you can do right away to see if you have problems in the works. For example:

- Replace the air filters in the furnace. A filter that will cost you just a couple of bucks can save you a small fortune in smoke damage or repair bills due to clogging or residue buildup.
- Oil the furnace and run a maintenance check. As a rule, you should run regular maintenance checks on all your equipment and appliances. As they say, "An ounce of prevention is worth a pound of cure."
- Replace the batteries in smoke detectors. Don't depend on your tenants to handle this key responsibility. It's fast, easy, and cheap. And you don't have to have a degree in industrial arts to do it.
- Turn on the stoves and water faucets to see what happens (or doesn't). If there are any problems, call your plumber.
- Simply walk around and take a good look at everything. If something looks wrong, there's usually a reason. A quick fix can prevent a long and perhaps expensive repair.
- Use your nose and sniff around, too. If something doesn't smell right, there's probably an unpleasant reason for the odor. Find out and fix it before a tenant raises a stink.

> Even the most talented contractor can hire an untalented laborer or subcontractor.

Working with Contractors

First off, realize that everyone needs to be watched. Even the most talented contractor can have a bad day. He or she can hire an untalented laborer or subcontractor. He might be very good at his job, yet still be distracted by missing a ball game, his kid's piano recital, or by thoughts of the guy down at the neighborhood bar who left him holding the tab for the previous evening's revelry. Regardless of the kind of work needed at your property or who is doing that work, you have a responsibility to yourself, your tenants, your property, and your profitability to keep an eye on what happens.

Contract Essentials

When working with a contractor, you must address three key elements that will help you make sure the outcome works out in your favor:

1. Have a written contract. Don't allow a contractor or subcontractor on your property without one. Make sure the agreement is detailed, is easy to understand, spells out exactly what is to be done, and contains a hard deadline for completion.

2. If a deposit is required, make it a minimal one. Pay the contractor incrementally, based on performance. If the contractor misses a deadline, he or she will also miss a payment. Let them know that you pay on schedule when they deliver on schedule. You should release payment only after the contractor signs a waiver of lien, so that he can't declare nonpayment and tie up the title of your property, keeping you from moving forward with your plans.

3. Be prepared for unpleasantness. Inevitably, the job will be done improperly. It will cost more than estimated and it will take longer to complete. All that goes with the territory, so you had better consider these potential setbacks when you plan your budget and schedule.

A producer in the motion picture industry once said of his suppliers, "You know they're going to rip you off, so you just have to build the rip-off into your plan."

When you are prepared on these three fronts, you are prepared to move forward comfortably with having work done on your property. Don't allow all of these dire warnings of disaster frighten you off. The world is filled with very talented, ethical, and responsible contractors and subcontractors. You will meet, work, and build sound relationships with some of them. Just realize that the world is also filled with scoundrels, and you will get to meet your share of those folks, too. Many unscrupulous contractors just can't wait to get their mitts on an inexperienced landlord. For a while, that's going to be you.

> Many unscrupulous contractors just can't wait to get their mitts on an inexperienced landlord.

It's essential that you shop around for contracting services. Ask other landlords for recommendations and warnings. Ask for references from the contractors, and be sure to call those references. And until they earn your full trust, keep your eyes on them throughout the process.

Don't Bankroll Your Contractor

As a property owner and manager, you will have the opportunity to care for the full range of maintenance problems, everything from replacing a light bulb to rebuilding the foundation or roof of an entire structure. Problems don't have to become hassles, and hassles don't have to turn into major disasters. The progression of events from problem to solution is pretty much in your control, provided you decide to actually take control.

Evaluate Your Maintenance Needs

Every maintenance and repair job is different, but the task of completing it will involve three basic elements: the nature of the job, the costs involved, and the job's priority.

Before calling in the painter, plumber, electrician, or another specialist, define the job in very specific terms. "Fix the stairwell" isn't nearly as informative as "Replace steps one through four, match paint to existing color, cordon off until dry, and mark it 'wet paint' with instructions to use the back stairs." Without such explicit detail, your repairman might continue with costly but unneeded repairs, such as replacing the handrail.

The cost of the job will be determined by the job or hourly rate of your contractor, the hours worked, and by the materials and supplies involved. Get a good handle on all of these factors before hiring anyone.

Property management is frequently all about priorities. Where does the job at hand fit into the overall scheme of things? If those steps in the stairwell are just showing a little wear and tear, they can probably wait until something more important is handled. If they're cracked, they could represent a health hazard and possibly significant losses through a lawsuit. Cordon it off immediately, put up the warning and the arrow pointing to the back stairs, and get to work.

You can eliminate a lot of problems with a little forethought. Find and work with the best contractors in your area. Chances are that any major work will require hiring a licensed, experienced, bonded (insured for damages to property) contractor who has a worker's compensation plan. *Don't become a contractor's bank.* Make sure the company or the individual has the money to buy the equipment and supplies needed to complete the job for which he has been hired. Some contractors use their advance payments to complete an ongoing project and will use your money for someone else's job.

The Bait-and-Switch Game

The old bait-and-switch game isn't limited to unscrupulous used-car dealers or furniture stores in the seedy part of town. You'll find many contractors doing the same thing. Here is how it works.

You meet, negotiate, and conclude a deal with the local account executive of a contracting firm. He or she is a bright, intelligent, friendly, and knowledgeable representative who clearly knows the business and is interested in doing a good job. The brochure you're shown is full of color photos of important jobsites filled with good-looking, hard-working men and women in clean uniforms and brightly colored hard hats. You agree and shake hands over testimonials from satisfied customers printed on the back of the brochure. You look forward to writing your own testimonial on their next ad.

While you're basking in the glow of your negotiating success, the contractor is off selling your contract to another contractor or individual who will actually complete the work. This company or person just might not have all those powerful testimonials, and perhaps for good reason. This is the old bait-and-switch routine. You pay for product A, but end up with product B, which is something entirely different. The next day, instead of seeing a team of professionals in clean uniforms and brightly colored hard hats, you find Moe, Larry, and Curly.

This is why we have lawyers. Always have your attorney look over your contract. If you have a friend or trusted associate in one of the contracting industries, have him or her take a look at it, too. Make sure that the contract isn't assignable, which means making

> Always have your attorney look over the contract.

An Underused Maintenance Resource

Have you ever walked into a local "mega-store" to be greeted by a friendly senior citizen? Many senior citizens are hired as sackers in grocery stores, assistants in fast food restaurants, and in other occupations not commonly associated with retired folks.

There's a good reason for this practice. These folks get hired because they're dependable. They show up on time, and they give a day's labor for a day's wages. They know, practice, and expect basic courtesy in business transactions.

Some of those senior citizens are retired electricians, painters, plumbers, or carpenters. That often unused pool of talent can be a great resource for the smart landlord and property owner.

sure that it can't be turned over to a third party. The laborers are probably great guys, but do you really want them trying to follow the instructions for the right mix of concrete, sand, and stone for the foundation of your building?

Work with City Hall

"You can't fight city hall" is a truism if there ever was one. As you may have heard somewhere, governments just love to govern, and they really love to govern landlords and property managers. Landlords make such good targets because there are so many elements of property that "need" governing. Don't misunderstand the meaning here. Some of all this governing is important, even essential, especially that dealing with construction projects.

Get Construction Permits

Trying to get around this requirement is a foolish gesture, and it will come back to hurt you. Only an amateur property manager would try to save a few dollars by avoiding something so basic as a construction permit. The few dollars you "save" will not equal or even approach the amount of legal fees and penalties you will accrue for your poor judgment. Undoing a municipality's "Stop Work Order" is a painful, slow, and costly process. It's not worth the gamble.

That's because the work done on property affects the structural integrity of a building. Often the health, safety, and even the lives of tenants are at stake. A poorly handled construction job could cost a lot more than dollars. In these cases, a city watchdog agency is needed to make sure the work was done in full compliance with the applicable safety codes. This is for your own good as well as that of your tenants. Never hire a contractor who promises to get the work done without a construction permit. You can't save money this way.

Of course, rebuilding a roof or foundation, rewiring, or replumbing a structure is a time-consuming financial burden. Spend the money, get the permit, and do it right. Getting the permit should be the responsibility of the contractor, subcontractor, or general contractor, but make sure the contractor does get it. See that they provide the original permit, currently stamped and dated, for your files.

Having the permit doesn't guarantee that your contractor or subcontractor will do the work according to city code. That's why it is important, even critical, that you only pay a contractor after you know for sure that the work was done completely and in full compliance with the appropriate city codes.

Technology and mechanics are changing daily. Rapid advancement in techniques, processes, and materials require new codes and changes and upgrades in existing codes. Your contractor should be on top of these changes as they occur. As a property manager, you don't want to hear, "Sorry, but that pipe you used just isn't up to spec anymore." The reference could apply equally well to electrical or fiber optical wiring, structural materials, sensors and detectors, roofing materials, and virtually anything related to building construction. You might have to go to the expense of ripping out something, that pipe for instance, only to replace it with material up to code specifications.

Work with your city and not against it. Local government is really not the enemy. Work with them to help keep you up-to-date and fully informed on any changes affecting your property. You'll find your business proceeds a lot easier, faster, and more profitably if you view your city as a partner in progress.

In Summary

Three hundred million people live in a variety of dwellings in this nation. As a result, there is a continuing need for new and existing housing. Young people are moving up the ladder of success and therefore moving up to bigger and better housing. Older couples are always downsizing their homes as their children grow up and move out. Families are always expanding and in need of homes and apartments. Immigrant families come to this country to share in the American dream, and they need homes as well. As landlords and property managers, you have a constant supply of customers! This is a great business, and residential property gives you an excellent way to get started.

> Families are always expanding and in need of homes and apartments.

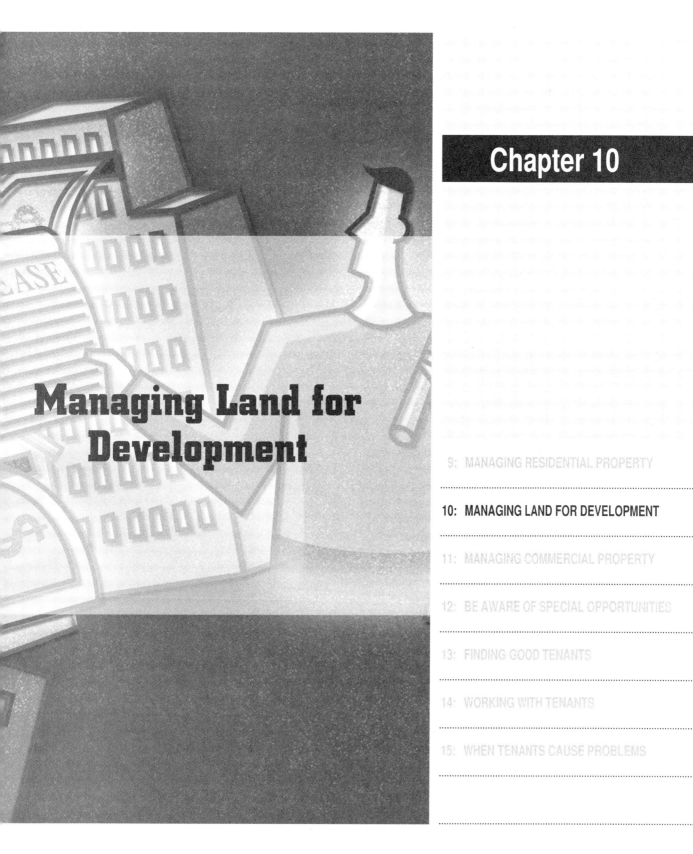

Chapter 10

Managing Land for Development

L and is defined as a portion of the earth's surface. Undeveloped land (which may or may not have been previously developed) is known as raw land in real estate. Most land in America has seen some development, although that development may date back centuries or more.

For example, while driving through downtown Phoenix, the observant traveler might notice the occasional ancient ruin among high-rises, commercial offices, and homes. People have lived in the Valley of the Sun for thousands of years. In fact, about a thousand years ago the population there is estimated to have been 50,000 or so people. After those folks left, the population didn't hit that level again until the twentieth century. If you dig beneath the streets and buildings of most of America's cities, you will probably find some evidence that ancient men and women saw the significance of that old adage—location, location, location.

Lots of Parking Profit

Although this book really doesn't focus on parking lots, the need for parking is a major concern for commercial property owners and for the people who rent from them. You might want to investigate parking lot ownership for that very reason.

Parking lots are great investments. They require little or no maintenance, and the landlord gets a high return on a short-term rental. It's something you may want to consider, but whatever your plans for owning and managing commercial property, diversify your investment. The opportunities are incredibly varied, from miniature golf courses to car washes to retail outlets. Diversification spreads your risk, increases the stability of your business, and enhances your profitability. Plan your business carefully, act wisely, become a good landlord, and you'll discover one of the real secrets to the "ins and outs" of commercial property.

Meanwhile, the next time you drive by or visit a row of restaurants offering valet parking, consider where all those cars are taken. Somebody somewhere is making a lot of money renting slabs of concrete. In most cases, that's almost pure profit. Once you get in, you'll never want to get out.

Look for Potential

Potential is what raw land is all about. The ability to see the land and at the same time visualize what it could be is the key to success for the real-estate professional. A healthy imagination is invaluable to a property owner who is considering investing in raw land.

Land use changes with time and as population changes. At one time, the downtown area of your community was raw land. As people moved in, it might have become the location of a trading post, a fort, or a religious mission. Later it probably became farm or ranch land. As more and more people moved in, the area became urbanized. Americans are infatuated with change and progress. Chances are that your downtown has been torn down and rebuilt several times during the last century. It is very likely that your downtown doesn't even resemble its old self from fifty or so years ago.

For those of you interested in purchasing and developing raw land, you will encounter a number of tough challenges that are balanced by very real opportunities. You may see some property and have a vision for its use, but you will still have to jump through a number of hoops to turn that vision into a reality.

Determine the Zoning

You may have a great vision for land use, but the property must be zoned by the city for that type of use. A zone is an area set off by local ordinance for specific uses. Certain restrictions and/or conditions must be met before the property can be put to use. This is a legal mechanism used by municipalities to control the use of private property, to prevent conflicting uses, and to promote orderly development. Even though the land is privately owned, the municipality may use its police authority to enforce these conditions and restrictions. In other words, you may have the property, but they have the power.

A zoning ordinance is an act of a municipal government, a county, or another recognized authority that specifies the type of use permitted on a property. The ordinance defines the reason the ordinance was adopted in the first place; the various zoning

For those of you interested in purchasing and developing raw land, you will encounter a number of tough challenges that are balanced by very real opportunities.

classifications (land uses) permitted within the zone; any restrictions, such as building height limitations; the procedure for handling nonconforming uses; the correct procedure for granting amendments to the ordinance; the appeals process; and the penalties for violation of the ordinance.

Examples of different zones are residential, commercial, light industrial, and industrial. A single block may contain several different zones. For example, one corner could be zoned for light commercial use, such as a convenience store or gasoline station. Another part could be zoned for single-family dwellings and another for high-density apartment buildings. Your city will have a zoning map, which will indicate the current zoning status of each area. Keep in mind that zones can change, and that, in some cases, you may be the agent for such a change.

There are areas in Chicago that are designated specifically for manufacturing or commercial use. These different zones keep industry in designated areas, commercial properties in others, and residential areas in still others. That way you don't end up with a husband and wife trying to raise two little kids next door to a meat-rendering facility, a jet-engine factory, or the manufacturer of saw blades.

Combine Properties, Increase Value

Sometimes the land you want is just too small to use for your desired purpose and something called an assemblage may be needed. An assemblage is simply the combining of two pieces of property into a single unit. Joining the two properties may enhance the value because the new property may be worth more than its separate parts. For example, let's say each piece of the pie is worth $10,000. Combined into an assemblage, the opportunities for that property are expanded. More can be done within the same space now that they have been joined. The total value then could be $25,000 or more.

Your Use Must Fit Your Zoning

If you tried to place a residential property in land zoned for industrial use, you would most certainly meet with failure. Again, that's not to say things won't change. As more people move into an area, industry tends to move away, so an industrial zone may eventually give way to commercial or even residential property. But why wait? There's already plenty of raw land for developing whatever you want to develop.

Regardless of your vision, the first thing you must do is find out how the property you want is zoned. If the zoning doesn't meet your needs, then find out if there's the possibility of changing that zoning.

Combining a Large Number of Properties

An assemblage isn't restricted to city blocks. The area brought together can be quite large. Walt Disney had to assemble 38,000 acres outside Orlando, Florida, to build Disney World, an assemblage the size of San Francisco. You can imagine the volume of paperwork involved in that purchase, which brings up a good point. Putting together an assemblage creates a lot of paperwork and a lot of "noise." Depending on the nature of your proposed land use, you may find it in your best interest to keep that noise as low as possible. If landowners get wind of the big project, they may demand more for their property, perhaps more than it is worth. There are confidential ways to assemble property by approaching the owners as individuals rather than as a group.

Sometimes people will hold out for reasons other than financial. For example, construction for the Presidential Library of for-

Define the Neighborhood

Land is defined as the surface of the earth or any part of the earth's surface. A neighborhood on that land is generally described as a specific geographic area containing a defined population base and a fairly common use of the land. Certain characteristics of the area can define rather strict boundaries. For example, a neighborhood could begin or end at a river, lake, an interstate highway, railroad tracks, city park, mountain or hill, valley, business structure, or another feature.

There are no official size limits on what defines a neighborhood. It usually evolves somewhat on its own over time. One city block or even one side of a city block in a large metropolitan area can easily become a legitimate neighborhood. An entirely different neighborhood with different characteristics could exist on the opposite side of the street. Sometimes neighborhoods are defined by the people living there, like Little Italy or Chinatown. In rural communities a neighborhood may cover miles of land.

All of these definitions are important to the property manager considering buying property in a particular neighborhood. Proximity to an interstate or railroad could be a plus for your commercial property. But if the neighborhood is residential, you might have to look elsewhere.

Raw Land as Commercial Property

Technically, if you buy undeveloped land, you can use it to build residential housing, office buildings, stores, restaurants, or an amusement park. However, unless you actually do build a residential house, investing in raw land is generally considered as investing in commercial property. For more details on how to finance a purchase of commercial properties and the types of tenants you might expect to deal with, see Chapter 11.

mer President Bill Clinton hit a snag when one landowner refused to sell. His stated reason wasn't that he objected to the library but rather to how the city was participating in financing the structure. What's the point here? If you run up against someone holding out, do a little research and discover the true motivation. If it's something other than money, you'd be wasting your time negotiating from that basis.

How Much of Your Land Do You Own?

What, exactly, is your land? The question is a lot more serious than you might think. "The Man Who Sold the Moon" is an old science-fiction story about an industrialist's attempt to be the first man on the moon. It's a fascinating tale, more about capitalism than rockets, orbits, and landings. The hero hedges all his bets and covers all his bases. It seems the moon actually passes over very limited, very well defined parts of planet Earth. To avoid earthly claims on "his" moon, the wealthy industrialist buys those parts of the earth. Why would he go to all that trouble? He did it for a very good, practical, and legal reason.

Theoretically, a plot of land exists in a wedge shape extending down from the surface of the planet to the center of the earth and outward in an expanding wedge to the heavens. When and if the space aliens arrive, they may have something to say about that, but until they get here, this is pretty much how the rules are applied. When buying land you must be sure of how much land you're actually buying and how much you can actually use.

Buy All the Rights

Many a person who has discovered oil on his or her land has also discovered that the original owner kept the mineral rights. Great. They've found oil (or gold or whatever) *under* their property, and they can't get at it. In such a case there is little the owner can do other than perhaps setting up a toll booth to charge an entrance fee for the oil rig trucks.

There may also be height restrictions. A proposed sports stadium in Phoenix was tripped up over this very matter. Some time before construction began, but well along the way in the planning stages, somebody noticed that the structure, equivalent to a twenty-story building, was in the middle of the approach to Sky Harbor International Airport a mile or so down the road. Let's see: Jets at low altitude taking off and landing right over the stadium. Why is this a good idea? What happens if a plane loses an engine? What happens if it gets hit with wind shear or a significant downdraft? Can a 747 land on the fifty-yard line? Eventually the Federal Aviation Authority stepped in and the project had to be rethought, from the ground up.

For more information on this topic, visit our Web site at www.businesstown.com

Chapter 11

Managing Commercial Property

Look out your car window as you drive through town. Almost everyone you see owns or at least plans to own residential property. But a few of those folks, a lucky few, have moved on to ownership of commercial property. This isn't a route for everyone to follow. But for those willing to take a chance, make a move, and invest in their own future, owning commercial property offers a proven way to success and security. Again, commercial property management isn't for everybody, but if you're so inclined and if you have the drive and stamina to handle the problems and take advantage of the many opportunities, you might want to give this area of real estate some serious thought.

Commercial Rental Property

Major industries get most of the press in America, but the backbone of the American economy, and therefore the backbone of the world economy, is small business. The local diner, carwash, mini-mart, drycleaners, and the repair shop are small business enterprises that require real-estate property. Business owners must have land and structures on that land to conduct business. Customers need a place to go to spend their money. Even phone orders or orders through the Internet must go to some physical place.

Take some of the time you're investing in research and drive through the commercial and industrial areas of your community. You'll see businesses manufacturing everything from cars to cardboard, food to fuel, tools to timber, and books to B-1 bombers. You'll find banks, insurance agencies, large conglomerates, and mom-and-pop shops all reaching for their piece of the American dream. They all need a place to make that dream come true, and that's where the landlord comes in.

Commercial Management Flexibility

If you're investigating the potential of commercial property ownership and management, you'll find a different set of sensibilities compared to those associated with residential property. For one thing, you won't have to follow the dictates of a tenant's bill of rights

> Take some of the time you're investing in research and drive through the commercial and industrial areas of your community.

or set of tenant's ordinances. Cities take a more hands-off approach when it comes to commercial and industrial properties. Their attitude is that business is business. Unlike housing, people (or companies) don't physically need a given piece of property the same way families need a roof over their heads.

Arrangements with commercial-property tenants are as varied as the needs of the property owner and his or her negotiating ability. Often the tenant is responsible for repair and maintenance. In many cases, the real-estate taxes and insurance are paid by the tenant too. As a rule, the owner of commercial property has considerably more flexibility in dealing with tenants than the owner of residential property does.

Financing Commercial Property

Buying commercial property usually requires more equity and cash paid up front. For example, multitenant apartments will generally require a 20 percent equity payment. Commercial property payments will generally run in the 25–30 percent bracket. Rates and costs vary according to the community and region of the country in which you make your purchase.

Start with Multitenant Buildings

The old saying about not putting all your eggs in one basket certainly applies to commercial real estate. If you've read the business section of your newspaper over the past few years, you've seen story after story about businesses closing down. Home improvement stores and discount book chains seem to have been prominent lately. At first glance, these tenants may seem like great opportunities. Many companies appear to be financially sound, backed by strong management, and built up on a solid base of satisfied customers. But often the picture isn't nearly as rosy as it appears in the business press or in the company's brochures and annual report.

If the company fails, you will be left with a vacated property, unpaid debts, and a "bad luck location" image, and it could take you

The Key to Success

Commercial property as an investment is as good as your tenant's ability to pay. Your best bet, especially when you're just starting out, is to own and manage a multitenant building so that you can spread the risk over different companies and organizations. In other words, it's best to have those eggs in many different baskets.

a lot of time to dispel that idea. Until then, potential tenants will look at your property and say, "Well, if XZY company couldn't make it there, I doubt that we could either. Better look somewhere else."

It's best for those new to commercial real estate to begin with a small, multitenant commercial property. They come in all shapes and sizes, and you'll find them everywhere. Industrial multitenant property often includes incubator space for more than one business. In the same way, a shopping center or strip mall allows you to spread your risk over many clients. If one or more fail, then you can structure your rents so that the rest can still cover your expenses and keep your property profitable. You want to create a situation where you have maximum flexibility in the event of a downturn in the economy, a shift in population, bad management by a tenant, or any other issue that could cause a tenant to fail.

Run Credit Checks

Running a credit check on your prospective tenant is another one of those essential tasks for a smart property owner/landlord. For those of you a bit skittish about looking into someone's "private" business, remember that if they're to become your tenant, much of their business becomes your business. You have a responsibility to make sure your commercial property is profitable.

Running a credit check does not imply that you are accusing anyone of being a deadbeat or anything like that. You're just taking care of business. If someone objects, there's probably a reason he or she wants to keep that business private. This is a lesson you should learn early and from this book before you have to learn it the hard way on your own.

Just because someone is in business and appears to be a success doesn't mean they have good credit. One of the reasons these folks may appear so "flush" is the fact that they don't pay their bills on time. Many a deadbeat tenant wears expensive clothes, drives a luxury car, and lives in a fashionable part of town. All that's easy when someone else, like their landlord, is footing the bill.

Your tenant must be able to pay his or her bills, especially the rent. Use a credit form or application that includes their history with

> Just because someone is in business and appears to be a success doesn't mean they have good credit.

other landlords. You should ask for the business's Dun & Bradstreet rating, copies of bank statements, accounts receivable, and any other articles necessary to prove that this company is a good risk as a tenant. You want to have maximum assurance that your prospective tenant is capable of paying the rent and has a record showing a willingness to meet his or her responsibilities as a tenant.

Commercial Leases

As a manager of commercial property, you will most likely have to pick one of three different types of leases for each property you rent out. If you have several properties, you will probably end up working with all three: gross leases, net leases, and triple net leases.

The Gross Lease

A gross lease requires the landlord to pay for all the expenses in a building (except for the utility costs). Obviously, this is the kind of lease least favored by landlords because all the expenses come right out of your profit margin. This is not to say that you can't make money or even very good money by using a gross lease. You just have to be very cost-conscious to do it.

> A net lease requires the tenant to pay some of the expenses in operating the building, although the landlord still has some exposure to costs.

The Net Lease

A net lease requires the tenant to pay some of the expenses in operating the building, although the landlord still has some exposure to costs. In addition to the rent for the space, the tenant pays other expenses such as taxes, insurance, and maintenance. For example, if Mark leases retail space to someone in a net lease arrangement, he will receive his full rent without having to deduct operating expenses, which are paid by the tenant. In sum, the net lease is a flexible lease in which who pays what is a matter for negotiation.

Tenants in a net lease cover the lion's share of the building's operating expenses, such as taxes, insurance, or interior repair of heating, air conditioning, and ventilating systems. The landlord doesn't get off completely free and may still be required to pay for certain repair and maintenance costs.

The Triple Net Lease

A triple net lease is most favored by landlords because tenants are required to cover all of the repair and maintenance expenses. Many of the major business tenants in the country, such as Walgreen's or Safeway, work with a triple net lease. Any expense incurred related to the property is borne by the tenant; the landlord just collects the rent.

Part of the triple net lease must indicate that, in addition to paying rent to the landlord, the tenant must also pay in advance, every month, one-twelfth of the real-estate taxes. The landlord holds this money in an escrow account to be paid when the tax bill is due. Be very careful about structuring this part of your lease. You don't want to deal with people or companies who have gone into

The Elements of a Lease

A lease is a contract and its elements are similar to that of other contracts. Here is a brief look at the eight key factors:

1. Full and legal name of each party, as well as legal signatures.
2. A legal description of the property. As with a contract, this will be written in the special format described in "Elements of a Contract" (Chapter 7).
3. Specific details, such as the length and options for renewal.
4. Valuable consideration, a trade made between the two parties; for example, rent for space.
5. Definition of how the property will be used. Your rental for standard office use does not give a tenant the right to open a fast-food takeout operation within the premises. Many landlords now include a boilerplate (standard) clause stipulating that the use of the property for illegal purposes, such as manufacturing or distributing illegal narcotics or any drug-related activity, is prohibited.
6. The rights and obligations of each party, which should be clearly spelled out. For example, tenants can expect access to the property and the owner can expect that his or her property will be respected.
7. The tenant's right of possession, which states that the organization has the right to occupy the property under the conditions of the lease agreement.
8. The amount of the rent and the timeframe for paying it. Sometimes the amount is expressed as a specific dollar figure "per square foot per year."

bankruptcy or out of business, or who are refusing to pay these real-estate taxes. If they don't make the tax payments, you could be forced into tax delinquency and incur penalties levied on you by your city. You pay enough as a property owner. There's no reason to pay for someone else's negligence, lack of business skill, or flat-out dishonesty.

Think Long-Term

Unlike residential property, commercial and office properties lend themselves to regular rent increases over time. Whereas a residential lease may be for a year or two or even month-to-month, commercial leases can run up to ten years or more. If structured properly, this is a win/win situation. The tenant has the stability of a good location locked in for a long period of time, and the landlord has a steady income over the same time period. If you negotiate a long-term lease, make sure you insert a clause in your agreement that permits you to raise the rent regularly. Usually the increase follows inflation and is set to ensure profitability and maintain the value of the property. If you don't take care of this, you could find yourself collecting this year's rents well into the next millennium.

Office Buildings

Office buildings add a nice variety to any real estate portfolio. Diversity is a key element to real-estate success. (There are those eggs and baskets again.) By definition, you almost always have multiple tenants in your office building. A single tenant may "anchor" your building just as a large department store might anchor a shopping center, but generally you will have other tenants so you can spread the financial risk of ownership. Leases may be structured much the same as with commercial property: gross leases, net leases, or triple net leases.

> Diversity is a key element to real-estate success.

Tenant Improvements

Make your office building as desirable as possible—without going off the deep end, of course. Mahogany paneling and beveled glass are nice for very upscale tenants, but they are completely unnecessary for most tenants serving middle-class customers. Tailor the look and feel of your building to the needs of the businesspeople who occupy it.

"TI" stands for tenant improvements—take care of them before the tenants move in. TIs might include carpeting, paint, wallpaper, drop ceilings, light fixtures, sub-offices within the rental space, and other amenities and options. Your goal is to make your tenants as happy as possible while staying within your budget.

The needs of the market vary. In some cases you will find yourself in a position to charge your tenant for all improvements. For example, if a major new employer moves into your area, rental space may suddenly be at a premium. You're in a good negotiating position because demand exceeds supply. If the reverse is true, say if you're in the community that a major employer just left, you may have to pay for these improvements yourself. Going to that expense is preferable to paying for an empty office building. If the market is really down or if there is a lot of rental space available, you might even find yourself in a tough negotiation. Sometimes landlords offer rent abatements or even free rent for a period of time just to attract good tenants.

No matter what the state of your market, bad tenants aren't worth the trouble. They'll be slow-pay or even no-pay, and they might even cause serious and expensive damage to your property. Renters are fickle, and they generally don't exhibit much loyalty to the landlord. If their business "goes south," they can usually pick up and move along. Some will do this without notice. It's important in any rental situation to check on the financial stability of your prospective tenants.

Know Your ABCs

Office buildings come in a variety of classes. Class A buildings are typically new high-rise office buildings downtown, the "best and the brightest" structures in the land. They feature the best locations, superior design and architectural style, modern construction materials and techniques, and state-of-the art high-tech services and amenities. Examples of Class A buildings are the John Hancock Building

> "TI" stands for tenant improvements—take care of them before the tenants move in.

and Sears Tower of Chicago and the large structures built in the tradition of Donald Trump's buildings. Take a look at what are considered the newest and most prestigious buildings in your community. They're probably Class A buildings.

Class B are structures built just after World War II, and so they are a bit older and may be showing a little wear and tear. Forty or fifty years ago, they would have been considered the "best and brightest" of their time. Although many are in excellent shape, they'll most likely be showing their age. The design will be post-WWII, as will many of the amenities and interiors. If the building has gone high-tech, it will have been through add-ons at a later date. Class B buildings are acceptable for business.

Class C includes structures built in the early part of the twentieth century or even earlier, at the turn of that century, although some may have been built as late as the 1950s. Unless considerable rehab has taken place, these will be obsolete structures. For example, if they're multistory, the elevator may still require the use of an operator hired to run it. Many were built cheaply and will lack access to high-tech amenities and services. Often there's no parking space provided for the tenants.

A building belonging to any of these classes may be good or bad. The definition depends upon your goals for the building, its zoning, market conditions, the economy, as well as other factors.

Older buildings could bring up images of continual maintenance and repair as ancient pipes, wiring, plumbing, and plaster wear out and need replacement. Of course, if you're charging rents that cover those expenses and still maintain your profit level, that's perfectly okay, isn't it? In fact, many Class C buildings, including those that look like "tear down" candidates, are finding a higher use and are being converted into residential condominiums. This is especially true of good downtown or urban areas. Again, this is where the real-estate professional with vision truly shines. He or she looks at an abandoned warehouse or old manufacturing plant, and sees upscale apartments. And upscale profits.

Always keep in mind that office buildings are very volatile with respect to the economy, more so than any other property. The building may be your "life," but to the tenant it's just a temporary place to

> Class B are structures built just after World War II, and so they are a bit older and may be showing a little wear and tear.

do business. If their business starts suffering, they can quite easily fold up their corporate "tent" and move on.

This very thing happened all over the country during the 2000 "tech wreck," when numerous high-tech companies suffered serious losses. When the big companies began to pull back, lay off, and downsize, their suppliers were forced to do the same thing. These losses naturally trickled down to the landlords renting those companies all that office space. Suddenly, a lot of landlords found themselves holding the keys to a lot of empty buildings.

So what's the lesson? Simple, and you've read it before in these very pages—diversify. Rent to different corporations and to different types of corporations. If the computer industry takes a hit, then the medical, satellite, or whatever other industry can take up the slack until you find replacement tenants.

Shopping Centers

Shopping centers are a central feature of the American economy. They come in all sizes, from the basic strip mall down the street to the huge Mall of America in Minnesota. Even small towns have shopping centers, and you'll find some small towns with rather substantial regional centers. This incredible variety of centers located from Dade County, Florida, all the way to Marin County, California, offers you an incredible variety of opportunities. Shopping centers truly "dot the landscape" of America.

This form of centralized shopping is a rather new phenomenon, which began to take shape (and take over) in the last part of the twentieth century. Basically, they have replaced the inner-city shopping experience, which was the norm prior to the 1960s. Several factors affected an explosive growth. Chief among them was the mass movement of families to the suburbs. The lack of downtown parking and the inconvenience that meant was another factor.

A center may have one or more anchor stores, such as Sears, J. C. Penney's, or Dillard's. Smaller centers will just be a cluster of different stores and shopping opportunities. Variety attracts customers who can buy new clothes, toys for the kids, gadgets for adults, books, candles, appliances, and bagels, plus send out mail or

Is There a Doctor in the House?

The medical profession, especially doctors, offers your best chance of office-building tenant stability. Think about it. How often has your family physician, dentist, or specialist moved his office? He or she is probably still located in the same building you entered on your first visit.

Stability in good-paying tenants is one of your chief goals as a landlord and property manager. Doctors and related medical practitioners don't make good landlords. They don't like to deal with the day-to-day maintenance, repair, and headaches of property management. They just aren't oriented that way, and that makes them good tenants. You rarely if ever hear from them; they maintain the property well; and they pay their rent on time. Better still, they never move.

even join the armed services. Whatever the consumer wants, there's a shopping center that has it.

Shopping centers range in size from 4,000 square feet to hundreds of thousands of square feet, depending upon the location and the needs of the market. Shopping centers are great for property managers and landlords because the tenants pick up most of the expenses related to the investment, including taxes and insurance. As with other commercial investments, diversity is a key to success. Try to get a good mix of tenants. If one tenant experiences a downturn, the others will be able to pick up the slack.

Study Traffic Patterns

A famous thief was asked why he robbed banks. His reply was elegantly basic: "That's where the money is." With shopping centers you want to be where the money is, too, and that's wherever people are located. Heavy-traffic areas are always the best locations.

Even in times of economic slump, people spend money to make themselves feel better. Music and clothing stores continue to do good business even when times get tough. People will always shop and today they do most of their buying in shopping centers.

Another real advantage to owning shopping centers is that they are so easy to manage compared to other commercial properties. The tenants have most of the responsibility for daily upkeep. Because they must deal with a fickle public, tenants generally take pretty good care of the property to keep the shoppers coming back.

Dining Establishments

The profit margin for a restaurant owner is always slim. The public is famously fickle, and every day is a challenge. Yet for the property owner who rents space, restaurant owners can be some of your best tenants.

Yes, there is an increased risk of a fire. After all, the tools of the restaurant trade include fire and oil. Yet city ordinances have pretty well mandated safety measures, so a fire shouldn't be an overriding concern.

> Another real advantage to owning shopping centers is that they are so easy to manage compared to other commercial properties.

However, the attraction of restaurant property is stability. Here is why. A restaurant owner will generally invest thousands of dollars preparing the facility for the public, getting specialized equipment, and really dressing up the look of their business. This is a real benefit for the property owner.

Even if the restaurant goes out of business, the facility remains in excellent shape. The location is still in a high-traffic area and another restaurant owner will most likely become interested in moving in. The real heavy expenses such as stoves, ovens, refrigeration, heavy-duty wiring, and gas piping have already been paid for. A failed restaurant for one owner represents a new opportunity for another.

Often the present owner, who is in trouble, will make significant efforts to find that second restaurant owner so that he can recoup some of that capital expenditure on equipment, furniture, and fixtures. The bottom line is in your favor. Even if the name on the sign changes, your rent payments continue.

There's often an added benefit to having a restaurant, a really good one, as your tenant. If you're a good landlord, you'll find you don't need to make reservations, even if the waiting line is out the door.

Ranches and Farms

We often associate ranches and farms with undeveloped land. After all, there's little out there except weeds, grass, trees, and a crop or two. But it's hardly vacant land, even though it may appear that way. The property should contain some barns, farmhouses, and outbuildings, as well as other specialized structures, depending on what type of agricultural activity is conducted there.

If you plan to own farm or ranch land, keep this in mind: Earning a living off the land makes owning a restaurant look lucrative. It's a tough life. If you do think that this is something you are interested in, however, make sure you buy with an eye to the future.

> If you plan to own farm or ranch land, keep this in mind: Earning a living off the land makes owning a restaurant look lucrative.

Because farming or ranching is so difficult, your chances of earning a decent profit are very limited. Therefore, if you buy this type of property, buy it in the line of growth of a nearby city. In other words, plan to make your real profit off something other than ranch or farm income.

As the city approaches, the people will need land for housing developments. That's where the money is. Use your ability to visualize the future. Select your land carefully and in the path of growth, and be financially secure enough to wait it out until those city folks come knocking on your door.

For more information on this topic, visit our Web site at www.businesstown.com

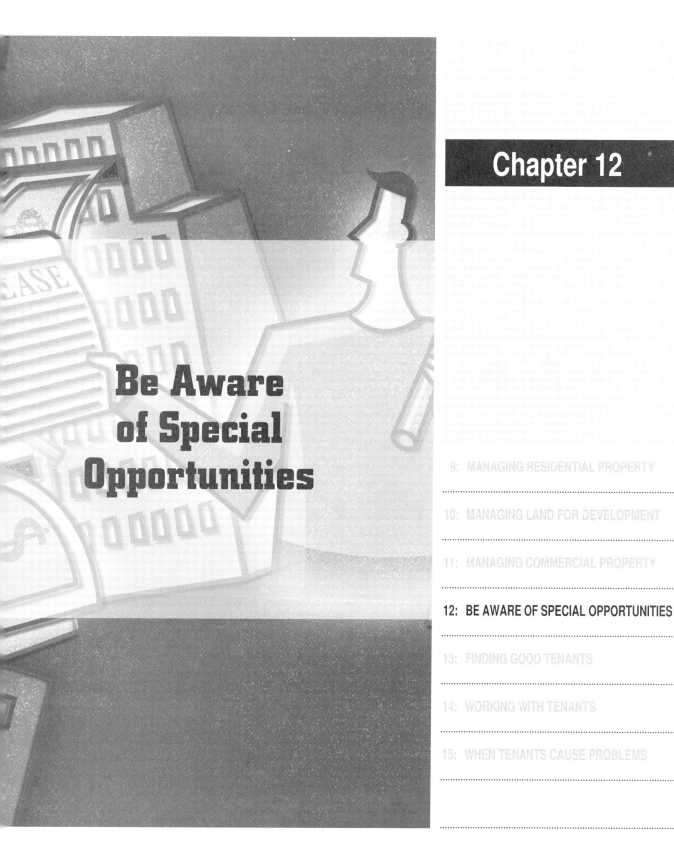

Chapter 12

Be Aware of Special Opportunities

The field of property management is full of small opportunities and many have the capacity to grow or help grow substantial businesses and even empires, which will then produce even more opportunities. In fact, there are so many prospects for growth in real estate that they are far too numerous to mention all of them here. This brief chapter devotes itself to explaining two key principles that apply to all special opportunities.

What Are Special Opportunities?

Special opportunities are atypical, that is to say, they offer a decidedly different set of options, obstacles, and opportunities when compared to more traditional real-estate businesses, such as apartment rentals or commercial real estate. Here are a few samples of special opportunities:

- Golf courses
- Hotels
- Motels
- Cemeteries
- Parking garages
- Recreational properties
- Resort properties

The list can go on and on. Again, these types of operations are far removed from the areas most people consider when they hear "property management" or "landlord." Still, these types of businesses can provide profitable, rewarding, and stimulating experiences, provided you follow the basic rules outlined here.

This is not to say that special opportunities discussed in this chapter are in any way preferable to the more conventional areas. As with all types of property and all opportunities, the smart manager or owner should evaluate not only the business, but also the market, market trends, and especially his or her own abilities and attitudes in that field to determine the most profitable area for him or herself. Special opportunities require a special set of skills and a special

> The smart manager or owner should evaluate not only the business, but also the market, market trends, and especially his or her own abilities and attitudes in that field to determine the most profitable area for him or herself.

desire to operate within that type of business environment. If you have what it takes—a particular area of expertise, for instance—then you should definitely consider using your special skills in an applicable area of real estate.

Don't Forget: It's a Business

You may be the world's greatest property manager or landlord, but how much do you know about running a profitable motel? Managing special-opportunity properties requires special expertise, knowledge, and skills. In this area of real estate, you purchase more than just a property—you acquire a business. You can't buy a cemetery and expect to visit your property once a month to collect the rent checks. A golf course green requires considerably more care than the lawn of a rental home. The demand for "people skill" is greater on the

Evaluating Special Opportunities

Where can you find a special opportunity in real estate? Consider the advice of Francis Bacon: "A wise man will make more opportunities than he finds." In other words, they are everywhere. You just have to seek them out. Here are the types of questions you should ask yourself as you consider the possibilities:

- Is the property easily accessible to the people who will be served there? Can the cars coming for gasoline get in and out? Do the walk-in customers have a place to park their cars? Can delivery trucks pick up and deliver? Even if a location is considered "good," consider if it is right for the business that's in place or the one you're planning on setting up. A great location for a fast-food restaurant may not be appropriate for a light manufacturing shop.

- Will the location remain profitable with the passage of time? Where is the neighborhood, the community, or the area economy headed? How will the shifting demographics affect your property?

- Who are your competitors? If there aren't any, why not? How would a new competitor affect your business? Would you still be able to make a profit?

It's true that opportunities are everywhere, but you must make sure that the operation's customers have the opportunity to trade there. Atypical properties typically require a lot of research and evaluation as well as careful planning.

manager of a resort than for the manager of a small commercial property in a strip mall.

Before you take advantage of one of these special opportunities, make sure you know exactly what you are getting involved with. If you buy a motel, you will need to staff it with a variety of people possessing a variety of skills. In addition to maintenance and repair personnel you'll need maid service, pool and recreational service personnel, desk personnel, and suppliers of soap, toilet paper, locks and keys—and the list goes on. Many of these needs and functions are out of the normal experience range of your average property manager. If you lack the know-how to manage these special needs, you'll have to hire someone who does. Of course, that expense impacts your bottom line.

Special opportunities operate by a different set of rules than traditional real-estate properties. Find a friendly expert in your chosen field, and get as much advice and counsel as he or she is willing to provide. Be sure to get sound advice on the peculiarities of the local situation.

Realize that it is in the interest of the person selling you the special opportunity to say how easy the operations are and how profitable they have been. This may be absolutely true, but it may be an exaggeration—or an outright pack of lies. You are tasked with the responsibility of finding out before you sign the check. If you don't conduct proper and in-depth research, you will learn the meaning of the old adage "Let the buyer beware."

Even if the glowing reports of easy work and huge success are true, will those conditions remain when the present owner hands you the keys and heads off to Retirement City? The previous owner may have been an expert in that field. How will the business fare without that expertise? You will most likely have to survive through the learning curve, so you must determine in advance whether or not you have enough time and operating capital to profitably get through the process. It may not be impossible, but it is extremely difficult to create a success from a special opportunity if you are learning as you go. The key to your success in conquering the learning curve will be your enjoyment of the job and its challenges, as well as your passion for the work.

> If you buy a motel, you will need to staff it with a variety of people possessing a variety of skills.

What Are Your Options?

The options you will have to choose from are numerous, limited solely by your skills and aspirations. If you really desire to own and manage a particular type of property and business, then you can truly make the experience into something special. The following sections will take a look at the most common special opportunities that are available for real-estate investors.

Retail Stores

The categories of retail stores include the following:

- Appliances
- Apparel
- Automotive and automotive supplies
- Boats and boating supplies
- Beauty shops and upscale hair salons
- Food and beverage
- Home supplies and hardware
- Repair facilities of all kinds
- Moving and storage
- Toys and games
- Recreation
- Service stations and convenience
- Department stores

This list of possibilities is neither exclusive nor permanent—it changes along with the growing needs and desires of the population. When entering the retail field as a property manager and business owner, always consider the existing market. Can you carve out a piece of it for yourself? Is there enough business for another operation? Do you have a unique offering that will bring in trade?

> Do you have a unique offering that will bring in trade?

Shopping Centers

Shopping facilities are expensive to build and maintain. They are therefore usually considered suitable for high-dollar investors or groups of smaller investors. Most shopping centers fall into one of three categories. A neighborhood shopping center, like a modern full-service supermarket, serves the smallest amount of customers—as many 40,000 people or as few as 2,500. Next in size is the community shopping center, which may serve as many as 150,000 customers. An example of a community shopping center would be a large discount store. The third type of facility is the large, regional shopping center, which can be enormous and encompassing dozens of stores. Often large department or variety stores, even competing stores, act as anchors to each end of the center.

Shopping strips are not as popular as they were in the past, and they are commonly being replaced by large indoor suburban malls. Depending upon the area and proximity to such malls, a strip center can still be a good investment. The traditional shopping strip is usually anchored by a large store, such as a supermarket or a department store. A piggyback shopping strip is placed to take advantage of the traffic heading to and from a large suburban mall. The neighborhood shopping strip serves a smaller and more local customer base.

Office Buildings

Individuals, corporations, and organizations of all types need office space. A property manager should consider a number of key factors before getting involved. Overbuilding can cause a glut in the market, resulting in low rents or empty offices. Shifts in population can pull renters from one area to another in a surprisingly short amount of time. Note which way the population wind is blowing. Downturns in the economy can force downsizing and even business termination. Also consider offering concessions to your renters, such as paying for moving expenses into your facility, temporary reductions in rents, or even free rent for a limited period of time.

> Downturns in the economy can force downsizing and even business termination.

Medical Office Space

Obviously, you'll want to locate or find properties near a major medical facility. Hospitals often move considerable distances to build new facilities. Stay on top of the medical business world so you'll be the first to know if any major moves are in the planning stages. Also, be aware that some medical facilities will require specialized properties to handle certain types of patients.

Hotels and Motels

Your best bet is to contact a major chain and interest them in leasing your property. That way, many of the headaches associated with this industry end up as someone else's responsibility. Hotels and motels are expensive and labor-intensive, and they require continual maintenance and repair, as well as a lot of on-site management. Furthermore, seasonal fluctuations in traffic can have a significant impact on the overall profit picture.

Service Stations

Location is key. You'll need to be visible and in a high-traffic area near a major traffic artery. As with a hotel/motel operation, your chances of success are much improved if you hook up with a well-known and respected national organization. Watch proposed changes in streets, highways, and roads, and be prepared to go where the traffic is flowing.

Restaurants

This is an industry with a low profit margin (around 6 percent, by some estimates). Fortunately, the property manager has a number of options. Provided the facility fits the specific need, it can be used as a mom-and-pop café, a fast-food outlet, a family restaurant, or an upscale facility for fine dining. Individual restaurants can do quite well on their own, but you should also investigate leasing to a national chain.

> Watch proposed changes in streets, highways, and roads, and be prepared to go where the traffic is flowing.

Movie Theaters

This business (space rental) is totally dependent upon another business (making and distributing movies). In this area of real estate, success depends on many factors. You should be located near a major population base with good traffic patterns and easy access to your property. Although there are still independent free-standing movie theaters around, the trend in recent years is toward large, multiplex cinemas with a central lobby. Be aware that if Hollywood has a bad year, so will the movie theater.

Industrial Properties

"Industrial" covers a lot of territory. An industrial site can be a single business devoted to light manufacturing, a large factory with huge smokestacks and lines of trucks delivering raw material, or entire parks designated exclusively for industrial production. All of these areas are generally high-dollar investments, paid for with capital raised by groups of investors.

Parks, strips, and some factories will require extensive amounts of raw land. You'll also need to check the need for access by street, road, interstate highway, and perhaps rail and water. Proximity to an airport may also be a major consideration. Streets and parking will have to be constructed to handle large vehicles and heavy day-to-day traffic.

The industrial market is another area where the success of the property manager may be dependent on the success of an entirely unrelated industry, as well as the ups and downs of the local, regional, and national economy. Business can be booming worldwide, but if your tenants are making vacuum tubes when the whole world is going digital, your business may be taking a big hit when they take a nosedive. Carefully examine a prospective tenant's credit rating. A number of companies, such as Dun & Bradstreet, provide this service. Get to know the industry's management team. Can they successfully run the business, or do you think they'll run it into the ground?

Check the Zoning

A zone is an area within a municipality that is defined by local ordinance for a specific use or a specific set of uses. For example:

- A C-1 Zone is for commercial use, such as a convenience store or a car wash.
- An R-2 Zone is defined as low-density residential for single-family housing.

- An R-4 Zone is a high-density residential area and would include apartment-style housing.

Zoning is simply the legal means by which local governments regulate the use of private property. If necessary, they have the authority to use police powers to promote an orderly development of the area and to see that there are no conflicting property uses within it.

A typical zoning ordinance defines the following :

- The purpose of that particular ordinance.
- Classifications and permitted uses within the zone.
- Restrictions, such as height limits.
- Proper procedures for handling nonconforming uses.
- Proper procedures for applying for amendments, variances, and appeals.
- Penalties for violating the zoning ordinance.

It should be obvious that if you plan to put up a parking garage, you wouldn't buy property zoned R-2, but some folks have made that exact mistake. Do your homework before you make your purchase. You need to know what the zoning ordinance is, at least so that you can attempt to amend it. An application for a zoning amendment to the zoning ordinance may or may not be granted by the local governing body. Amendments generally require a public hearing and a recommendation by the municipality's planning commission. Check with your local government for the correct procedure in your area.

The Realities of Rezoning

If rezoning is a consideration, remember to prepare your sales contract contingent on the property's being rezoned. Otherwise, you could end up with a desirable piece of property, but without the right to place your establishment on it. Rezoning requires time, planning, and often a good bit of skill in the public relations arena. Altogether, the process will take at least six months; sometimes, however, it can take years—it all depends upon the scope of the rezoning appeal.

How to Determine a Particular Property's Zone

Your municipality will have a zoning map, which is available to the public. This is a basic map of the city, with each block marked with sections of different zones. Using a zoning map is a fast and reliable way to scan the market and to determine whether a given property meets your zoning needs and decide whether to apply for rezoning. The map can save you a lot of time and energy. For example, if all the blocks around the property you want are zoned low density, there's very little chance you'll be granted rezoning for that goat cheese factory you want to open in the neighborhood.

Realize early on that the community might not welcome you or your ideas with open arms. Folks in the neighborhood may not be nearly as enthusiastic about your project as you and your partners are.

As you prepare your rezoning appeal, remember that public relations must be a key element of your strategy. You're not only dealing with rules and regulations and government bodies, you're dealing with a wide variety of human personalities. Some might welcome your project. Others will be skeptical until convinced by the logic of your arguments and the pleasing aspect of your personality. Still others might oppose you simply because that's how they get their "kicks" out of life. Keep your cool at town hall or community meetings. Show your best side at all times. Like other pioneers, you may experience arrows in your back for presenting new ideas and changes to the community.

Neighbors Who Aren't

Lots of towns have once-exclusive areas that have fallen or are falling on hard times. These areas can become an interesting mix of very upscale mansions and crumbling ruins. You would think the residents would welcome changes that would maintain the integrity of the neighborhood in tough times. In some cases, however, this does not occur.

In one such town, an ambitious young man purchased a crumbling mansion and turned it into an upscale bed-and-breakfast. Many in the neighborhood went wild with outrage. "How dare some young upstart bring a *business* onto our street!" People wrote letters to the editor of a local newspaper, letters to the owner of the property, and letters to each other. They protested, called the young entrepreneur, and knocked on his door and interrupted the pleasant atmosphere of his business environment.

Of course their actions were futile. The man already owned the property and had completed all the renovations. The angriest neighbors didn't care. When the owner explained that without his purchase and rehab of the property it would have fallen into disrepair and would have become an eyesore, he was told that such a state of things would have been preferable to having a business in the neighborhood.

The point here is that you can please some of the people all of the time, and you can please all of the people some of the time, but some people are just jerks. Be ready and be prepared for anything.

Win Some and Lose Some

Nobody wins all the time. That's just the nature of the beast called rezoning. It is important that you always keep your cool and maintain your professional demeanor. The rudeness of protestors and the inexactitude often found in their arguments must not throw you or dissuade you from making a professional presentation.

Appearances are important. Don't make yourself the target for those who oppose your business plans. Make a positive impression on the governing body and the audience, and they will likely give you a fair chance. If you lose your composure even once in front of an audience, you will lose face in the community. You'll be labeled as an unprofessional developer and property owner. As former President Nixon once said about a series of television interviews in which he felt he was poorly used, "I gave them a sword." Don't give those who oppose you the sword of poor demeanor. They'll use it to hack you to pieces.

Consider a slow approach that will allow the community to review your proposal and get familiar with it while you are still resolving your detailed plan. Of course, the slow approach will allow your opposition time to mount their arguments, too. That's why it's a good idea to give the community something in return for their support. You are asking for their cooperation, so it's fair to offer them a green space, lighting, a parkway, a water fountain, anything that will be genuinely appreciated by the people in your new neighborhood. Get to know the people. Find out what they need.

Despite all your efforts, you may nevertheless lose one or even many zoning issues during your career. To prevail, let the objections roll off your back. Let the project go and move on to the next one.

Talk to Those Who Can Help

Always consult with your councilman or alderman before attempting a zoning change. These people have their finger on the pulse of the neighborhoods. They can save you enormous amounts of time and money by letting you know their opinion of your project before you're too far along. They can also direct you to influential community leaders, people you can approach first to gain their advice and support. This is a far wiser course than just springing your ideas on the community without preparation.

For more information on this topic, visit our Web site at www.businesstown.com

Chapter 13

Finding Good Tenants

As you have heard, the key to success in real estate is location, location, location. Other key factors include expenses, income, financing, the type of property, and so on. Yet, if pressed to name the most important element to long-term success, the answer would be "people and the ability to work with them." As a property manager, you want to find good tenants who will not cause trouble. You owe it to yourself, your business, and the other tenants.

Working with Rental Agents

For rental agents, the important factor is commission, commission, commission—and that's fair, because that's how rental agents make their profits. The need for rental agents varies, depending on market conditions. A landlord trying to find tenants for an apartment that has remained vacant for some time will find it in his or her best interest to pay commission, rather than losing months of rent checks. Remember: The commission amortized over the term of the lease justifies the income that the rental agent is now providing you.

Earning that commission should be a direct result of excellent service, not merely going through the motions. Rental commissions are usually set at half a month's or a month's rent.

Prepare a Detail Sheet

It's important that you have a detail sheet, that is, a sheet accurately describing the unit you have available. This puts you and the agent on the same page. Make sure the agent signs off on a copy, acknowledging exactly what it is that he, she, or they are leasing for you. It is also important that you supply the agent with the credit form and application that you want to use to verify the tenant history and credit history. Remember that once the rental agent leaves, you have the sole responsibility for living with the representations that the agent made on your behalf to the tenant. If those statements are not accurate, whatever situation develops is still your responsibility. If the agent is sloppy in researching the tenant's credit or rental history, you get to pay for that mistake, too.

Set Tough Standards

To avoid potential problems with your rental agent, you must set an operating standard. The agent must be someone who can and will fulfill your needs as the landlord and property manger. All too often the rental agent will to some extent embellish the features of the apartment, or leave out details, such as lack of air-conditioning. Avoiding the problems will get the prospective tenant to sign the lease faster, but it will probably create more problems for the landlord in the long run, as the disgruntled tenant decides to move out or demands costly renovations to fix the problem that the rental agent avoided disclosing in the first place.

Misrepresentation Is Dangerous

Here is an example of how a rental agent's misrepresentation of facts can cause problems for the landlord. After completing a "gut rehab" on a building in 1987, Mark was anxious to have the building rented. He'd gone to considerable expense and the property had been vacant for a full year. When Mark advertised the rental, many agents called, asking for a fee if they delivered a tenant. He was overjoyed when one Chicago company brought in a group of tenants for one of the units. Soon, however, that joy turned into an ugly, unpleasant, and costly nightmare.

It turns out that the agent had misrepresented the building to the tenants. The unit was not centrally air-conditioned and the agent knew this before making contact with potential renters. The tenants were a group of four girls from suburban Cleveland. They moved in

Avoid Unscrupulous Agents

Here's another horror story of an unscrupulous rental agent causing problems for both the tenants and their landlord. Mark was doing renovations in an apartment building, and everything was complete except for one last apartment. While much work still remained to be done, a rental agent was already on the case, and had found a lovely couple moving to Chicago from Boston. To seal the deal, the rental agent told the couple that the renovation would be done a month sooner than the actual completion date.

Mark was enjoying a Labor Day weekend at Walt Disney World when he received a frantic phone call from his office. The apartment, which was scheduled to be completed for October 1, had a tenant standing outside next to a stuffed U-Haul truck. The couple had driven all the way from Boston and were waiting to move in during September.

Again, the rental agent took the money and ran, and it was Mark's responsibility to provide temporary shelter for a very unhappy new tenant. The financial loss was more than $8,000, not to mention the aggravation and a bad start to a landlord/tenant relationship.

However, Mark learned his lesson. He now requires agents to fill out a clear and detailed rules of behavior form before they show his units to prospective tenants and sign the property description sheet. Also, he does not pay the agents until after the tenant has moved in and is in the apartment for one month.

during the middle of summer. The weather was hot and humid, a typical Chicago summer, and the girls had never in their lives lived in such a condition.

Chicago summers can be brutal without air conditioning. Soon, angry parents were calling to complain about the poor treatment of their daughters. Eventually, Mark had no choice but to terminate the lease and let the girls move out. What else could he do? The misrepresented situation wasn't the fault of the tenants. It wasn't the landlord's fault either, but guess who took the blame—and the loss?

Mark had to find a new tenant, but the rental agent no longer wanted to cooperate. He became defensive and claimed that Mark had said the entire building was centrally air-conditioned. It turned out that this agent was new to the business; his lack of professionalism and greed for earning his commission with minimum effort had led to the misrepresentations. Unfortunately for Mark, the rental agent was paid when the lease with the girls from Cleveland had been signed. Mark ended up with having paid commission for a lot of trouble and an empty apartment.

How to Screen a Tenant

When your rental agent does find prospective tenants who would like to move in, you need to exercise great caution in screening out the problem tenants and troublemakers from the quality tenants who pay their bills on time, follow the rules, and do not create hassles for the neighbors or the property manager. Making sure your potential tenants fit into this category is a relatively quick and painless way to save yourself a lot of long-term agony. Here's what you should check when you are looking at prospective tenants:

- **References.** Your prospect should provide satisfactory references from landlords for the past three years.
- **Income and employment.** The tenant's household monthly income should be three times (or more) the monthly rent. Please verify that they do have a permanent source of income.

> You need to exercise great caution in screening out the problem tenants and troublemakers from the quality tenants who pay their bills on time, follow the rules, and do not create hassles for the neighbors or the property manager.

- **Evictions.** The prospective tenant should have a clean record.
- **Criminal record.** It seems obvious that you should check your prospective tenant's criminal record, but you'd be amazed at how many property managers ignore this key issue.
- **Identification.** Your prospect should produce a valid social security card and at least one other source of identification, such as a driver's license.
- **Collections.** The applicant's record should be free of collections for the past year.
- **Credit.** Your prospect should have a good record with no outstanding balances. The only way to know is to check the credit history.
- **Verification.** Make sure that the people moving into your property are the same people who filled out the application and not someone else who could never qualify.

Furthermore, the applicant must sign a document that shows his or her agreement to all your rental stipulations, such as the policy on pet ownership.

Meet Every Applicant

Meet the entire household, without exception: wife, husband, kids, roommates, mothers-in-law, and hamsters. If you run into a problem meeting someone, there may be a very real and unpleasant reason. "My, uh, husband was called away on a job unexpectedly, heh-heh." Well, that may be true, but it may also be true that the job was a stickup down at the local convenience store, a moonshine run out to the hinterlands, or a lecture at the local branch of the Anti-Landlords Club. Without meeting these people, there's no way of telling what kind of nightmares they'll bring along. Watching the police and FBI surround your building while your tenant shouts "Come and get me, Copper!" isn't exactly good for business.

Even if you depend on a rental service to find customers, make a point of meeting every prospective tenant. Remember, you can't discriminate—that's against the law—but you can investigate.

> Without meeting these people, there's no way of telling what kind of nightmares they'll bring along.

A criminal and credit check can help you eliminate trouble before it takes root in your building.

The Four Personality Types

You will find it much easier to screen applicants and deal with tenants once you understand that people fall into four specific personality types. These are rather basic, but everyone you meet will belong primarily to one category. (There will be some overlap, obviously, but one trait will always dominate.)

The analytical personality. Analytical people are task-oriented, focused on the job at hand. Their thinking process might go something like this: "We're here. We want to go there. This is the shortest route, so let's go!" Tenant negotiations with these people may be quite straightforward and without a lot of byplay.

The driver personality. A driver is pretty much self-directed and controlling, good at quick thinking and a very capable negotiator when it comes to repairs, redecorating, or lease renewals.

The amiable personality. These folks are attentive, supportive, loyal, and focused on relationships. For them, the negotiation process is often as important (or even more important) than the outcome. The amiable personality wants to make sure all sides are heard and that fair discussion has taken place.

An expressive personality. Expressive personalities are spontaneous, friendly, outgoing, and good at making conversation. Be warned: Conversations about rent, maintenance, and other related topics may drift off to all kinds of discussions. If time is important, the landlord will have to direct the flow and pace of the negotiations.

Conduct Background Checks

You should take all the necessary steps to try to avoid problem tenants, and your best tool is a thorough background check. Don't be

---

How to Read People

People are part of what we do. Every endeavor involves an individual, a family, or a group of people. Everybody is different and, as noted earlier, people react differently at different times. A good property manager must be able to adapt to dealing with an ever-changing cast of characters. It's not an exact science and much of your interaction with other people will be guided by your instincts. Often, you have to "feel" your way through a given situation.

Most people are good folks who want a safe place to live or in which to conduct their business. The troublemakers are the exceptions to the rule. All types of tenants, good and bad, must be dealt with. When interviewing prospective tenants, check out their backgrounds and, if possible, get a history of how they have behaved as tenants in other properties.

hesitant or shy about this necessary task, even if a potential tenant makes a fuss. You're entering into a business arrangement involving cash payments in exchange for property rental and maintenance and repair of that property, and you need to know exactly who you are dealing with.

When you do a background investigation, be sure to follow the applicable rules and regulations—to do otherwise means risking the unpleasantness of a discrimination lawsuit. Your local real-estate offices should have forms that are acceptable, comply with local statues, and that may be safely used within your community.

How People Relate to One Another

Most people you meet will fall into one of three categories of behavior. People will be dominated by one of the following:

- What they see.
- What they hear.
- What they touch.

It's important that you realize which type of individual you are dealing with. Just by knowing what sense dominates a person's behavior and awareness will allow you to communicate much more effectively.

Look for clues in a person's speech. About 60 percent of everyone you meet will be oriented visually. They will relate best to pictures, even word pictures. "I see." "Do you see what I mean?" "Get the picture?" These are some typical phrases that indicate a visually-oriented person.

Phrases such as "I hear you," or "Listen to me," or "Let me tell you something" are clues that you're speaking to someone who relates best to what he or she hears. Sometimes these people may avert their eyes or look down when speaking with you. It's not that they're being rude, rather they're blocking out visuals so they can better listen to what you have to say. When dealing with this type of personality, be careful to speak clearly and precisely, and choose your words and phrases carefully.

The third type is a "hands-on" personality. People in this group are "touchy-feely" people. Human contact, a strong handshake for example, is important to these folks.

Possible Strategies

The less time you spend investigating, the more time you will probably spend dealing with difficult tenants and the problems they will soon cause. How do you find out whether somebody is a difficult or problematic tenant? Check whether this person was a difficult tenant for another landlord. Get a list of the applicant's previous landlords and make a few phone calls. Remember, you're not asking for privileged information. You just want a basic tenant history so you can make a fair and impartial judgment about your prospective tenant. By investing a short amount of time on the phone with previous landlords, you'll save yourself days, weeks, and months of hassles by eliminating problem tenants before they become *your* problem tenants.

Set your standards high and keep them high. That's your right as a landlord and property manager. Your basic standard should be that the applicant has a sound credit history with no collections problems. Of course, even good people have bad problems. A lot of hard-working people miss a payment now and then. What you are looking for is a good record over time. Obviously, the individual or the head of the family should have a stable job. The information the prospective tenants provide should be accurate and up-to-date.

Get Permission for Credit Checks

A credit rating or credit report is an objective evaluation of an individual's history of debt repayment; credit reports are generally available from a local retail credit association. (Business histories are available from such sources as Dun & Bradstreet, Moody's, Standard & Poor's, and Fitch's.) Credit reports are your only way to check whether a prospective tenant is capable of making timely rental payments. Don't just ask the tenant how well he or she manages personal finances—request permission to see their credit report. You don't have to be sneaky about this. Tell the prospective tenant that you run a credit check on each applicant, hand over the form, and ask that it be signed. Be sure to get written authorization to look into someone's credit records—personal and business privacy are generally protected by law.

> Credit reports are your only way to check whether a prospective tenant is capable of making timely rental payments.

Some red flags that may require additional inquiry include a bad credit history, a lack of a credit history, repossessed automobiles or appliances, bad check writing, high-balance credit cards, no credit cards at all, foreclosure on a home, bankruptcy, a record of making late payments, a lot of requests for credit information, and a lack of a checking account or a savings account.

Evaluate the Facts

You just can't tell who will be a good tenant and who will be a bad tenant from how he or she looks, speaks, and acts during an initial meeting. The most responsible, easy-to-work-with tenants in the world may show up wearing jeans, scruffy shoes, and shirts that are frayed at the edges. Some of the biggest crooks you'll ever meet wear expensive clothes, drive nice cars, and take long vacations to exotic places. Although instincts are important, it's wise to rely on background and credit checks when considering potential tenants.

Check Before Taking a Check

Mark was very anxious to rent out an apartment in the first building he owned. When a real-estate broker called him and told him he had a good tenant who was ready, willing, and able to lease the apartment right away, Mark wanted to hear more. The broker told him that the prospective tenant was an attorney with a strong financial background, and Mark felt even better.

Unfortunately, problems began before a lease had even been signed. The tenant made frequent phone calls, demanding changes and adjustments of the apartment to suit his needs and tastes. Annoyed and suspicious, Mark took the initiative to phone up the man's previous landlord. From the previous landlord, Mark learned that the tenant was very high-maintenance. Being an attorney, he always hinted at the implied threat of tying up the landlord in legal proceedings to add force to his demands. The man could easily pay the rent, but was the income worth the likely hassles? Mark decided that he did not want to find out.

Discrimination Is Illegal

If you have prejudices against certain people or certain cultures, property management probably isn't for you. The Civil Rights Act of 1964 as well as additional acts and numerous fair-housing laws make it clear that discrimination based on sex, race, disability, and other criteria will not be tolerated in this country. Those landlords who fight this trend—and some still do—find themselves facing the full force of the law. They also face the force of the community, which is made up of different races, creeds, customs, and cultures. Outside of the fact that discrimination is just plain wrong, it's illegal. Justice these days can be swift and severe.

Someone else came along and rented the property before the attorney signed a lease.

Accept Nothing at Face Value

Here's another example from Mark's "dodged a bullet on that one" file. One bright day, a well-dressed man walked into Mark's office wanting to lease an apartment. He was polite, professional, well-spoken, and appeared to be a completely responsible person. He showed his place of employment, filled out the lease application, and even brought in the promised deposit money when he said he would. This "book" had a very shiny and attractive cover.

Unfortunately, this was a dirty book. A credit check revealed that the man never paid a bill on time. He skipped his rents, hadn't paid his alimony, and had a long line of bad credits and even a series of lawsuits related to not paying his bills. Many of these lawsuits lagged on for years . . . but it gets worse. When the man was informed that his lease would not be accepted, he became abusive. He made threatening phone calls, and Mark eventually had to alert the police and get a temporary restraining order against the man. Imagine what kind of problems Mark could have gotten himself into if he didn't run a credit check on this apparently well-behaved man. Never accept people at face value. Only a thorough credit check will allow you to determine fact from fantasy.

Tenant Inspection Tours

One of the best techniques for heading off potential maintenance, repair, and even decorating complaints is to do a complete walk-through of the property with your tenants. Make this an inspection tour and make sure that you express it that way to the tenants. Look at everything. Make notes (or use your own inspection form) on anything that needs to be repaired or replaced.

Once you've completed the tour, ask if the tenant is satisfied. Get specific. Naturally, you don't have to repaint the walls just to

> Once you've completed the tour, ask if the tenant is satisfied. Get specific.

please the vanity of a tenant, but if those walls really do need painting, agree to do so and place a timeframe on keeping that promise. Have the tenant sign the form. Keep a copy for yourself and give one to the tenant.

Some landlords take a photograph of each room during the inspection. Others have even been known to conduct the tour with a hand-held videotape recorder. Consider having the tenants pose in one of the shots. This provides proof that the photos were really taken at the time of the tour. Cameras, film, and even those film/camera kits are so inexpensive these days that this is a very cheap way to protect your assets.

Sign the Lease

When you finally find an applicant who you believe will make a good tenant, you will need to sign a lease. A written lease should protect the rights of both parties. The owner provides a safe and sound living space for which the tenant pays a fair market value. If both uphold their part of the agreement, everybody wins.

Be sure to have an experienced person review the lease with you. All kinds of obligations could be hidden in the document. These things can turn into destructive "land mines" during the term of the lease. One more piece of advice: Never deposit a tenant's security or cleaning deposit without a signed lease. To do so begins a lease by implication.

A Month-to-Month Lease

Most often, residential properties are rented under a one-year lease, but some landlords do offer month-to-month leasing terms to their tenants. With a month-to-month lease, the tenant can, at any time, give notice the he or she is leaving. Tenants love this agreement because it offers them more freedom of action. Avoiding the month-to-month lease often sways the rights more in favor of the property owner. You may have very little notice at all that you now have a vacant apartment on your hands.

How Should You Determine the Amount of the Deposit?

Check with your local rules and regulations to determine any limitations you may have, and then structure a system that is fair to the tenant as well as to your business's well-being. Here's how Mark handles it. When the lease is signed, the tenant is required to pay one month's rent as the deposit, and an additional half a month's rent if there are pets. At this time, the first month's rent should be paid as well. Some landlords also require the tenants to pay the last month's rent before they actually move into the apartment. This is an extra precaution in case the tenant decides to pack up and leave town.

Nevertheless, some landlords actually prefer the month-to-month leases. Because the lease works both ways, it also allows the landlord to terminate the lease at the end of each month, and landlords like the ability to give their tenants immediate notice that it's time to move out. If the owner is planning a change, say to convert the apartment into condominiums, he or she may not want to wait six months or a year for all the leases to come to an end.

However, even with the month-to-month leasing terms, the owner still has to be aware of the tenant's rights. The city will probably frown on a landlord putting people out on the street in the middle of a winter snowstorm. That being said, the month-to-month lease certainly gives that owner a lot of flexibility in planning the conversion to condos.

Negotiating Lease Renewals

Here is what you should keep in mind for the future, when the lease you have just signed has expired and is up for renewal. Lease renewals at higher rates or longer time periods aren't automatic. This is especially true when dealing with good tenants.

Many factors must be weighed. If your local economy is strong and growing, and demand for good housing is high, you might have no trouble at all asking for higher rent. If, on the other hand, the economy is on the downslide, you will probably be much more willing to negotiate just to keep your property occupied.

Renewing a lease provides each side of the negotiation with a comfort factor and that's good. The tenant knows the landlord as someone who takes care of the property and the tenant's needs. The landlord knows the tenant as someone who respects the property and makes his payments on time. A comfort factor can contribute significantly to a successful negotiation.

> The tenant knows the landlord as someone who takes care of the property and the tenant's needs.

Lease renewal negotiations generally revolve around three elements:

1. A landlord will want to extend the length of the lease, while the tenant will most likely want to keeps his or her options open and will push for the same lease length or for going on a month-to-month basis.
2. The landlord will want a rent increase, but the tenant will want to keep the monthly rate the same or to reduce the amount of the proposed increase.
3. The property may be in need of maintenance or repairs, and the tenant may use this as a bargaining chip.

Consider each point carefully, and negotiate in good faith. Remember, good tenants are worth their weight in gold.

For more information on this topic, visit our Web site at www.businesstown.com

Chapter 14

Working with Tenants

Dale Carnegie pegged it right when he said, "When dealing with people, let us remember we are not dealing with creatures of logic. We are dealing with creatures of emotion, creatures bustling with prejudices and motivated by pride and vanity." The way humans think and act will have a tremendous effect upon your business. Whether that effect is positive or negative mostly depends upon your knowledge and understanding of how they think and act combined with your "people skills." Regardless of the location, location, location adage, you will always be dealing with people and with their widely diverse personalities.

Situations can be complex. Personalities and moods change. Think about the people you know. Are they all the same all the time? Of course not. Even the most cheerful of your acquaintances probably feels down in the dumps once in a while. In property management, your ever-changing world is the ever-changing human personality. Human beings are predictable only in the sense that they are always unpredictable. This chapter provides a general road map to help you navigate that fascinating, frustrating, and sometimes frightening territory of working with your tenants.

Basic People Skills

As a property manager you are running a business. Your principle duties are collecting rents and maintaining property. Like it or not, people are and will always be right in the middle of those chores. They can be allies or obstacles, and in most cases the choice is really up to you.

You will probably find yourself dealing with some people and situations that you do not find personally acceptable. You will certainly have to overlook some things in the name of good business practice. For example, you may not like cats, dogs, or other pets—you may even be allergic to certain animals—but that's not the fault of tenants and potential tenants. Pets are for the most part benign and are very important to their owners. Many of these owners are in search of pet-friendly environments. A smart manager gets over his or her aversion to cat hair and runs "pets are welcomed" in his or her newspaper ad.

The Pet Policy

Property owners who exclude pets because of their own prejudices are just cutting themselves out of a large and profitable market. However, make sure you have a clear policy when it comes to pets that are acceptable. Comedian Bill Cosby used to tell a story in which he got a pet rhino just to see what other folks would say. Even the most ardent pet-loving property manager would say this is over the line.

Provided the animals do not interfere with the orderly conduct of your business or public safety, it's best to allow your tenants to be who they are and to live the life they want to live—Fluffy included.

Maintain Good Rapport

A good landlord nurtures good tenants. Here are a few simple, yet powerful ways to build strong relationships.

- Pay interest on your tenant's deposit (a requirement in some states). Let the tenant know you do this up front. The amount of interest is so small, it won't have a serious negative effect on your bank balance, but it will have a powerful effect on your tenant/landlord relationship.
- Provide a maintenance request form. Not only will this show that you are a concerned landlord, the specific information will help you prioritize the jobs and allocate appropriate personnel and materials. It's also a good idea to provide a general complaint form, which would be applicable to other, nonmaintenance situations.
- You can also give your tenants a maintenance guarantee in the form of a document that promises prompt attention to maintenance needs. As a good property manager you want to do this anyway, so why not put it in writing?
- Send thank-you notes. It's a simple and inexpensive gesture, but it goes a long way toward cementing a relationship. People just love to be courted.
- Explain basic maintenance. Encourage tenants to solve minor problems themselves by providing the necessary equipment. If you want to encourage them to use a plunger on a stopped-up toilet, it wouldn't hurt to provide that plunger.
- Give your tenants information they can use. A simple, typewritten sheet with emergency phone numbers, your phone number, the number of your maintenance person, emergency evacuation routes, tips on living in an apartment, tips on equipment and appliances, and any other information your tenants will find valuable.

> Give your tenants information they can use.

In general, keep your eyes open for opportunities to show that you are a concerned landlord and exploit those opportunities every chance you get.

Practice Aggressive Listening

When most people "listen" to someone else, they're actually focused on things like what they're about to say next, how much they'd rather be someplace else, or what to make for dinner that night—anything except what the other person is saying. In property management, this attitude is a sure path to trial, trouble, and tribulation. *Most people are not effective communicators. A good property manager knows how to make up the difference by employing effective listening skills.* Call it aggressive listening, to differentiate the process from the glazed-stare nodding that often passes for listening. A good property manager is a good aggressive listener.

Sometimes your conversations will be purely social. You want to build and maintain a good rapport with all your tenants. The rapport is the grease that keeps the wheels of our society rolling. You don't have to have long, boring conversations with a blabbermouth of a tenant either. You always have the perfectly natural exit line that you have to take care of another tenant's problem. Just keep it friendly and move on. That gets you out of the situation and at the same time confirms that you're a good and attentive landlord.

Other conversations will be all business. Of course, keep these as friendly and as pleasant as the situation allows. Aggressive listening is key because a tenant may not be able to express himself or herself clearly. "We have a heating problem over here" may mean the pilot light has gone out or that the building is on fire. An inconvenience to one spouse may represent a major disruption of lifestyle to the other. Some people may even minimize a bad situation. "No . . . gasp . . . problem . . . gasp . . . I can hold out . . . gasp . . . until you call the gas company." It's your responsibility to discover the true nature of any complaint before you decide on a course of action.

Ask Good Questions

One of the keys to aggressive listening is to ask good questions so that you get accurate and up-to-date information. In case you have trouble coming up with direct questions, here are a few:

> You want to build and maintain a good rapport with all your tenants.

- Could you give me a better description?
- What exactly do you mean?
- How bad is it right now?
- When did this start?
- How extensive is the damage?
- Are you the only one affected?

The nature of the complaint will lend itself to all kinds of questions and follow-up questions. Be sure that you ask them.

Dealing with a Crisis over the Phone

As you will eventually find out, some tenants like to call up their landlords in panic mode. They may make all kinds of demands for immediate action—primarily that "you get over here right now!" Don't fall into the trap of dropping everything and running across town to resolve whatever crisis they've gotten themselves into. Instead, try to establish whether the situation is really as dramatic as they are making it sound. You might say something like, "I'll take care of this right away, but first I really need to get some more information from you."

Reassure, but make sure you get the facts straight, because a crisis situation may be nothing of the sort. A catastrophe to a tenant may be nothing more serious than a clogged drain. You would be showing rather poor time management skills if you break off your meeting with the mayor, take a cab across town, and rush into your rental only to find a popped circuit breaker. Ask first, then act accordingly.

A Fast Response

Whether you have one tenant or hundreds, you will have responsibility for maintenance and repair of your property. Sometimes these matters require immediate attention. There are two very good reasons for a fast response to tenant needs. One is to protect the value of your property. Sure, it may be an inconvenience to drop whatever you're doing to handle fire, flood, or a freak storm, but immediate action may be the only course available if you want to prevent even

Assign Tenant Responsibilities

Let the tenant know that he or she is responsible for a certain level of basic maintenance. If someone doesn't understand how a circuit breaker works, take a moment to conduct a demonstration. If you live in an area where ice can be a problem, make sure the tenants keep a bag of salt handy to sprinkle the driveway and sidewalks during winter storms.

more damage. It's possible that a fast response to a situation may be the only way you can maintain property to manage.

The second reason is to maintain good relations with your tenants. If you're in property management for the long term, you'll need good tenants. More than that, you'll need the word to get out that you're a good landlord. Word does get around, and good people, the kind who are responsible and who pay rent on time, are attracted to good landlords. Taking good care of tenants who respect your property is one of the best ways to take care of and preserve its condition.

Control Every Situation

Many of the situations you will face are like a boiling pot on a stove. Your control of the situation will determine whether that pot boils over or simmers down. Property managers walk a fine line between serving the needs of tenants and holding their own ground to protect and maintain their property. The story of the tenant who let a boiling pot overflow in one of Mark's buildings makes a perfect example.

The damage to his building from the burned mess and the resulting smoke was bad, but not significant enough to make an insurance claim. Clean up and repair still cost him a good bit, and he wanted to recoup those expenses from the tenant who caused the problem. He consulted an attorney who provided him with options and a recommendation. Mark should serve the tenants with a lease termination notice unless they paid him a fee to cover the cost of clean-up and repair.

Deducting the amount from their security deposit was neither prudent nor legal at that point in their lease. The tenant's rights rules and regulations in Chicago prohibited such action. Fortunately, Mark sat on the idea for a while. His instinct told him to hold off, and it's a good thing he listened.

The rental market in Chicago was soft at that time. His monthly income of $1,850 was significant, and would be hard to replace. Mark's intuition said that if he sent the letter of termination, the tenant might become angry or upset and refuse to pay the rent

> If you're in property management for the long term, you'll need good tenants.

altogether. That would have led to an expensive and time-consuming eviction process, which would be a definite lose/lose situation.

Mark sought counsel from his older and wiser colleagues at a local builders club meeting. Their advice was golden. Send a letter to the tenant stating that, although legal counsel had advised him to pursue the situation through legal channels, he would instead absorb the costs of clean-up and repair. He would further explain that he appreciated the tenant and the tenant's business and wanted to continue the relationship. It worked. The letter released a lot of tension and created a significant amount of good will. And it really didn't cost Mark that much. Breaking the expenses down, his loss was only $75 a month.

That's how a smart property manager looks at a situation. Mark was well within his legal and ethical rights to evict his careless and foolish tenant, yet he did something else. He "lost" a mere $75 a month, but kept a nice $1,850 check coming in at the same time. That's dealing with the human element!

Role Playing Keeps Things Rolling

Property management is a people business. Every time you enter a new lease with a new tenant, you are starting a new relationship. Being able to play different roles effectively will help you maintain it as a good relationship.

The roles landlords have to play vary wildly, from the passive good listener to the active surrogate parent. Just which role you play and how you play it will vary according to the situation, the property, and the people involved. Often you'll be called upon to play these different roles at a moment's notice. To be successful you'll need to become a master of the art of improvisation. "Thinking on your feet" will become a way of life, or at least a way of conducting business.

The character Schneider in the 1970s television show *One Day at a Time* is a perfect example. The show was about a divorced mom and her two daughters who lived in an apartment. Schneider was the building's janitor, but he was often called upon to be more than that. In many ways the character became a surrogate parent, uncle, big brother, and best friend.

Most of the time you'll find yourself playing the role of landlord, but if you take your responsibilities as a property manager seriously, you'll find yourself playing other roles, too. Teacher, counselor, good guy, bad guy, and friend are just a few of them.

When All Else Fails, Negotiate Compensation

Here's a true story about a tenant with an electric stove that stopped working. The problem wasn't serious, but no repairman could get out to fix it for some time. The family living in the apartment had no way of cooking the evening meal—or any other meal, for that matter—and had to go out to eat every night until the repairman at last showed up and fixed the stove.

The family claimed that the landlord was responsible for covering their eating-out expenses. The landlord realized they had a good point. Repairing the stove was his responsibility, and the family had incurred unplanned costs as a direct result of his faulty appliance. These were good tenants who paid their rent on time and who really weren't the complaining and whining sort.

The landlord didn't really want to pay for days of fine dining, so he decided to negotiate compensation with the family. He asked them what they thought was a fair deal, and they asked for a $50 gift certificate for a nearby grocery store. From the landlord's perspective, the request was more than reasonable and he accepted immediately. This policy works really well with good tenants because they will generally ask for less than you'd be willing to give them, so make sure you let the tenant speak first.

The Five Basic Types of Tenants

As noted previously in this book, everyone is different, with diverse wants and needs. Still, if you stay in this field long enough, you will come to distinguish all tenants as belonging to one of five categories: watchdogs, complainers, helpless tenants, slow-payers, and those who refuse to pay at all. As you might guess, the first three of these categories are okay to deal with, while only the last two can be considered legitimate problems.

Watchdog Tenants

The term "watchdog tenant" may sound problematic, but these tenants really aren't. Watchdog tenants always call to alert the property manager to fix a problem. They are the "squeaky wheels" that demand immediate attention. If you think about it properly, the people are anything but problematic.

The watchdog tenant wants to live in a good, clean, and safe environment. Isn't that what you want for your property and your tenants too? If there's a real problem, you want to know about it right away so you can fix it and perhaps prevent an even greater problem down the line. Wouldn't you rather know about that tiny leak before it bursts the pipe and has your tenants impersonating Noah and his family trying to survive the flood?

Certainly, these folks can be a bit trying, and often you'd rather be on the phone with someone else—anyone else. Try to overlook your aggravation and keep this in mind: Watchdog tenants are valuable people, and you want to have them around. They can tell you what's really happening in and around your property and can prove to be some of the most reliable tenants you'll ever have.

Complainer Tenants

Unlike the watchdog, whose calls are warnings, the complainer calls for one reason only: to complain. That's his or her purpose in life. Complaining is like their hobby or, worse, the centerpiece of living. It's important to realize that regardless of what you do, how well you do it, or how fast you get it done, it's never going to be good enough for the complainer. The act of complaining, and not the problem itself, is the real focus of attention.

Handle complainers by setting up rules very early on. If you don't, they'll feel free to call you up any hour of the day or night with mostly imagined problems. Every ping, bump, squeak, or normal house-settling noise becomes an excuse to pick up the phone. Again, set the rules early or be prepared to lose a lot of sleep.

Helpless Tenants

A helpless tenant appears to be, well, helpless. These folks will tell you with a straight face that they don't know how to change a light bulb, plunge a toilet, or reset a circuit breaker. They are often the personality type in need of a surrogate mother or father and you, Mr. Schneider, have been selected. Why? Because you're there.

> Handle complainers by setting up rules early on.

Address these issues in your lease papers. Let your tenants know up front the extent of their own responsibilities in your building. If you encounter someone who really doesn't know how to change a light bulb or who doesn't understand the need to spread salt on an icy sidewalk, invest a few moments to instruct them in the basics. In your list of tenant responsibilities, include such things as costs for excessive service calls, lock changes, or lost keys. Essentially, you have to create a fee schedule for tenants who create cruel and unusual requests.

Slow-Paying Tenants

Slow-paying tenants really do cause problems. Although you'll eventually get your money from these individuals, the process will be a major hassle. You'd think that a slow-paying tenant would make irregular payments. Curiously, most people who pay late maintain a schedule. They won't pay on time, but they pay regularly.

These folks establish a payment rhythm. For some reason, they'd rather pay during their second paycheck cycle, the second two weeks, and fork over the penalty for being late. Often, they've just scheduled all their payments inconveniently. Maybe the car bills, credit card bills, and educational loan bills come at the same time as the rent is due.

In these cases, and after you've investigated the tenants carefully, it's best to accept the situation. A slow, but regular payment is better than no payment at all. And as long as you're charging that late penalty, the tenant is paying extra for the privilege. It may be slightly inconvenient, but it's at least a win/win situation.

> A slow, but regular payment is better than no payment at all.

Tenants Who Refuse to Pay

This final category represents the tenants who will cause you the most problems. As a property owner you must set standards of business practices and then rigorously maintain them. One element must be the immediate serving of delinquency notices to tenants who do not pay their rent on time. Certainly you will determine that some pay, although they can never manage to pay on time. If that schedule plus the penalty payment is acceptable, then it's okay, but you should still maintain your standards.

Automatically serve notice within the time prescribed by law on anyone not paying his or her rent. If you do not receive your rent after the service of notice, without delay have the file sent to your eviction attorney or do the filing yourself in the appropriate court for possession of the unit and a money judgment in your favor for the rent owed and the balance owed according to the terms of the lease. Allow no room for flexibility in collecting your rental payments. You must set a strict standard here to be successful in the property management business. If you make exceptions, you will create exceptional problems.

The tenant who will not pay rent is usually cunning and knows the rules and how to delay eviction. Believe it or not, you're not the first property owner that this tenant is taking for a ride. Somehow in your checking references, you missed something. It happens. What separates a good property manager from a weak one is how you handle the situation.

Please don't think property owners and managers have to be cold and harsh. You just have to conduct business in a businesslike manner. In most cases, the collection of rent will be as easy as opening an envelope at the beginning of the month. But don't waste time protecting yourself, your property, and your investment as quickly as possible.

Like Attracts Like

Most people are pretty decent folks if you treat them decently. Every once in a while, however, you run into someone, even entire families, who thrive on causing trouble. These are the people who have no respect for other tenants and certainly not for themselves. They hold late-night parties. They keep illegal pets. They clash with other tenants. They trash your property. Basically, they just don't conform to approved ways of conducting themselves around other people.

These are the people you want to get rid of as quickly as possible. Like attracts like. If you're not careful, one bad tenant can run off a lot of good ones. Worse than that, the bad tenant will attract

---

Storytelling at Its Best

When the tenants do not pay their rent, they will come up with various explanations to justify their delinquency. Some of these stories will be quite remarkable. If your avocation is writing, you might want to collect these excuses as sources of inspiration for your science fiction and fantasy novels.

Never hesitate to start the eviction process, and don't listen to excuses and tales tenants create to dodge their obligations to pay the rent. The longer you wait before processing the eviction of tenants who are not paying their rent, the longer it will take you to get to get possession of the unit as well as collect money owed to you.

people with similar attitudes. Instead of one problem tenant, you could find yourself with an entire nest of them. Do not underestimate how much trouble or how much physical and emotional damage these people can cause.

There's no nice way to handle problem tenants like these, yet you just can't kick them out. Again, your community will have very specific rules and regulations regarding this matter. Tenants, even bad ones, have rights. Begin by building a paper trail of their wrongdoings. Put them on notice for every lease violation. Cite every violation, paragraph after paragraph, and note that the issues were specifically covered in their lease agreement. Play by the rules, but don't allow bad tenants any "wiggle room." Once you've established a solid paper trail, get together with your attorney and begin the eviction process. For more details on dealing with problematic tenants, see Chapter 15.

Tenants, even bad ones, have rights.

For more information on this topic, visit our Web site at www.businesstown.com

When Tenants Cause Problems

Trouble will inevitably come your way. It's part of the job. You will most definitely encounter problem tenants. That comes with the territory. Some of them will come at you out of the blue, but you can improve relations with some tenants and fix the problems before you realize you have troublemakers residing in your property. In some cases, a little forethought and some prompt action will go a long way.

Again, your people skills in handling troublesome tenants will to a significant degree determine your success in this business. They will certainly control to an equal degree your professional and personal peace of mind and the number of antacid tablets you consume.

Ask for Feedback

Some tenants will begin to cause problems to get your attention because some issue that is important to them has not been addressed. Asking for the thoughts, opinions, and suggestions of your tenants is a great way to keep the lines of communication open. Often a little advance notice or your own insight into personal behavior can prevent a problem from developing.

In addition to speaking with them, put up a suggestion box so they can leave you messages when you're not around. Sure, you'll get the inevitable "Dry up and blow away" or "Go fly a kite" response, but you might also get some good ideas and interesting feedback. When you get a good suggestion, thank the tenant for being concerned and for taking the time to provide you with the suggestion, even if you don't act on it.

Put up a tenant bulletin board. The tenants can use it to post notices of property for sale, advertise baby-sitting services, announce club meetings, and so forth. Your tenants will appreciate the gesture. You can also use the board to solicit comments and suggestions. Just post a simple notice about whatever subject you'd like to hear about. Be sure to note the means of replying to your request, such as your phone number or e-mail address.

> Some tenants will begin to cause problems to get your attention because some issue that is important to them has not been addressed.

Consider developing a regular newsletter for your tenants. You don't have to be professional about it, although with many desktop publishing software programs producing a top quality newsletter is easy. Include any information that could affect your tenants, such as your vacation schedule and who to contact while you're away. Note improvements you've made or are making to the property. Be sure to state the benefit of those improvements. For example, a new sidewalk isn't just concrete. It's increased convenience, increased safety, and an aesthetic improvement.

Always seek out new and better ways to get information from your tenants. They're the lifeblood of your business. Keeping two-way information flowing will do wonders for your financial health.

Defensive Measures for Offensive Tenants

A lot of tenants are borderline—they are neither perfectly behaved nor intrinsically evil. With a little planning and some early work on your part, you can bring a lot of those people around and build a positive relationship throughout the length of the lease. It's worth the effort. A wise manager places as many problematic tenants in that category as is humanly possible. How? By working as effectively as possible with the tenants to handle situations before they evolve into real problems.

However, there are bad tenants out there. Don't allow them to get under your skin. You will have a natural pride in your properties, in your ability to manage them, and in your continuing success. When a tenant shows a lack of respect for your property, for the other tenants, and for the property manager, that insolence can cause you emotional damage. There will always be such toxic people out there. Some of them actually enjoy hurting other people, especially those in a power position such as a landlord.

Avoid these types whenever you can. If you must deal with them, don't give them any power or allow them any control over you. Be professional and act in a businesslike manner at all times. Keep your cool. If they get through to your emotions, they've won the battle. Never forget that the property is *your* property and you are in this business for the long term. Avoid foolish actions that could burn bridges or come back to haunt you.

Problems Can Hide Other Problems

Problems aren't always what they seem. And some problems can mask other problems, which might even be more severe or troublesome. A good property manager knows how to ask questions to get answers. And a really good property manager knows how to continue asking questions, really listen to the answers, and then ask follow-up questions to get at the real source of the problem or issue. Mark ran into a situation that perfectly illustrates the point. Here's how it went and what he learned in the process.

This situation took place in a five-bedroom, three-bath apartment rented by four roommates. One day, Mark received a phone call from one of the roommates. This man called to complain that their oven was not working, and that his calls to the maintenance man were left unanswered.

Mark called the maintenance man himself but could not get through. He left a message, and a couple of days went by before Mark followed up on the problem. It turned out that the maintenance man had quit his job and wasn't doing maintenance for that building anymore—in fact, he had been out of town for weeks.

Take the Time to Investigate

After calling the tenants to apologize about the problem, Mark finally realized that he should have begun the process of fixing the problem by figuring out what the problem was. After a question or two, Mark figured out that most likely the problem was with the oven knob. It was installed upside down, and baking temperatures were all wrong. The tenant's buttered toast came out looking like a blackened roofing tile while his baked lasagna remained a muddle of lukewarm tomato sauce and un-melted cheese.

Yet more problems were to come. The next day, the tenant called back, ranting and raving. The oven had stopped working entirely, and the gas burners had stopped functioning too. The tenant claimed that this stove was always a problem and that this situation had gone unresolved for too long. He was going to complain to the city about paying for but not getting a working stove.

> A really good property manager knows how to continue asking questions, really listen to the answers, and then ask follow-up questions to get at the real source of the problem or issue.

Complaints to the city, whether justified or not, are always a problem. Bad feelings, unnecessary paperwork, and additional expense are sure to follow. It's best to make a genuine attempt to resolve a negative situation with a tenant before others get involved. Mark, with good reason, thought he had provided an answer to the tenant's problem. He learned a valuable lesson—make a follow-up call or visit to make sure the problem really is being or has been solved.

To avoid complications, Mark quickly made arrangements for a replacement stove. It would be delivered and installed the following Saturday, the earliest possible date. He left a message to the tenant on their message machine to that effect. That same evening a call came from one of the other roommates. This roommate called to say thanks for the replacement stove in advance. He was quite happy that after all these months their need would be met. However, he mentioned that now half of the apartment had lost its heat.

Having learned his lesson, Mark began to ask questions. He knew that the apartment had gas heat, and he wondered whether the oven that stopped working and the heat loss could be connected. He asked if the floor without heat was in fact the same floor where the kitchen with the broken stove was located. By gosh it was. He quickly advised the tenant of the possibility that the reason the stove would not bake and the burners would not light just might be due to the fact that the entire floor did not have gas. After a long silence, the tenant said he understood the situation. Here is what happened.

Earlier in the week, this tenant had called the gas company to complain that they were receiving two bills for gas utilities each month. The gas company informed them that they had two gas meters supplying gas to their apartment due to the zoned heat in the unit. The unit they were living in was previously two units that had been combined into one apartment years earlier, so there were two meters for each different floor. The tenant felt that if they received only one bill rather than two they would save money in utility costs, so he directed the gas company to remove one of the gas meters, thus ceasing the flow of gas to half of the apartment. He got exactly what he asked for. No gas (and no gas heat) in half the apartment.

> Complaints to the city, whether justified or not, are always a problem.

The Follow Up

Mark immediately called the gas company, which reinstalled the meter. Heat was back on and the oven started working again, so Mark cancelled his order of the new oven, saving himself the money and the trouble.

A few days later, Mark visited the apartment to see if the stove still worked. Miracle of miracles, gas was flowing, burners were lighting, and toast was toasting. The tenants felt embarrassed that they had caused their own problems and then blamed Mark for them, and he never heard about any minor problems from them again.

> Don't avoid your problem tenants.

Avoid Childish Behavior

As the landlord, remember that you don't have to resort to threats or revenge. You are a professional; no matter what, deal with your problems in a professional, responsible manner. Although it might be tempting, don't avoid your problem tenants. Slipping threatening messages under the door, leaving angry voice messages, or sending scathing e-mails won't get you where you need to be—these are just ways of skipping out of a confrontation. The tenant will do nothing but ignore you, or respond in kind, leading to an escalation of troubles.

Remember, you can be powerful and polite without being a bully or by sticking your foot in your mouth. Losing your cool only plays into the hands of the offending tenant. Chances are he or she is much more experienced and is a much better player at that game than you.

Furthermore, trying to get back at a bad tenant by withholding a right, such as interest on a deposit, will get you in jeopardy with the applicable tenants' rights. Penalties can be severe. Revenge, even against a truly troublesome tenant, just isn't worth your time or effort.

Never let a tenant force you into losing your temper. The only way to maintain control is to be in control. Explosive situations have a way of getting out of hand and sometimes that's exactly the plan of the troublesome tenant.

Handling Hard Luck Stories

You will get to hear them all. Just when you think you've heard every possible excuse and hard luck story, someone will throw you a curve with something entirely new. The least imaginative people in the world can suddenly become creative geniuses when it's time to pay their rent. If some of these folks could just channel that creative spark, they could make a fortune in Hollywood. Unfortunately, their focus is not on making. It's on taking.

Hard luck stories come at you from two angles: prospective tenants who *will not* pay their rents, and existing tenants who *don't*. Those two angles cover a lot of territory, but the sooner you familiarize yourself with it, the less likely you'll fall victim to the strategies of the people coming at you from these angles.

A red flag should be waving or a buzzer or bell should sound if you start hearing hard luck stories during your initial meeting with a prospective tenant. They're probably just setting you up for a fall. You can't discriminate on the basis of a hard luck story—that's illegal—but that red flag should encourage you to conduct a thorough investigation into this person's or this family's credit history.

Popular stories include losing a job, having a death in the family, or encountering some large and unexpected expense. If you know the people, if they have a good credit record, and if you feel okay about cutting a tenant a little slack now and then, that's fine. But never forget, their problems aren't your problems—unless you make them yours.

> Never forget, their problems aren't your problems—unless you make them yours.

Keep a Record of Hard Luck Stories

Some tenants discover a really good hard luck story that seems to work better than all the rest. Like an actor who discovers a terrific role, he or she continues to play the same part year after year. That's fine for the arts, but you're managing an apartment, not a theater.

Take notes on every hard luck story you hear from every tenant. Keep the notes in a file so they'll be handy. You'll be surprised how many people experience the same tragic event over and over. There are tenants who have "lost" seven or eight parents, dozens of aunts and uncles, and uncounted family friends and coworkers.

Of course, the failure to pay the rent is due to these tragic events and not to the tenant's own laziness or greed.

If you have kept a history of such excuses, you can give the performance the bad review it deserves when you hear that poor Uncle Joe has passed on for the fourth or fifth time.

Bad Luck or Bad Attitude?

Not all hard luck stories reflect bad luck. Sometimes people will attempt to turn their good fortune into a hard luck story just to avoid paying their rent. Here's an example, a true story. One of Mark's tenants worked for a very successful company that manufactured cookies and crackers. Although she had originally worked at their headquarters in Chicago, she was promoted to a position that required extensive travel. The only time she returned to her Chicago apartment was during the weekends.

Her salary was pretty good, and she had received a hefty bonus to sweeten the deal involving the transfer. The new job allowed her to stay for extended time periods in some of the finest and most elegant hotels in the country. Unfortunately, her rent payments no longer arrived on time and eventually stopped. Perhaps she felt that since she wasn't really living in the apartment that much she shouldn't have to pay for it. Of course, there were the little matters of the lease she had willingly signed, her legal obligations, and her word.

After Mark served her a notice of termination, suddenly the payments started coming back in—on time, too. With remarkably few exceptions, the trials and tribulations and the successes and triumphs of your tenant are not your concerns. Don't allow your tenants to turn them into your problems. Essentially, a deal is a deal. If the stipulations change, they should change only at your discretion.

Management Rule #1

This rule is simple and basic: Rent must be paid on time. Most people are good and decent folks who act responsibly. You can work with these people. It's the few rotten apples in the barrel you have to worry about. You'll discover people who will try to manipulate you

Rent must be paid on time.

into agreeing to changes in the lease after they've signed it. Some do it because they're poor money managers. Others do it for the sheer joy of getting away with something.

A good property manager is a strict manager. If rent doesn't come in on time, you must immediately serve the tenant with a rent delinquency or termination notice. The moment you vary from this policy is the moment people will start to take advantage of the situation. This is especially true when you are renting to commercial or industrial clients. When a business is late with their rent, cut them loose and move on. Find a more solid business, and rent to an organization willing to be responsible.

The Exception to Rule #1

There are exceptions to every rule, and this management rule is no different. Some tenants sign a lease without realizing that a lot of their bills will be arriving at the same time. If they are like a lot of people out there, they're living from paycheck to paycheck, and one check can't possibly cover all those bills. They decide to hold off on the rent, pay late, and accept the late fee as part of the cost of doing business.

These people aren't deadbeats. They can afford to pay rent, and even the penalty, but they've just scheduled their finances poorly. If you have a tenant who can pay regularly, and pay the late fee without griping about it, then you have an exception to rule number one. Basically, you have someone who is acting responsibly. In a situation like this, you'd be far better off if you skip a costly, time-consuming, and possibly emotionally-charged eviction process.

Invest in Common Sense

Realize that genuine hard luck comes along now and then. For example, if a tenant is called to active military duty, and he or she is the sole supporter of the family, under law the landlord must honor the tenancy even if the rent isn't forthcoming. That's why it's so important for you to meet and get to know all your tenants. You'll be able to weed out the actors from the decent and responsible folks who may be experiencing a legitimate run of bad luck or who have

> If you have a tenant who can pay regularly, and pay the late fee without griping about it, then you have an exception to rule number one.

met with an unexpected change of fortune. This is where your common sense comes in to play.

Here is a story of how the landlord and the tenant can work together to avoid a problem. Back in the 1980s, Mark was in the retail business and owned a store. When the economy took a downturn, his business followed. Fortunately, Mark knew his landlord, who had invested the time to meet and get to know him. When Mark approached him with the truth, the landlord suggested the following plan. Mark would pay a reduced rent, and payments would be staggered and structured so that over time, Mark would pay back every cent he owned. Mark agreed, and they were back in business.

This is a perfect example of a landlord using common sense. He knew his tenant was being truthful. The economic downturn was all over the newspapers and was affecting everyone's business. He knew the local real-estate market was soft and finding a new tenant would be difficult at best. He also knew that Mark was a serious businessman who would handle his responsibilities. Having a tenant paying something is a lot better for the landlord than paying the bills on an empty building. Common sense created a win/win situation.

Keep Move-outs Moving

A lot of tenants don't become problem tenants until they decide to move out. Here are a few tips on how to make the transition a smooth one for both landlord and tenant.

- Get the tenant ready for move-out when they move in. Tell them—better still, provide written information—about the move-out procedure you expect your tenants to follow. Leave no room for ambiguity or misunderstanding. Ill defined or "fuzzy" items have a tendency to rear their ugly little heads at the most inopportune and costly time.
- Inform tenants of your deposit return policy. Leave nothing to chance and make sure there's no "wiggle room" for the

> A lot of tenants don't become problem tenants until they move out.

tenant to avoid his or her obligations. Again, this isn't just good business. It's good public relations.

- Include a "Notice of Intention to Vacate" form with your other printed information handed out to new tenants. When they decide to move, the tenants just fill out the form and hand it over. A form is considerably more "real" than the spoken word, both in tenant/landlord relationships and in court, if necessary.
- Provide a list of all the possible charges related to move-out. For example, list all landlord-furnished items and the expense of replacement. Cleaning charges should certainly be noted.
- Define the meaning of "move-out." You'll be surprised how many interpretations of two simple words your tenants can come up with. The only definition that matters is yours, but you have to share it.

When it's finally time to move out, make sure to do the following:

- Conduct a thorough inspection of your property, preferably with the tenant. Make sure you have noted all items or situations that require deductions from that deposit. Make sure the tenant has paid up his or her utilities.
- Get your keys back. If a previous tenant returns to your property and uses a key you once provided to enter and cause mischief, you could be held responsible. Ask if the tenant had additional keys made and get those, too. An excellent time to hand over the keys is during final inspection of the property just prior to the move-out.
- Promptly return all deposits and the interest payments on them.

Be Fair

Act fairly when charging your tenants. Define "wear and tear" versus "damage." Sun-bleached drapes fall under the category of normal wear and tear. A cracked or shattered mirror is damaged. Be warned: You can't charge a tenant the full amount of replacement on a damaged item. You can only charge according to the useful life remaining in that item. If the mirror is thirty years old, don't try to make your tenants buy a new one at their own expense. Fairness is essential to good business practice. Besides, the word gets spread pretty quickly about rip-off artists.

Lease Termination

Sometimes the tenants choose to move out, but other times you come to a conclusion that you need to tell them to do so. In many communities how you serve termination notice on a tenant can be just about as important as the notice itself. A lease termination notice comes in many shapes and forms, depending upon your community. In Cook County, Illinois, a tenant who does not pay his or her rent gets a five-day notice of lease termination. A month-to-month tenant has to be notified thirty days in advance. Whatever form and whatever advance notice is required, you must make sure the notice is delivered according to the statutes in your area. Posting it on the doorway may be perfectly okay in one part of the country, but completely wrong in another. In some areas you must physically hand a notice to a tenant, sometimes in the presence of a witness.

Evictions

Eviction is a legal proceeding in which a landlord seeks to regain possession of property from a tenant. There are several different types of evictions:

- **Actual eviction** occurs when the force of law or a legal process is used to remove a tenant from a property.

Giving Notice

A "notice" is an official communication of a legal action or of someone's intent to take a legal action. For example, Landlord A may need to move bad Tenant B out of his building, so a legal notice of termination is given. The landlord will probably be required to allow a set number of days for the tenant to leave as part of this process. This isn't only a practical matter of allowing sufficient time for the move. It's also good public relations—you don't want to make yourself look like a villain throwing someone out on the street with a day's notice.

The notice must be served on the tenant. It shouldn't be left in the door or handed to a friend, although in some states it is permitted to give notice to a family member or to another tenant residing in the space. The safest procedure is to deliver the notice to the tenant yourself.

Make sure you know the law. For example, if a witness is required, but you present the notice without one, legally you haven't given notice. An improperly serviced notice is no notice at all.

- **Constructive eviction** happens when the landlord allows the physical condition of the property to deteriorate to a state where it is unfit for the purpose for which it was leased. For example, if a landlord allows the roof (or basement, floor, or another part of the property) to go into disrepair so that the property is no longer safe to inhabit, the tenant may be able to terminate the lease through constructive eviction.
- **Partial eviction** happens when a tenant is deprived of a portion of the rental property. For example, if the landlord wants to repair a floor in a rented office space, the tenant and landlord agree to a partial eviction while the repairs take place. An appropriate reduction in rent is normally part of the process.

Partial eviction h
when a tenant is
deprived of a portion
of the rental property.

For more information on this topic, visit our Web site at www.businesstown.com

PART IV

Enlisting Professional Help

Topics covered in this part:

- Where to go when you need help.
- How a good attorney can protect your business.
- Why you need to work with your accountant.
- Who can help you figure out your finances.

Find a Good Lawyer

Chapter 16

T he best attitude to take in finding a good lawyer and in building and continuing your landlord/attorney relationship was
best expressed by Robert Schmitt in the Spring 1984
Americans for Legal Reform newsletter: "The average lawyer is
essentially a mechanic who works with a pen instead of a ball peen
hammer." A good lawyer, like a good mechanic, is essential to maintaining a smoothly functioning society. Perhaps if there weren't so
many bad people, we wouldn't need to have so many lawyers.

An Important Role

The need for sound, experienced, and readily available legal advice
cannot be overstated. You will need critical and unemotional analysis
of legal forms, contracts, and offers of all kinds. The waters can be
especially treacherous for those of you entering a field in which you
have little or no experience.

Remember, your attorney will be working with you closely on
some of the most important business and financial decisions you
will ever make. His or her ability to provide good legal advice will
have a dramatic impact on your ability to earn a living as a property
manager.

What You Need in an Attorney

Your attorney or legal firm should have a lot of different skills and
experience, but two are key to your success: a sound reputation, and
a proven track record in closing real-estate transactions. A good reputation and real experience aren't necessarily reflected in the hourly
rate of an attorney or law firm. How do you find a good attorney?
One of the best techniques is to ask for referrals. Get a lot of names
from a lot of people, preferably people in real estate, and make a lot
of calls. Meet with different lawyers and firms. Research and interview your legal representative as you would your doctor, your suppliers, or the kid with the nose ring about to take your daughter to the
prom. This is serious business. If you're meeting with a firm, be sure
to meet with the individual or team who will actually be handling

Hired to Do a Job

Upon approaching an attorney for the first time, many
people wonder if they should
bow, curtsy, genuflect, or just
meekly hand over a blank
check. That's not a good business attitude. True, a good
lawyer is worth every penny
he or she charges. They'll
keep you out of more trouble
than you can possibly imagine
if you work with them. They'll
rescue you from bad situations or at least help prevent
bad situations from becoming
disasters.

However, despite all the
wondrous things your attorney can do for you, always
remember that your attor-
ney's role is not much different from that of your
plumber, electrician, carpenter, secretarial service, bookkeeping firm, and every other
contractor or supplier—
lawyers are men and women
you hire to do a job.

your work load, not just the high-powered "brass" whose pictures appear in the newspaper.

Mark notes that he's never seen a lot of difference between a thousand-dollar and a ten-thousand-dollar attorney when it comes to real job performance. If you do your homework, check out those references, and conduct serious interviews, you'll find someone who charges a day's wages for a day's work.

You Need a Real Estate Pro

Don't be "penny wise and pound foolish." Some folks are so cheap and their focus on saving pennies is so concentrated that they end up losing much more in the process. Do not make that mistake in regards to your legal affairs.

Too often, property managers and landlords try to get by "on the cheap" by avoiding the expense of legal counsel or by settling for a lawyer who is unfamiliar with real estate. In today's business climate that's not only foolish, it's downright insane. When you are buying, managing, and selling property, you need a good real-estate attorney.

Keep in mind that states have different real-estate laws. For example, people in Louisiana live under a unique legal system called the Napoleonic Code. If you don't buy, sell, or manage property in the Bayou State, you won't have that dramatic difference to deal with, but you can count on significant differences between California and Connecticut, Montana and Mississippi, or New York and New Mexico. As a landlord, you are just too busy to learn—much less stay on top of—the changing laws in your own state, much less the other forty-nine. You will need the services of a knowledgeable attorney to put together the paperwork on your transactions. That applies whether you are working with a property across the country or just across town.

Your attorney should be someone you trust to put partnership agreements, contracts, and other deals together, and someone you believe to have a lot of experience in this area. The attorney should also be familiar with the current tax laws. This is important. Should your accountant make a mistake, you may need your attorney to

Be Forewarned

Before signing or even verbally agreeing to any contract, you must know precisely what you are signing or agreeing to honor. The language used in legal documents, sometimes called "legalese," can be tricky for the uninitiated. It's important to have someone available who can make sure you are signing what you think you are signing. People who try to save money by avoiding the services of a qualified attorney usually end up losing a lot more of their money in the long run.

defend you in court, and the lawyer must have a basic understanding of accounting in order to build a credible, intelligent defense.

Again, it is critical that your attorney be a real-estate attorney. The greatest divorce lawyer, criminal defense attorney, or corporate wheeler-dealer may prove to be useless in real-estate matters.

What about the up-and-coming young lawyer who hasn't had time to develop experience? You can still check this person's academic accomplishments. Perhaps he or she worked part-time for a law firm during school and gained some real-world experience. That's helpful and good to know. However, if the young attorney lacks experience, you must be assured that an experienced lawyer will be supervising the newcomer's every action. Keep an eye on how things are going. You never know; sometimes the rookie goes on to become the most valuable player.

Specify a Completion Date

Here's an example of how things can go wrong when someone chooses the wrong type of attorney. A man was in the process of buying a new-construction home, and he found an attorney who was skilled and experienced, just not in real estate. The man had his life precisely scheduled. He would live in his apartment until the lease ran out, at which point he'd need to spend one month in temporary residence (for which he made plans) before he could move in to his new house.

Things didn't exactly happen that way. The developer had a problem of some kind with his city alderman and could not get the permits he needed to build the house. The developer's problems quickly became the buyer's problems. There was just no way the house could be built within the specified time.

An experienced real-estate attorney would have inserted a clause in the contract specifying a completion date. This guy's attorney didn't know that he needed to do that. The only completion date was expressed in a nonbinding, nonlegal verbal statement between the developer and the buyer. As a direct result of hiring the wrong type of lawyer, the client lived in that "temporary residence" for a year and a half, trying to get his money back from a developer who had neither the capability nor the enthusiasm to finish the project.

> An experienced real-estate attorney would have inserted a clause in the contract specifying a completion date.

Don't Overlook Overcharges

Overcharging can be a real problem in the legal industry. Find out your prospective attorney's rates up front. Do they charge by the hour or by the transaction? Also ask about the attorney's existing clients. What problems had the attorney solved for them? How were they solved? Get a list of client references and call them. Another strategy is to check with the local bar association to verify that the individual attorney and the legal firm he or she represents are in good standing.

You will need an attorney who will not get defensive or angry when you call up to ask about a specific charge. On the other hand, when you have questions about a fee, you also have the responsibility not to overreact. Simply ask for clarification. It may be that the attorney tried to rob you blind, but you may have also forgotten a request for services you've made. Another possibility is that the

Mark's $1,024 Letter

Mark was recently involved in the sale of a condominium. During the process, a heavy rainstorm led to a flooded basement, and the negotiations stalled. The buyer claimed that Mark had not disclosed that the lower level of the building was prone to flooding. Mark did, in fact, address that issue. To deal with the situation properly, he hired an attorney to respond to the buyer's complaints.

The buyer's lawyer often did not speak with Mark, and therefore communication had to go from buyer to attorney to attorney to seller and back again through the same clumsy procedure.

Mark's attorney reviewed the buyer's two one-page letters. He also reviewed the real-estate contract and invested some time checking the appropriate case law. He also brought in an associate on the case. After all this, the lawyer prepared and sent a letter to the buyer's attorney stating that everything about the transaction was proper and all appropriate disclosures had been made.

The bill for this letter was $1,024. That's a pretty hefty fee for a one-page letter. Mark—or any property manager, for that matter—could have dictated the same letter in no time at all. Of course, other factors were at play here. A letter from a lawyer has a greater impact than a letter from a property manager. Is any letter worth more than a thousand dollars? Will the impact of the legal firm's logo on that letter be worth your investment compared to handling the situation yourself? Only you can decide that.

overcharge may simply be a bookkeeping error that can be quickly rectified. The point here is that you need the kind of attorney with whom you can communicate without creating doubt, confusion, or mistrust. The more open and honest you are, the easier that is to accomplish.

Evaluate Time and Money Skills

When you are still negotiating with a prospective attorney, consider his time-management skills. Does he or she return phone calls within a reasonable time? Will you be charged for every little phone call? Or will the attorney cut you a little slack when you need sixty seconds of his or her time? Does the individual or firm have a good reputation for being on time during all phases of a transaction? Transactions should never linger because of a lawyer's lack of due diligence.

Attorney Scams

As with every group on the planet, there are good and bad lawyers. There are numerous ways the bad ones can take your money. The most common is the practice of inflated billing—simply charging for work that was not actually performed. When a lawyer or a firm is being paid by the hour, there is a tremendous temptation to bill for more hours than the attorney actually spent working on your case. Some companies even have hourly billing quotas. If the work doesn't meet the quota, then, by golly, the invoice will. Furthermore, in a contingency case, in which the attorney's fee is one-third of the settlement, expenses are taken off the top *before the money is divided*.

Another problem is when the attorney commingles funds by collecting a client's money designated for an escrow fund and placing it his or the firm's own account. This lets the attorney use the money free of charge: he or she can even collect interest on it.

A lawyer may also get involved in a scam with a second party. For example, let's say a lawyer agrees to a $10,000 settlement. A compliant adjustor tells the client the adjustment is for only $9,000. The lawyer takes the extra grand or splits it with the adjustor.

Finally, an attorney may tell you that in order to win a case, a specified sum of money must be passed on to an influential person (for example, the judge or the prosecutor). The problem with this little scam is that the attorney only does it on a case that is a sure bet. No one is actually bribed, and the lawyer pockets the money.

Also discuss payments for assistance with deals that end up falling through. Will you be charged on the same level as if the deals had been concluded successfully?

Beware "Flash"

Which of the following do you think would make the best real-estate attorney for your needs?

- The tall man with the southwestern drawl, long and well-groomed hair, buckskin jacket with fringe, large silver and authentic turquoise belt buckle, highly polished cowboy boots, and a small tribe of assistants catering to his every need.
- The well-dressed woman with a suntan, polished nails, starched white shirt with French cuffs, an expensive thin brief case, and a small tribe of assistants catering to her every need.
- The local attorney dressed in a suit from Sears, wearing the Rotary Club pin on his three-year-old shirt, sporting a haircut from one of those places down at the mall, and without the small tribe of assistants—just an answering service.

Which one's for you? Do you have any idea? Of course not. There's no way of knowing without conducting some really serious research. A lot of flashy attorneys wearing expensive clothes are excellent practitioners of their craft. Unfortunately, a lot of attorneys so attired are all flash and no show. Others may express their individuality in colorful regional styles of dress and speech, and that's all right. As you will learn, there's a place for showmanship in business. The point for you is to discover whether there's a quick-thinking and attentive mind behind all that showmanship. The local guy may lack flash and showmanship, but he may be the best attorney for your needs—or the joke of the local bar association. Again, you can't tell until you really get to know these people.

For your first real estate transaction, you'll probably need a "downtown" attorney. This is someone in your community with a

> For your first real estate transaction, you'll probably need a "downtown" attorney.

Learn the Ropes

The services of a good lawyer will make your life much easier, but it's important that you know exactly what's going on as it happens. If your attorney says or writes something you do not understand, ask for clarification in layman's terms. If you don't get it, and get it quickly, chances are this isn't the attorney for you. Sometimes the best legal representatives are the low-key, almost invisible people in the field. To find out for sure, you have to do your homework. Learn the ropes or, to borrow a phrase from boxing, you could end up on the ropes.

good reputation who knows the ins and outs of your market. If you're purchasing a property for under $1 million, you will probably not require the services of a two-hundred-person legal firm. Don't give an attorney more credit than due just because his or her rates are the highest in town. Rates and fees don't automatically translate into competence, a commitment to taking care of clients, or the willingness to return urgent phone calls.

The Hiring Process

When checking out attorneys, you'll want to look at many things, but chief among should be the following:

- **Knowledge of current real-estate law.** Real-estate law can change with amazing speed. Try to find the kind of lawyer who makes a practice of staying on top of local, regional, and national changes in real-estate law. An attorney who is prepared and knows what's going on will always outperform the one who needs to go and research the answers to any questions you might have.
- **Familiarity with the local market** (however you, the client, define "local"). An all-encompassing knowledge of national real-estate law is fine, but that won't necessarily do you a lot of good when you are filing to rezone a plot of land downtown.
- **Good references.** Any good property manager will ask for references and check into a lawyer's background. This is no place to slack off. Making those calls or visits is an investment in your future. You'll be placing the fate of your business into the hands of your attorney or legal firm. Make sure they're strong enough for the task.

If you are dealing with a legal firm, make sure that you meet the actual people who will be handling you account, and discuss the potential fee arrangement. If you feel confident that this individual or firm is on your team, an active partner interested in promoting and maintaining your success as a property manager, you've got a good lawyer on your hands.

Working with Your Attorney

The key is to work *with* your attorney, not for or against him or her. Your attorney works for you, but you are on the same team and should have mutually compatible goals. Share the load and share it with good spirits, courtesy, and respect.

Before any important meeting, have your attorney give you a checklist of items you need to prepare or have ready for that meeting. For example, you may need to produce legal proof of your citizenship or age. It's better to have that material available for the meeting than to break up the meeting and reschedule while you go back to your home or office and try to scrounge up what you need. You don't want any delays of any kind when consummating a deal.

Losing Lawyer-Client Privileges

It can happen, and with surprising ease. Communication between a lawyer and a client is generally privileged. That is, it must be kept strictly confidential, because the lawyer must protect the client's privacy. Legally, no one, not even law enforcement or the courts, have a right to inquire into your dealings with your legal representation.

A lawyer can't go off and talk or write about confidential matters, either. This is a two-way street between you and your attorney. However, there is an exception. A third party, such as your banker or accountant, who happens to sit in on the conversation between you and your attorney cannot claim the lawyer-client privilege. You lose your confidentiality. The way around this is to have the lawyer speak to the third party separately. Of course, when confidentiality is not a concern, you would not want or need to claim attorney-client privilege, and you could have any number of parties involved in the communication.

The thing to remember is that to ensure confidentiality, keep the information between you and your lawyer and involve no one else. If a third party needs to be involved, see that the party becomes an employee of the attorney, such as a consultant, or conduct the third-party conversations separately. If in doubt, ask your lawyer to make sure the privilege is at all times maintained.

Make sure your attorney is aware of local laws and disclosures that are related to the negotiations at hand. If you are preparing to sign a contract, have your attorney give you a sample contract so you can read, review, and ask questions before the day for signing arrives.

Make sure to meet with your attorney face-to-face, even if you have to make the trip yourself. Do not cover important material over the phone, by fax, or through e-mail. Although your legal representative should not charge you for that meeting, if you are billed, you have a pretty good idea of what you may run into in the future with respect to fees.

Seek Good Rapport

Good rapport is essential. Remember, your lawyer or legal firm is working for you. A good lawyer, like a good doctor or financial consultant, has to be available for your calls within a reasonable amount of time, to provide the accurate and up-to-date information you need, and to answer your questions without being condescending or aloof.

Good rapport is an essential element of the client/attorney partnership. You may have found the world's greatest lawyer with the most experience in real estate, but if you can't get along, you will not be able to maintain a satisfactory working relationship. Listen to your instincts. Regardless of his or her qualifications, if you feel uncomfortable, find someone else. You will save yourself a lot of time, energy, money, and frustration by moving on. America is loaded with lawyers. There are hundreds of thousands of them nearby (wherever you are) who can satisfactorily meet your property management needs. Find one with whom you can establish and maintain a good rapport, and each of you will be richer for the experience.

You don't have to become best buddies. You don't have to meet for drinks at the friendly neighborhood pub. You don't have to invite each other over for dinner on Saturday. You should like your attorney, feel comfortable discussing your private business, and feel that your needs as a human being are being met.

> Good rapport is an essential element of the client/ attorney partnership.

Accept Your Responsibilities

Your work with an attorney should be considered a partnership. Certainly, it is an unequal partnership. You are, after all, the boss. But it should be a mutually beneficial relationship and a win/win situation. A good lawyer is not only someone who is knowledgeable in real-estate law. He or she is also someone who takes the time to work with you and your respective situations, who checks and verifies that you are getting exactly what you are supposed to get and that you are fulfilling your legal obligations, and who provides you the necessary legal services.

Robert Half, a well-known personnel agency executive, once said, "Delegating work works, provided the one delegating works, too." As a businessperson you can't neglect your own responsibilities. You may not know the intimate details of local laws and regulations, but you should be familiar with local laws and how they are changing. A good basic knowledge of applicable law will make communicating with your attorney much easier, simpler, and faster, because you absolutely must invest the time to read and to understand every document you sign and every verbal agreement you make.

Build Time into Your Agreements

It is a common practice to include a period of time for the attorneys involved to approve, disapprove, or suggest changes in the contract. This attorney approval period generally lasts five days. This gives you ample time to consult with your legal counsel to see if there are any nasty surprises hidden in the fine print.

Most real-estate sales are "as is, where is" transactions, which means that the day after you close, anything having to do with the physical nature of the property is your responsibility. Language in the contract may not include this specific phrase, but the meaning will be in there someplace.

Usually, representations of the physical soundness of the property or warrantees having to do with the property expire at the closing. If you sign the document and thirty seconds later the roof collapses, the basement cracks, or the plumbing springs a leak, the

> Most real-estate sales are "as is, where is" transactions, which means that the day after you close, anything having to do with the physical nature of the property is your responsibility.

Free and Clear

If you do not acquire clear title to your property, you could be liable for delinquent real-estate taxes, state taxes, or money owed to contractors and suppliers. These amounts can be significant, so all such items must be accounted for and cleared up. You want to take possession of the property, not someone else's obligations. If there are any encroachments or easements or restrictions on the deed, you must be made aware of them through the legal description and survey of the property.

previous owner can smile, offer a friendly goodbye wave, and say "I'm outta here." In a lot of ways it's like buying a used car. All warrantees are off and the responsibility for repair and maintenance sits with the purchaser. (And that's all the more reason to thoroughly investigate your purchase before you make the purchase.)

Know and fully understand your responsibilities before closing so you can have some leverage before you lose the ability of gaining recourse. Remember the old adage of "Let the buyer beware," and be very wary. On the other hand, if the seller guarantees that the physical condition is in a certain shape and it is not when you reach the closing, you want to make sure you are adequately protected, covered, and that you get what you are supposed to get out of the transaction. This same point also applies should the seller guarantee a certain amount of income from the property and that income doesn't materialize. A good lawyer will not only help set up your agreements so that there is recourse in such matters, he or she will be able to guide you through and handle the often complicated legal process of actually getting that recourse.

Get Clear Title

Any property you purchase must be delivered with a clear title. A title search is an examination of the public records to determine the actual ownership and any encumbrances and/or past claims affecting a piece of property. The attorney should be responsible for conducting a title search and then providing the client with an abstract of title, which is a historical summary of all the recorded instruments and proceedings affecting title to that specific property. This step is taken so that any obligations from the previous owner will not become your responsibility.

Problem-Solving Tips

Here are a few short answers to a few common problems that may come up in the course of your working with attorneys. To help you avoid problems to begin with, remember that as a general rule, the more open you and your attorney keep the lines of communication, the fewer problems you will encounter.

- The fee seems too high.

Solution: What happens when you discover the price of your toothpaste is too high? You shop around. Do the same thing with your legal services. Shop around, and don't be shy about negotiating for a lower fee. After you've found a new lawyer, get a contract or a letter specifying all fees and rates, how they will be calculated, the services covered, and the payment schedule.

- You just can't afford the fee.

Solution: Say so, and say so up front. If you really want to work with this attorney, ask if he or she will reduce the fee or extend the payment period.

- The fee appears inflated compared to the amount of work done.

Solution: Get more information. Ask for a breakdown of the work performed on your behalf, the amount of time required to do that work, and the charge for it. Often lawyers, and other suppliers, put in many more hours on a project than the client ever realizes. If you can't get a satisfactory answer, approach the local bar association and bring the matter to their arbitration board. If there's a lot of money being disputed, you may want to hire another lawyer just to help you in the arbitration. As a last resort, you can always take your attorney to court.

- The lawyer is neglecting your transaction.

Solution: Speak up. Voice your concern and ask for an accounting of work on your project. If you don't get a satisfactory response, tell the attorney that you might report him or her to the bar association and the lawyer review board. Of course, you can fire the lazy lawyer and find someone who'll represent you with more energy and professionalism.

- Your lawyer mishandles your property.

Solution: This may be cause for a malpractice suit. Investigate that possibility with another attorney who has expertise in that field.

> If you just can't afford the fee, say so, and say so up front.

If the settlement doesn't cover all your losses, you can appeal to the client security fund of the bar association, which reimburses clients victimized by lawyers. You can avoid this problem before it happens by insisting your lawyer provide you with regular, detailed accounts of the assets placed in his or her trust.

When to Sue for Malpractice

If you conduct your search for a very good lawyer properly, malpractice is not a problem you should encounter. However, lawyers and situations can change. Consider suing for malpractice if you believe the following:

- That recent litigation with which you have been involved would have ended in a more favorable decision/resolution for you were it not for the neglect of your attorney.
- That your attorney fell below the commonly accepted standards of skill and knowledge possessed by lawyers in similar situations. An attorney cannot claim that the standards should be lowered by locality and custom, but these reasons can be used as a defense to illustrate why a law or procedure is not settled. Also, standards may be raised by the specialization required by the case or situation. To prevail in this situation, you will need to present expert testimony.

The easiest way to avoid a malpractice situation is for you and your lawyer to maintain clear lines of communication. Try to avoid situations in which the attorney is handling serious cases or procedures for personal friends. Keep business all business. While no one, not even the best lawyer, can guarantee a successful outcome, your attorney should be confident in giving you an objective opinion. Lawyers frequently use the phrase "You have an arguable case."

Make sure all fees and costs are spelled out in advance and in writing. Have the lawyer note any exceptions or special cases where additional costs could be incurred. It is okay to specify a cap on how

> The easiest way to avoid a malpractice situation is for you and your lawyer to maintain clear lines of communication.

much you will be willing to invest in the given situation. Make sure the attorney clearly states the extent of his or her responsibilities, including any appeals if appropriate. Your agreement should make provision for periodic payments to your attorney. The exception would be a case where the lawyer is working on contingency. The best way to avoid such expensive and time-consuming situations is to speak openly and honestly. Eliminate situations before they turn into legal problems.

These days lawyers are the only people who can read, understand, interpret, and put to use laws, regulations, contracts, and agreements. That's especially true in real estate. If you want to be a successful property manager, listen to the advice provided in an ancient and oft-proven proverb, "What the large print giveth, the small print taketh away." There's no better rationale for finding, hiring, and maintaining a good relationship with a very good real-estate attorney.

> These days lawyers are the only people who can read, understand, interpret, and put to use laws, regulations, contracts, and agreements.

For more information on this topic, visit our Web site at www.businesstown.com

Find a Good Accountant

Chapter 17

A quick glance through the appropriate pages of your telephone book will reward you with a long list of accountants and accounting firms, but finding the right one to handle your specific needs is another matter altogether. This chapter will explain why you need a good accountant on your side and suggest where to find this elusive creature.

What Is Accounting?

An accounting is a financial statement of income and outflow that keeps a detailed record of your receipts and disbursements during a specified time period, such as a year. It is the practice of keeping, analyzing, and explaining commercial accounts. If the business is a new one, the accounting period would cover the time from when the business began to the present.

The record can be prepared by your internal accounting department, an accounting firm, or an independent accountant hired for this purpose. This record should detail your financial transactions in some appreciable detail, including cancelled checks, invoices, and bills. Accounting procedures, when conducted properly, are clear, strict, and formal. Of course, we've all encountered examples of accountants bending the rules; you need to be aware of the rules and basic principles of accounting so that you will detect instances when these rules are trampled.

Accountants Aren't Property Managers

Robert Townsend, author of *Up the Organization: How to Stop the Corporation from Stifling People and Strangling Profits* (Fawcett Books, 1984), wrote: "Accountants can be smarter than anybody else or more ambitious or both, but essentially they are bean counters—their job is to serve the operation. They can't run the ship."

Harsh words? Not really. Townsend is just speaking from experience. Before writing his best-selling management book, he turned Avis Rent-A-Car into the top contender for the number-one car rental company, Hertz. Remember the "We're Number Two. We Try Harder" advertising campaign? Townsend's point is that it's far too easy to allow experts in other fields to make management decisions in your field. Good accounting is a necessary part of your business, and an accountant is an essential member of your business team. You just have to remember who really runs the show.

Managers Should Manage

The temptation to let your accountant take on more responsibility than is prudent is easy to understand. Accountants speak a different language, and the mass of numbers they generate for you can be overwhelming. On top of that, there's an entire body of law associated with those numbers.

It's important to remember that management is your job and that you and accountants live in two different worlds. Accountants live in the world of hard numbers, precise rules, and strict procedure. In that world, if there's a problem, you just apply the appropriate formula and the answer comes spewing out of the calculator or the PC. The labor and thought behind that labor may be intense, but there's very little—if any—room for doubt. Accountants do not guess, nor do they have to. If speculation is called for, it's labeled as such, although, if you think about it, it is still based on specific formulas.

You live in a world that's half real and half fantasy. There is no single right answer, and there are many possible outcomes to any problem or situation. Terms constantly change on you with every new tenant, adjustments in the law, economic forecasts, changes in your community, and any other number of ever-changing factors. Half the time you're guessing.

As a property manager, much of your business life depends on the future. Your job is sometimes not too different from the medieval kings who based their predictions on their fortunetellers' predictions. What part of town will be hot in the next decade? What neighborhoods will face a decline? How will the economy ten years down the road affect my rentals? Is there an economic potential in that run-down and abandoned warehouse? All these questions require answers that are nothing more than instinctive. A landlord has to work with hard numbers all the time, but the job also requires constant use of intuition, a bit of luck, and scientific guesswork. You can't put any of that down on a balance sheet. Those things aren't numbers that can be "crunched."

> It's important to remember that management is your job and that you and accountants live in two different worlds.

As with your attorney, you hire an accountant or an accounting firm to do *a* job, not *your* job. They provide the data, but you have to take the responsibility to make the decisions.

Accountants Aren't Bookkeepers

What do accountants do? They keep the books, don't they? Most people think accountants and bookkeepers do the same things, but nothing could be further from the truth. These are two entirely different business functions, usually handled by two entirely different groups of people.

The property manager or landlord usually handles the bookkeeping function. This entails compiling and tabulating the income and expenses for each property you manage. It's an important job, but it's not accounting—it's merely keeping track of what you had already done, that is, income you already received and expenses you already covered.

Your accountant should be in charge of performing the following:

- Making sure that you are allocating your expenses correctly.
- Filing proper tax forms with state and federal governments.
- Making sure you're depreciating assets appropriately and not subjecting yourself to any federal penalties for not paying applicable taxes and disbursements to your real-estate holdings or your investors.

What to Seek in an Accountant

As with any other supplier, your accountant or accounting firm will need to have a number of skills and considerable experience. Here are a few areas that are essential:

- Experience in real-estate accounting and in handling real-estate transactions. Your cousin, brother-in-law, or next door neighbor may be a great accountant, but without "real"

Estimating Your Profits

Basically, accounting is the procedure that lets you know whether or not you're making money from your properties. If you are making money, accounting will help you decide how to redirect your attention in order to increase those profits. If there are losses, the financial data should point them out as well. This information provides you with the opportunity to make changes, such as raising your rents or sprucing up your property, so that you can move your notations from the loss column into the one labeled "profit."

real-estate experience, he or she has the power to do you much more harm than good.

- Familiarity with applicable real-estate law is important. A good understanding of the rules and regulations is important as background, but the accountant should keep an eye on where things appear to be going, too.
- Fee structures that are appropriate for the market or the job and that are easily understood are obviously a major consideration. Again, the highest hourly rate doesn't always translate into the best service. Unlike many attorneys, accountants don't usually charge for a basic phone call. Still, it's a good idea to get a clear picture of rate and fee structures before you make your final decision.
- A client list will reflect the caliber of work by the caliber of clientele. You can also get an idea of the accountant's area of expertise and perhaps a hint of the connections this supplier may be able to make for you. Remember, a top-notch "mom-and-pop business" accountant with a list of good clients may or may not be the ideal choice for your ten-story high-rise apartment building. That's why you need references (as explained in the next point).
- Any professional should be willing to provide you with a list of references, and accountants are no exception. Take the time to call at least some of them to get the full story.

More Complicated Than Quantum Physics?

Albert Einstein possessed the twentieth century's most brilliant mind. A far-ranging thinker, his ideas shaped his era and will have a tremendous impact on the direction of the twenty-first century. But after all his probing into the complex mysteries of the universe, he said, "The hardest thing in the world to understand is the income tax." If Einstein couldn't hack it with a balance sheet, how much luck do you think you or I will have?

Hire Knowledge and Experience

An accountant who is a credible individual with experience in real estate is as important a member of your team as a savvy real-estate lawyer. You need both sets of skills and experiences. Just as you would expect and need your attorney to have some basic knowledge of tax implications from real-estate transactions, you should expect your accountant to have some legal knowledge as well. For instance, he or she should know how depreciation schedules work for residential buildings versus commercial buildings. (Depreciation is over 27.5 years for residential properties and over 39 years for commercial properties.)

Accounting for a building with multiple owners differs significantly from accounting for a single-owner property. Your accountant needs to understand those differences. Equally important, the accountant must stay on top of the ever-changing set of local, state, and federal laws and regulations governing property ownership and management. This task is something best left up to someone who really knows the business. As a manager, you have neither the background to understand those changes nor the time to try to keep up with them.

Is Your Accountant Accountable?

A very good accountant will do much more than help you file your taxes and send an invoice once a year. As a businessperson, you should expect excellent service, which should at least include coming up with new ideas or suggestions throughout the year. Think ahead of the financial curve. A very good accountant will be looking out for your welfare this year, next year, and the years beyond right into your retirement. Areas he or she should be aggressively researching should include the following:

- Tax preparation
- Evaluation of your business insurance coverage
- Evaluation of your personal insurance, including life insurance
- Retirement and estate planning
- Professional financial statements for loans
- Investment advice
- Credit advice
- Record keeping
- Acting as a "sounding board" for your ideas

Seek Objectivity

You don't want a "yes man" handling your finances. In the recent past, a number of financial scandals that made the national news involved accounting firms that were all too willing to jump to the command of the companies that hired them. The accounting

> As a businessperson, you should expect excellent service, which should at least include coming up with new ideas or suggestions throughout the year.

companies' greedy and short-sided actions led to a number of large, embarrassing bankruptcies; in some cases, the scandals ended in the court room.

Your accountant should explain the pros and cons related to any of his or her advice. Risks and rewards should be explained in detail and without bias. You should also expect to be warned against unsound investments or risky deals, regardless of your personal excitement about them.

Working with an accountant is just like any other business relationship. If both parties will work together, and if each tries to make the other's job a bit easier, it should be a win/win relationship that lasts.

Concerning your end of the partnership, you should provide your accountant with accurate and up-to-date information, open communication, information that is well organized and easily accessible,

Four Helpful Financial Documents

Landlords and property managers are sometimes inundated with financial paperwork. Some of it is standard, and some of it is extremely useful. Here are four documents you will find most valuable in evaluating your daily, monthly, and long-term operations. It's a good idea to study these, and other financial forms, in some detail.

1. An income statement, also called a profit-and-loss statement, summarizes your profits and losses during a specified period of time, such as a quarter or a year. The statement itemizes all revenues and all operating expenses for that time period.
2. A balance sheet is a financial snapshot of your business operations at any given moment. Usually, an accountant will put together a balance sheet at the end of an accounting period. Among other things, it lists your assets, any items of monetary value, and liabilities, which are monies owed to creditors of the business.
3. A cash flow analysis compares the cash flowing in to the cash flowing out in order to determine whether or not you're making a profit, a handy fact to know in real estate.
4. A quick asset ratio compares your current assets (assets that can be sold within the year and are therefore liquid) to your current liabilities (short-term liabilities that can be eliminated within the year). Obviously you want a good assets-to-liabilities ratio.

and complete data. Don't put yourself in the position of having to say, "Oh, darn! I forgot . . ." Remember, the ultimate responsibility for the success of your real-estate success lies within your own hands. See that you keep a firm grip.

Understand Tax Considerations

Our government's tax code changes with as much regularity as do laws and regulations governing everything else. We are all subject to taxes, and the amount of taxes we owe varies from year to year. As you buy and sell properties, your tax situation will vary considerably.

If you are invested in a partnership, your group is required to file a tax return with the government. The return will show your income, expenses, and taxable gains or losses. The partnership must be real. Income must be dispersed properly to all partners, even if those partners are your spouse and children. This is why accurate record keeping is essential.

> The attitude of some tax and regulatory people seems to be that the landlord is guilty until proven innocent.

The attitude of some tax and regulatory people seems to be that the landlord is guilty until proven innocent. That's something like the old custom of discovering whether a person is a witch by tossing her into the lake. If she floats, she's a witch and is burned at the stake. If she drowns, she's innocent. Unfortunately, she dies in either case. Be duly warned: If the IRS ever comes knocking, you'd better be prepared.

The Tax Reform Act of 1986

The most significant change in the U.S. tax code in recent history was the Tax Reform Act of 1986, instituted during Ronald Reagan's administration. The act brought major change because it facilitated the following:

- Greatly reducing your ability to acquire tax shelters from real estate investments.
- Lengthening the depreciable lives of assets.
- Eliminating favorable treatment of capital gains.
- Restricting the use of installment sales.

- Creating the Real Estate Mortgage Investment Conduits (REMICs) to help the issuance of mortgage-backed securities.
- Significantly reducing the number of tax brackets for individual taxpayers.
- Eliminating or phasing out certain itemized tax deductions.

The act had an immediate effect on the stock market, which plunged in October of 1987, and on the savings and loan debacle of the 1990s. It has been revised every year since it was instituted, and no one knows whether or not it will undergo a complete overhaul. In other words, things remain in a state of flux.

The Tax Reform Act gives two definitions for "passive activity income": first, any trade or business conducted for profit in which the taxpayer materially participates; second, any rental activity, regardless of the taxpayer's material participation. In other words, rental property was made passive, and the federal government disallowed passive losses. Owners may not use losses to shelter other types of income. If your accountant had continued to deduct losses from your passive real-estate investments after 1986, you would then be subject to serious fines and problems with the government. This is a very good reason for having a competent accountant who stays on top of things working with you. A good accountant will allow you to adjust to the changes that will inevitably come your way, so you can keep buying, selling, and managing your properties—profitably.

> As a full-time property owner or manager, you have the privilege to deduct your real-estate losses against your ordinary income.

Appreciate Your Depreciation

As a full-time property owner or manager, you have the privilege to deduct your real-estate losses against your ordinary income. (Please note the modifier to property manager in that sentence. It must be "full-time," and that's a serious legal distinction.) You can use the depreciation in your buildings to offset your personal income. If you have a loss at the end of the year, you may be able to save thousands of dollars on your income tax return. A very good accountant will be monitoring these factors for you all year long.

The tax code doesn't prohibit you from owning and operating other businesses, but you cannot take the deduction if your side business generates your primary income. But if your primary income as described by the IRS is property management or property ownership, you can take the tax advantage. This income can easily exceed the IRS limit of $3,000 a year, which all your partners and investors are required to adhere to.

Property Is More Than a Shelter

A smart property manager gets into real estate for more reasons than just sheltering taxes. Take the tax shelter as the *additional* benefit to property ownership. Take all the depreciation and losses that are due you, but essentially you should look at property ownership as a means of building your personal income. Why just take losses when you can build a fortune? Again, a good accountant can help you achieve your maximum goals in both areas.

Get the Accountant on Your Side

As noted, your lawyer is an important partner in your success, as you are in his success. The same is true for your accountant. He or she should be willing and able to work with you and your lawyer to keep your business running smoothly. In fact, a good accountant can provide a good referral to a good attorney (or vice versa).

You can often find accountants who are lawyers and lawyers who are also accountants. There's nothing wrong with having one person handle both responsibilities, but your checklist of needs includes someone who knows tax law, real-estate law, partnership, and contract law. That's a lot of responsibility for one person. If the individual makes an accounting mistake, there is no lawyer to catch it. Checks and balances have served the U.S. government well for more than 200 years. They can serve you just as well in business. As a general rule, don't put all your eggs in one basket. Share the wealth—and the responsibility.

A good accountant is someone you hear from at least once a quarter, not just at the end of the year. He or she checks in periodically to make sure you are keeping up with your bookkeeping and to see that you are filing all the documents you are required to submit

> You can often find accountants who are lawyers and lawyers who are accountants.

on time and in good order. This is a basic service you should expect from any accountant or accounting firm. You do not want to be scrambling around in a desperate search for invoices, receipts, and financial records at tax time. That just puts unnecessary demands on your time and extra burdens on your accountant. Keep your records accurate and up to date throughout the year.

Prepare for Meetings

Once you've hired an accountant, remember that this professional is not there to help you organize your files. If you're paying an hourly rate, it's bad business to hand over a bushel basket full of unorganized papers and say, "Here, figure this out." The same will apply to working with accountants who charge a flat fee. Making a professional clean up and organize your files just wastes time that should be invested in reviewing your situation and finding ways to save you money.

When you plan to meet with your accountant, get organized. Here are some things you should have in hand when you arrive:

- A list of all your earnings.
- The amounts of any estimated state and/or federal tax payments and the dates on which they were paid.
- A list of any securities you have sold within the past year. You should have the date of purchase, date of sale, cost, and the proceeds.
- A list of items you know you can deduct on your tax return, such as medical expenses, interest on loans, contributions to charities, and your business expenses.
- A separate list (if appropriate) of income items, expenses, and losses that you are not clear about or have tax-related questions.
- If you have bought property, bring in your escrow or closing papers. If you have sold property, bring closing papers from the original purchase.
- A list of any improvements you have made to your properties, including the cost of those improvements.

> When you plan to meet with your accountant, get organized.

Furthermore, if you are meeting with your accountant for the first time, bring along your income tax records for the past five years. The accountant will need these for reference.

Computer Programs Aren't Accountants

Today you can walk into any number of computer stores, software stores, and even department stores and pick up any number of so-called computer accounting programs. These programs are designed to help you keep your books and run the day-to-day financial operations of your business—or so the advertising copy on the boxes says. Accounting programs are designed by top people in the business and produced by reputable firms. Many of them even do exactly what the ad copy says they do. There's just one little problem: These programs are not *accounting* programs.

These programs are not *accounting* programs.

"Current" Is Obsolete

Although the cover and advertising copy says these shiny disks really are accounting programs, there's just no way that can be true for the property management industry. The copy isn't lying to you. It's just that the laws and regulations governing accounting change so quickly, any program you buy will be obsolete before it can do you any real good. It is essential that you stay on top of all the changes that affect the accounting portion of your business.

A program that was completed January 1, 2002 became out of date by January 3, 2002. Somewhere some bureaucrat or lawmaker or regulator is already making changes in the laws and regulations covered in that computer program. It's just impossible for any software to be up to date. Do you want to risk missing out on a new tax benefit or risk a painful loss over a change in the tax code because that change was made after your computer disk was slipped in its fancy box, shrink-wrapped, and shipped to the neighborhood computer store?

Not Totally Useless

Don't misunderstand the point. Computers and computer programs are wonderful. They have proven their value in business applications in virtually every industry in the country. They have their place in the tool shed.

Years ago we used handwritten ledgers. Every building, every expense, every income dollar, every item had to be logged by hand. Then we had to go through the time and trouble to transfer those notes to typewritten pages, which often had to be run off on an old-fashioned copy machine. Talk about labor-intensive! Things are much better, much faster, and much more accurate these days, thanks in large part to computers and computer software. But to trust your accounting completely to technology, even the latest technology, is little better (and maybe a little worse) than trusting to the old-fashioned ledgers, paper, and ink.

Bookkeeping Software Is a Good Buy

While accounting programs really aren't the safest bet, there are numerous bookkeeping programs that can save you hours of toil and trouble and make the effort as close to effortless as it can be. While no specific product is endorsed here, there are numerous topflight software packages out there. Just be sure to tell your salesperson that you are interested in bookkeeping and not accounting programs. There's a world of difference.

The bookkeeping program should meet your needs and your computer skills (or the skills of your in-house bookkeeper). It should be comprehensive, but it should not be so complex that you have to add on staff just to load the darn thing in the computer. The information you generate will be invaluable to your accountant at the end of the year. In fact, you might consult with your accountant as to which software packages best meet your (and his) needs.

If you own or operate multiple buildings, make sure to have a bookkeeping system for each building. This is especially important if you have different partners in different real-estate ventures. It's illegal to commingle funds. If you didn't know that, you do now, so make sure you have separate accounts for each property. It's much easier to keep things separate, accurate, and up-to-date if you don't mix everything up at the beginning. Sorting everything out at the end of the year can be a real nightmare.

> The bookkeeping program should meet your needs and your computer skills (or the skills of your in-house bookkeeper).

Chapter 18

Find a Good Financial Advisor

T here must have been a lot of "good old days" because we hear so much about them. A key feature of those happy times was the friendly neighborhood banker. Many of you reading this book aren't old enough to remember the friendly neighborhood banker. This friendly banker didn't only stick to banking and making profits—he (there were no female bankers in the "good old days") also dispensed financial advice.

In fact, the friendly neighborhood banker was the financial advisor for the entire community. He knew business and finance. He knew who in town was a good businessperson and who couldn't manage money or pay bills on time. Financial matters were much simpler in the days before the global economy, so he knew a considerable bit about many aspects of finance. He was always glad to see you and would often grant a loan based on your trustworthiness and track record with the bank, even if you didn't appear sound on paper. How things have changed since those days of yore. Today, bankers are just people in the business of lending money, which doesn't make them financial advisors.

> Today, bankers are just people in the business of lending money, which doesn't make them financial advisors.

Banking Is Business

One major change since the good old days is the disappearance of the community bank. Like the herds of buffalo that once covered the plains, community banks are rapidly becoming extinct. The merger mania that has marked banking in the past decade has helped create stronger institutions with considerably more financial strength. An effect of this change has been the replacement of that friendly neighborhood banker with a man or woman who takes your financial information, punches it into a computer program, waits to see if you fit the bank's "profile" or "credit score" of a good bet, and then gives you their decision of whether to give you a loan or show you the door.

Banks these days advertise that they have financial advisors ready to help you with all your monetary needs. Many have separate departments devoted to that end. However, it's not clear how well they are able to do that. Many of these financial advising departments are really operating as investment centers for mutual funds, stocks, and bonds. Many are experienced in setting up 401k plans and retirement accounts. If you're thinking about approaching your bank for financial advice, you should find out if any of them have real estate experience. If your banker doesn't have a good handle on the ins and outs of real estate, he or she really can't offer much in the way of sound financial advice. Before seeking real estate advice from your banker, or anyone for that matter, check out his or her credentials.

Learn the Tools of the Trade

Two key words you'll hear when talking with your financial advisor are "financing" and "financial leverage." They're important terms and you should fully understand them. You'll run into them frequently, so be sure you understand what you're saying before you say it.

> **Financing** as it relates to real estate is the borrowing of money to buy property. Your financing options include getting a mortgage, assuming a mortgage, getting a loan from the seller to buy the property, or creating an arrangement to buy in installments.
>
> **Financial leverage** is the use of borrowed money to complete a purchase. There are many considerations involved, and you will most certainly need the counsel of a financial advisor if you are considering this route.

Other Financing Options

You don't have to invest directly in a building, a shopping center, an industrial park, or raw land to invest in real estate. You have a lot of options. Most investors rarely consider many of them. Here are a couple of areas worth investigating.

Think about making an investment in stocks and/or bonds of other real-estate companies. Lots of companies, including builders, real-estate development companies, mortgage insurers, and even building-supply companies make these offerings. Some companies only indirectly involved in real estate may make similar offerings. Banks, savings and loan companies, and insurance companies

Get References

Yes, get references, even if you are considering working with a financial advisor who works for the biggest bank or financial company in town. The biggest company around can do you no real good if they assign someone without the necessary experience or knowledge to handle your account, so the first question to ask is: Who exactly will be in charge of your account?

Insist on meeting and getting to know this individual before you commit to any firm. Investigate. Ask questions. Shop around. Then, follow your instincts.

financing real-estate deals may also be attractive additions to your portfolio.

Also review the holdings of large companies that are very heavily involved in real-estate transactions. You'd probably be amazed at the variety of companies owing substantial real estate that are open for investment. These include companies involved in farming, forestry, oil and gas development, mining, railroads, and other areas related to land and property.

Take the time to look around. Do your homework. Consult with your financial advisor. It's possible that investing in these areas will fit your portfolio needs.

More Uncommon Investment Opportunities

Don't stop looking for investments at companies involved or associated with the real-estate industry. There are lots more options available. Check out the government-backed securities that are issued by a number of U.S. Government agencies. These securities, backed by mortgage pools, may be ideal for your personal or corporate investment needs. Many publicly and privately traded companies offer the same type of securities.

Examine the variety of real estate–related trust funds open to investment. These include Real Estate Investment Trusts (REITs), certain mutual funds, and various trusts that offer real-estate specialization. You can also take a close look at certain limited partnerships with real-estate holdings. Many public and private partnerships are open to investment.

You don't need to limit your investment opportunities to just the popular or common options. Certainly, they're worth investigating, but think outside of the box, too. Work closely with your financial advisor, and be sure to investigate all your options.

> You don't need to limit your investment opportunities to just the popular or common options.

Seek Good Advice

The American author John Steinbeck once said, "Nobody wants advice–only corroboration." There's a lot of truth in that statement, which is something you need to be aware of. When you have to make important financial decisions, you want serious advice–not corroboration for the benefit of your ego. You need to be strong enough to pay attention to advice, and sometimes you need to be strong enough to reject it. When you start relying exclusively on others to make important business decisions, you're making a fundamental mistake. Your final decisions should be your own. You're the one who ultimately will have to live with them.

Interview people in the know. Seek them out. Ask questions, but in the end trust your own good judgment. Follow your instincts. Too many people in real estate fail to follow that "tiny voice" and live to regret it. If you're feeling uncomfortable about some one or some transaction, there's probably a sound reason for that feeling. Explore.

Find a Real-Estate Mentor

You don't do it on your own. Find a mentor, an expert who is willing to invest the time educating you in a particular area of real estate or property management. A good relation with a wise counselor will help pave your way to success. One day, you will find yourself providing the same service for someone else.

To find a good mentor, try the following: See who is selling the most properties in your area. You can tell by looking in your newspaper and seeing who is running the most ads. Drive around and take note of who has the most signs in your community's front yards. Check their credentials with the association of Realtors and the Better Business Bureau. Experience is important, but you should also try to find a person that you can easily get along with and would like to learn from.

> Find a mentor, an expert who is willing to invest the time educating you in a particular area of real estate or property management.

Talk with the Experts

A lot of people have a dream of buying a building, hiring a property manager, and then sitting back to let those monthly checks roll in. That can happen, but it's not the best way to begin a career in property management. Certainly it's a good idea to have an experienced property manager show you the ropes; in fact, someone who has experienced the ups and downs of property management can offer some of the best financial advice you'll ever receive.

The best way to learn the business is to learn on your own under the watchful eye of an experienced pro. Find such a pro, and hire him or her as a consultant. You need to learn how things work (and don't work) on your own. Having a counselor nearby allows you to do that, but with backup when you get into areas where you really need help.

After a while you'll discover something important. You're the only person who is completely focused on your real-estate investments. As you gain experience, you'll need less and less of that consultant's time. In fact, at some point you'll probably become a consultant or advisor yourself.

Leave Some Things to the Pros

Always have a second pair of eyes review any important document. As previously mentioned, the two key players on your team must be an attorney and an accountant. Both can provide sound financial expertise. But sometimes it would be wise to rely on a professional financial advisor.

Value Your Time

If you are managing a property that you do not own, how do you charge for your services? The time of your lawyer, accountant, and financial advisor is valuable, and you can be assured they'll bill you for it. Whatever their hourly rate may be, your time is just as valuable. After all, you're the one creating the work, right? If your lawyer charges $350 an hour, your time is worth at least the same amount. If your accountant charges $1,000 for a job, your time is worth that much—and more.

Make sure you charge for your own time as a property manager. A standard fee charged by property managers is 6 percent of the rents collected. That's a good rule of thumb. Naturally, there are variations throughout the country. A lot depends upon your local market, market conditions, the economy, and what the market will bear. If you are managing larger properties that require more time, energy, and expertise, you may be entitled a higher fee. Empty buildings still need managing, but they don't generate any income. In situations like that, you'll probably want to negotiate a flat fee.

Your chances for painful financial loss increase at exponential rates when you fail to use the professional expertise available to you. Remember the lesson of being "penny wise and pound foolish." These people know things you don't know. More than that, they stay on top of the changes, which you just don't have the opportunity to catch.

As a professional property manager, you want people on your team who are better at their jobs than you are. That's why you hire them in the first place. Certainly you will make your own decisions, but be sure to base those decisions on sound financial advice.

Keep This in Mind

Occasionally you may feel that you're out there alone. Your accountant, lawyer, and financial advisor accept the work you provide. They earn a good part of their living from your efforts. Yet, they're not around when you're out there pitching the business that makes it all happen. Where are they when you receive the late-night phone call from a partner with a case of cold feet? Do they go with you as you scour the city looking for new and better properties? Are they taking time from their family and friends on weekends to invest a few more hours at the office just to make sure the business is on sound footing?

It's a given that you'll put more time, energy, money, and heart into every project than your accountant, your lawyer, or your financial advisor. That's okay. It's part of the deal. These people work hard for you and deserve just compensation. Don't resent their attitude. Adopt it. As a hard-working, forward-thinking property manager, you deserve just compensation, too.

Financial Advisors Are Invaluable

When and how to put the talents, skills, and experience of a financial advisor to work for you is a decision best made on a case-by-case basis. When praised for his brilliant insights, Sir Isaac Newton said, "If I have seen further, it is by standing on the shoulders of giants." He realized an important point. Our achievements, no matter how much we personally invest in attaining them, are the result of teamwork. We all need each other to reach our individual goals. A very good financial advisor should always be part of your team.

PART V

Other Issues to Consider

Topics covered in this part:

- **The details you need to be aware of in your everyday landlording experience.**

- **The finer points of insurance, taxation, and finance.**

- **An explanation of the fine print in contracts and real-estate law.**

- **A valuable guide to advertising and public relations.**

Insurance
Matters

Chapter 19

When it comes to investing in insurance protection, many people are in denial. Stephen Leacock framed those people's argument succinctly when he said, "I detest life-insurance agents. They always argue that I shall some day die, which is not so." Accidents, injuries, and property damage always happen to the other guy. Of course, the other guy felt the same way right up until the little old lady slipped on his sidewalk, the roof collapsed on that nice family downstairs, or that asteroid finally landed on Apartment B.

Regardless of your position on the need for insurance or your opinion of insurance salespeople, insurance is a major element of property management. You have the right and the duty to protect yourself, your properties, and your investors, and insurance is one of the best vehicles for doing so.

> Part of your continuing education should be devoted to learning all you can about the business of insurance.

Educate Yourself

Yes, you need the services of a top-notch insurance representative, but the issue of insurance is so serious that you cannot completely hand over this responsibility to another person. Part of your continuing education should be devoted to learning all you can about the business of insurance:

- The theory behind insurance.
- Its principles and practices.
- Risk management.
- Types of policies.
- Special risks related to real estate.

You can find any number of good books on this subject at the library or your neighborhood bookstore. Surf the Internet, and look for any seminars or courses offered at your college or university. Don't hesitate to get real-world information from your insurance representatives, either. Make no mistake about it, insurance is a key factor in your continuing success. Protect that success with more knowledge about your insurance needs.

Required Insurance

The bank or lending institution from which you borrow the money to buy your property will require you to provide them with a safety net. This net is called insurance, and it is designed to protect both of you in the event of an unforeseen occurrence. If there is a fire at your property, you want to have the financial ability to rebuild and restore that property to its original condition. Few of us can afford that kind of expense on our own. Even partial damage can be too expensive to fix. The costs could drain your reserves, profits, and future earnings and still leave you with a ruined building on your hands.

Don't underestimate the amount of time, effort, and expense that reconstruction requires. Many factors can affect the timescale. For instance, suppose new construction is booming in your market. If the contractors are already booked up, you may have to wait weeks or months before a company can get to your project. Or your reconstruction could face a significant delay due to rain, mud, and washed-out bridges or roads. Depending on which part of the country you're in, your plans could be delayed by snow, dust storms, hurricanes, or tornadoes.

You can't anticipate everything. However, you need to be prepared. As you shop around for insurance, take the following advice into consideration:

- Shop around for the best prices and best terms.
- Make insurance a requirement even when there's no lender involved.
- Talk to other landlords and ask about their horror stories. Find out what kind of unexpected nightmares they encountered.
- Get liability coverage as well as replacement coverage. Somebody will have to pay the hospital bills of that little old lady who slipped on your sidewalk.

Finally, avoid using the size of your property as the sole basis for your insurance-buying decision. Evaluate other important factors that could affect your insurance needs. What is the value of the

> Avoid using the size of your property as the sole basis for your insurance-buying decision.

property? Will that value decrease, remain static, or improve? What is the income potential? Will you be required to make additional expenses or replace costly items? Does zoning limit what you can do with the property and possibly your income? For example, the replacement cost of a big building in a high-end part of a large city is the same as for an identical building in a low-rent part of a small town, yet the income stream from the small town is considerably less. Good insurance could make up the difference if replacement became necessary.

Following a fire or flood or whatever other disaster, your losses are far greater than just the physical structure. There's the matter of all those rent payments, which will go unpaid. Loss of that income could be devastating to many landlords. You want to be covered for the full time while your property is under reconstruction.

Shopping for Insurance

Salespeople, one of the cornerstones of our nation's economic success, don't have the best reputation. This seems to be especially true of insurance salespeople. Whether or not the image is fully justified, it's doubtless that there are shady characters out there, but if you look harder, you'll find honest, ethical, and hard-working insurance representatives as well. Finding top people in any industry is simply part of your responsibility as a property manager. In purchasing insurance you not only have to find good salespeople, you have to make sure these people represent good companies.

Does It Make Sense?

Always take time to analyze the facts, figures, and need of any major purchase. Never hesitate to ask yourself, "Does this make any sense?" If it doesn't, you need additional information from your insurance agent. Be honest and straightforward. Just say, "This doesn't make any sense to me" and ask for details. If he or she hesitates, suddenly develops a bad attitude, or starts "tap dancing," take the hint. It's time for you to waltz down the street to do a bit more shopping around.

Just as you shouldn't skirt the issue of lead paint in your apartment, for example, an insurance salesperson shouldn't skirt the issue

> Finding top people in any industry is simply part of your responsibility as a property manager.

of your need for a particular type of coverage. Make sure you have a clear understanding of:

- What is being covered.
- Why each item needs coverage.
- The amount of coverage.
- The actual cost of coverage.
- Any conditions affecting that coverage.

Shop Around

It's okay to get multiple quotes. In fact, it's essential. You must be comfortable shopping around, not only for insurance, but for all major purchases. That's just smart business.

Learn from the experience of others. Here is what happened to Mark. He owned a property on the south side of Chicago, a rough part of town made famous in a song about a tough character named "Bad, Bad Leroy Brown." The area had a reputation, but it wasn't all bad. In fact, it was a pretty good market for real estate. The University of Chicago, known as the "Harvard of the Midwest," is located there. Additionally, the area was undergoing a lot of development and a lot of active, upwardly mobile people were living and doing business there.

One day, Mark's insurance agent informed him that his carrier would no longer insure property on the south side of Chicago. He was told that he'd have to pay more to a new insurer, Lloyds of London. Mark bit the bullet and took the insurance at the higher premium. Later on, he wondered why he needed the world-wide services of a company famous for insuring the legs of film actress Betty Grable, the diamonds of Elizabeth Taylor, entire steamship lines, and the World Trade Center.

A few years later, the same agent returned with the same story. Lloyd's of London would no longer insure his property. Without notice, the agent presented Mark with a premium bill, increasing his payments from $4,000 to $14,000 per year. This agent had found a way to ratchet up the premiums by promoting a big name company totally inappropriate for this type of insurance need.

> Learn from the experience of others.

Careful Research Will Pay Off

Remember, insurance companies have their ups and downs. The excellent company of a few years back may have evolved into a shoddy version of its earlier self. Ask the people you know about their coverage, especially any horror stories. Log on to the Internet and take a look at their annual reports. Visit your library and ask the reference desk for a copy of the A.M. Best ratings (this company evaluates and rates insurance companies; it's an independent organization, and the facts and figures it presents will be quite helpful). Once you have narrowed down your final list of potential insurance companies, meet with the agents and then make your decision.

Be sure to investigate how and who to contact in the event of an insurance problem. Is there a local or regional representative? Can you contact someone through the home office at any time of the day or night? Is there a hotline? Sometimes speed is crucial. Make sure your insurance representatives will be available whenever you need them.

Mark was tired of playing this game. He contacted a fellow realtor who had property in the same geographic area. The man provided the name of a more reliable insurance agent. Mark made the switch and today is back to paying $4,000 per year for his insurance. Shop around. Get multiple quotes. Question everything and make the best deal possible every time you make a deal. Be extra careful with insurance purchases so that your money and assets don't end up in the pockets of a less-than-ethical insurance salesperson.

Only Buy What You Need

Here is an example of how you can unwittingly overdo it when it comes to purchasing appropriate insurance. An apartment-building owner bought insurance to protect his building. He was new to the business and didn't pay attention to details. He ended up buying a lot more insurance than he intended—or needed. The agent not only sold him protection for the building, he also included insurance to cover the appliances in the building. That sounds okay, doesn't it? Appliances are expensive. They're difficult to replace and costly to install. What's the problem?

The problem is simple: The appliances were already covered under the landlord's existing damage and liability insurance. This salesperson took advantage of the manager's lack of experience and carelessness to sell something the man really didn't need. The matter was later rectified with another, more ethical insurance agent, but in the meantime the landlord had wasted hundreds of dollars in an unnecessary purchase.

Types of Insurance

You'll need a lot of different types of insurance. Exactly what the mix should be depends on too many variables to make a specific recommendation. Here are a few thoughts on many of the options you have available. This is just a "bare bones" outline. Get the full details from your agent.

Liability insurance is a must. Period. Two factors make liability coverage essential. One, we live in a litigious society. People at times seem to be "lawsuit crazy," and the number of court cases has risen dramatically in the past decades. Two, the amounts awarded in those cases seem to be rising just as fast. Remember, in some instances the landlord doesn't even have to be proven negligent to lose the suit. Play it very safe. Protect everything you can for as much as you can.

Umbrella coverage is also known as blanket coverage. When you exhaust all your coverage in one type of insurance, liability for example, the umbrella policy takes over. For instance, your liability insurance could pay off $110,000 on a $200,000 settlement. If you had umbrella coverage, the second policy could pay out the additional $90,000. A good rule of thumb is to make sure you're covered for twice the value of your personal assets. Provided you get a good or comparable deal, acquire your umbrella coverage from the same company providing your liability coverage. This should reduce the paperwork and the time involved in settling the case.

Title insurance is proof that you really do own what you say you own. Purchase of title insurance is mandatory in many situations. For example, your bank or lending institution might insist on it.

A title search should determine if there are any claims on the property that could sour or ruin your deal. A case in New Orleans relating to the purchase of valuable downtown property was held up for months because an opposing attorney discovered an agreement on the property dating back to 1851. The past can be very much a part of today.

Fire insurance is another "must have." Consider all the conditions in your apartments that could start a major blaze: smokers, pilot lights, candles, inebriated cooks, frayed wiring, spontaneous combustion, lightning, and so on. There are just too many things that can go wrong to pass on fire insurance. Calculate your replacement costs and make sure you stay covered for that amount.

Flood insurance is needed by more people than you might think. Insurance companies sell this coverage separately from other types. Find out if your property is in a flood plain. This may not be as obvious as you think, so don't trust your eyes. Verify.

> Umbrella coverage is also know at blanket coverage.

Earthquake insurance is another area never considered by many of the people who need it. Look back in your area's history books. America's biggest earthquake didn't occur in shaky California, but in Missouri (in the early 1800s). The event was so powerful that it briefly reversed the course of the Mississippi River. Earthquake insurance is another item sold separately by the insurance companies.

Extended coverage offers protection on a wide variety of possibilities. Areas covered could be as different as an exploding water heater, hail damage, any problems with the roof, or smoke damage from a fire. This type of insurance is sometimes called "comprehensive coverage." It can protect you from a thousand "little" things with the capacity to escalate into major disasters.

Loss of rents protection should be very high on your list. Remember, in the case of a fire, your fire insurance will cover the replacement of your property, but what about all those monthly payments you miss during the reconstruction period? Loss of rents insurance can keep your business in business during those lean months.

Mortgage insurance will pay off the balance of the mortgage due in the event you cannot make the payments for a reason such as a disability. There are two basic types of mortgage insurance. One type pays off for the landlord. The other pays off the lender.

Boiler and machinery insurance is designed to protect the insured from claims relating to heavy equipment, such as an injury or death occurring while working on a large air-conditioning unit installed on the roof. Large equipment and machinery have the capacity for causing serious damage, which could result in large claims.

Contents insurance isn't designed to protect your tenant's property. It's there to protect your belongings that are used and/or stored on your rental property. This would apply to such things as your lawn mower, appliances, washers and driers, and the like.

Workers' compensation is necessary if you have any employees, even temporary ones. If an accident happens in the

> Loss of rent protection should be very high on your list.

performance of a task related to your property, you could be liable for that person's medical bills. The nature of the task can be as simple as running down to the convenience store for a can of oil for the lawn mower. If something happens along the way, you could be facing a lot of bills related to the incident. Workers' comp is probably a requirement in your state. Whether it is or not, it's still a good idea to purchase this type of insurance. Make sure you look into it.

Vandalism insurance is another form of insurance that, sadly, seems to be more and more a necessity. You can't "read" every tenant correctly, and some will turn out to be vandals and troublemakers. They could leave your property spray-painted, full of holes, with broken and torn furniture, ruined appliances, and worse. Proper coverage will pay for repair or replacement of the damages caused by the dregs of society.

These are the major areas you want to examine. Some may not apply to your situation, but be sure to verify that fact and don't go by tradition, instinct, or the desire to save money.

Insurance Myths and Scams

Every industry is cursed with con men and scam artists and beset with a lot of inaccurate and harmful myths. The insurance industry is no exception. Again, protecting yourself is primarily a function of doing your homework, paying attention to details, and shopping around. Here are a few considerations worth a little extra attention.

Buy from A-Rated Companies

Insurance companies are just like every other company. They rise. They fall. They go out of business. Always know the rating of the company that insures your property. Of course, it's important that you work with a good, ethical, and knowledgeable agent—that's a given—but you must know the rating of your insurance company as well. A great agent can represent a bad company, so don't confuse the two.

Sometimes Landlords Need Renter's Insurance

Mark believes in renter's insurance from personal experience due to an unusual occurrence. In 1982, while a tenant himself, he was living on the first floor of an apartment building. The property had just been sold. The new owner decided to sandblast the basement to prepare the existing work for interior tuck pointing.

The date chosen was the day before Thanksgiving Day, at a time when Mark was out of his apartment in school. The crew came in and started blasting away. The force of their equipment blew sand up through the basement ceiling, depositing a thick layer of dust on Mark's hardwood floor. And his stereo. And his stove, furniture, clothes, plants, ceiling fans, and virtually everything else in the apartment.

Fortunately, Mark had purchased renter's insurance at $250 per year. He filed a claim immediately and for his rather small investment was allowed to live in a hotel while all his possessions were being cleaned and his apartment was put back in order.

Work exclusively with insurance companies holding an "A" rating. Do not accept anything less. A company with a lesser rating may not have the money to pay when your claim is due, and all your payments will have been in vain. Worse than that, you'd be stuck with a serious reconstruction bill or a liability that could wipe you out if you don't get that claim money.

Discuss this with your agent. If he or she pushes a lesser-rated company, don't be shy about insisting on an A-rated one. In addition, do your own research on the companies your agent recommends. The information is readily available in company brochures and literature, as well as on the Internet.

Don't Pay the Agent

One of the most common scams in the insurance business is to have the insured person write the premium check to the agent rather than the company. If you don't think about this too hard, it makes sense. Unfortunately, it's twisted sense. Some agents simply pocket the entire amount and never pay the premiums. They're gambling that the insured will never have to make a claim and will never discover the deception. The ones that do find out usually find out the hard, painful, and costly way.

Always write your premium check directly to the insurance carrier, never to the agent. Don't get ripped off. If an agent asks you to write the check in his or her name, get another agent.

Hire an Adjustor

Even the best, most talented property manager can't "go it alone." At times we all need the services of professionals. If your property is damaged to the extent that you will need to make an insurance claim, hire an insurance adjustor as your representative in the negotiations.

An adjustor acts as a mediator or broker between you and the insurance carrier. Even the most ethical insurance carrier will make the best deal possible on its behalf, not yours. If you're not involved day-to-day in the building trades, you just don't have the know-how, the experience, or the current facts, figures, costs, and rates to take

> Some agents simply pocket the entire amount and never pay the premiums.

care of this yourself. An adjustor has that information because it's an integral part of his or her job. Most landlords don't know how to evaluate property damage, how to estimate the costs of reconstruction, or what other conditions might arise from the incident.

For instance, you may have a fire in Apartment B that is fully contained in that apartment. Still, smoke and water damage could easily affect Apartments A and C. It's possible that such damage could extend to other buildings and damage the property of another landlord. Smoke damage is worse than you can imagine. It gets in your drywall and carpet. In addition to causing damage, smoke

Sell Tenants on Renter's Insurance

Tenants can be very hesitant to purchasing renter's insurance. Some are just plain cheap, while others just don't see the need. Even if renter's insurance is part of the agreement, you might have to make a good case for the purchase just to maintain good relations. A few moments of explanation represent a valuable investment in public relations. Here are a few tips:

- You want the tenants to get renter's insurance because you're a good and considerate landlord. The insurance will protect your renters in a time of need, in case something should happen. Explain how much good insurance can cover and the events that could cause a need for coverage. For example, renter's insurance may cover losses incurred off your property, such as when someone's $300 tennis racquet is stolen down at the courts.

- Supply your tenants with a list of companies providing renter's insurance. Once you have conducted this research yourself, you could be passing it on to each one of your tenants. Encourage them to shop around and get the best deal. If they have Internet access, suggest they start surfing.

- Don't quote any rates, but have a fair "guesstimate" of a logical range of costs.

- Mention what your tenants can do to possibly reduce their premiums, such as having a fire extinguisher nearby. You may have already done some of this for them. Your deadbolts, fire sprinkler system, and the like could save them a sizeable amount of money on renter's insurance.

- Emphasize the cost of replacement. Prices rise, and whatever is lost will probably cost more than when the first item was purchased.

- Be sure to inform your tenants of their own liability. If they cause an accident such as a fire, they could be responsible for paying for extensive damages.

- Lastly, be sure to reiterate that renter's insurance is very affordable form of self-protection.

leaves a smell that never goes away. All of this becomes your responsibility. If you've handled your insurance business properly, the monetary cost can be borne by your carrier.

An adjuster is particularly important when the fire is a small one. That's because the damage caused by the fire fighters will be far more extensive than that caused by the blaze. You need a professional who can evaluate the actual damage, the true cause of that damage, and the real costs of repair.

Tenant protection is another major concern. Smoke, water, or other damage could ruin some or all of their possessions. Protect yourself from tenant claims. Include in any lease a rider that requires your tenants to purchase renter's insurance or recognize that they are at risk of having no protection in the event of an accident or destructive event. Place the responsibility for your tenants' belongings where it belongs, on the shoulders of those tenants.

Adjustor fees vary from area to area, but they will generally be around 10 percent of whatever the adjustor collects from the insurance company. Ten percent may sound like a lot of money. But if you're thinking about handling the negotiations yourself and keeping that 10 percent, your thinking isn't very clear. A professional insurance adjustor knows his or her business, pays attention to detail, knows to look in and around places that would never occur to you, and will check things you'd probably forget if you knew about them in the first place. In other words, the adjustor will get you more from the settlement than you could possibly get on your own. Another important benefit of working with adjustors is that they know how to get paid faster.

> Adjustor fees vary from area to area, but they will generally be around 10 percent of whatever the adjustor collects from the insurance company.

Insure Yourself

You can never know when you'll need insurance, so it's best to take care of that matter early in your career. To be properly insured should, in fact, be one of your first objectives. Here's an example of why it is such an important consideration.

Part of property management work can put you to work for other parties, including banks and lenders who are in the process of foreclosing or have already foreclosed on a property. This type of work might introduce you to some of life's less pleasant personalities, such as the belligerent property owner Mark once encountered. This man had gotten himself into trouble by not paying back a bank loan. He still owned his property, at least for the time being, but the court had appointed Mark as the receiver of the property.

Mark was now responsible for collecting the rents and maintaining the property. Unfortunately, the new situation brought out the darker side of the man who hadn't paid his debts. He would show up at Mark's office full of fury. His behavior was so irrational the staff actually thought the man might be insane or at least on the verge of cracking up. To say he was belligerent would be an understatement of some magnitude.

When confronted about his behavior, the man only became more and more angry. He said he didn't care how he behaved because he was suffering from a brain aneurysm. He was convinced that he was about to die and he just didn't give a darn what other people thought of him or his actions.

The man claimed that he had slipped and fallen in the hallway of his building, which Mark was managing now for the circuit court of Cook County on behalf of the lender. His knee was bruised and he was going to sue the property manager, the foreclosing lender, and everyone else involved in the matter—even his own insurance company, who was still the insurance carrier on the property! He didn't have much of a case and ended up roaming all over town trying to convince personal injury lawyers to take the case.

Before long, the man actually did die of his brain aneurysm. Of course, that's not the end of the matter. Before dying, the belligerent man did find an attorney. And after the man's death, this attorney planned on suing on behalf of the estate.

Upon hearing this, Mark hired a lawyer to settle the case with the insurance company. The attorney settled the case, and despite the fact the fact that the man was dead and therefore had no use for his knee, the insurance company awarded his estate $20,000. Fortunately, the property was insured for accidents of this type. The insurance paid the estate the hefty sum, which could have caused a major financial obstacle for Mark.

Make sure you are well insured. Regardless of the premium, it's cheap compared to the alternative.

> Make sure you are well insured. Regardless of the premium, it's cheap compared to the alternative.

Eliminate the Risks

Why wait for insurance protection against some loss to kick in when you can take measures to prevent the cause of the loss in the first place? Take an in-depth survey of your property—all of your property, including parking lots, sidewalks, and green areas. Look at any physical and health hazards and potential risks. Be completely objective in your evaluation. Don't think of a situation in terms of the expense of repair, but in terms of how much serious money you stand to lose if you don't make that repair. Hiring a professional to fix those loose bricks on the second floor ledge is far less expensive than the expenses and guilt incurred after one of your tenants is hit on the head by a falling brick. A quick comparison of the costs of repair against the expense of legal fees, court costs, and medical bills will

Handling an Accident

As they say, "accidents happen." You may be lucky, but chances are, someone someday will be injured on your property. If that happens, don't panic. Ideally, you have already played the "what if" game and are emotionally and intellectually prepared to respond in a calm and collected way.

A property manager's initial thoughts in this situation generally follow this progression: "I hope he's not hurt," which is followed by, "I hope he won't sue me," which is then followed by, "I hope I don't lose everything I own." Instead of giving in to your fears, here's what you should do.

Your first actions depend upon where you are at the time. If you're present or nearby, obviously you should seek immediate medical attention for the injured party. Call 911 if the situation is serious. Offer to take your tenant to the emergency room or to the doctor. Sometimes very serious injuries don't appear all that serious at all. It's best to get a qualified medical opinion just to be certain.

Next, and as quickly as you can, call your insurance agent and file an accident report and any other documentation necessary. Get the facts in writing right away. Memories fade with time. When a landlord can be sued, and if a lot of money can be gained, those memories can be changed through the filters of greed or revenge. Even good people acting out of the best motives can "remember" events in ways far removed from the truth.

Lastly, follow up with a visit to your tenant. Don't be afraid. If he or she appears hostile, well, you've done your best. In other cases, a simple show of genuine concern can dampen the fires of resentment and greed.

show you the wisdom of calling in your maintenance guy as soon as you possibly can.

A property manager has no control over floods, forest fires, snowstorms, hail, earthquakes, or other natural disasters. You can, however, avoid buying property in a flood plain, in an earthquake zone, or next to a smoldering volcano. When a snowstorm hits and your sidewalks ice over, you can salt them down and keep them safe for your tenants.

In many cases, there are some measures that can give you at least some control over a situation. Driving over to salt the sidewalk may be a pain, but it's not nearly as painful as facing in court someone who slipped and was injured on that sidewalk. Again, what is the cost of a little salt and your time compared to the expenses of a lawsuit?

Cut Your (Future) Losses

During your survey, look for ways in which to reduce or eliminate risk. Think to the future, and consider all the many things that might go wrong. What can you put in place to short-circuit potential dangers down the road? Here are a few suggestions to stimulate your thinking:

- Hire a security guard or a security company. Their presence discourages vandals and thieves and also provides a sense of security for your tenants.
- Install overhead water sprinklers. Some water damage in the hallways is far preferable to losing the entire building to a fire. Tenants will notice the extra protection, too.
- Post escape routes or provide printed handouts. It's a good safety and public relations measure.
- Create an emergency response program. This is where the "what if" game can be most useful. What could happen? How should I respond? Who should I contact first? How can I prevent that in the first place?
- Store equipment safely. Lawn mowers, hedge clippers, rakes, hammers, electric saws, and other tools can be extremely

> Create an emergency response program.

dangerous in careless hands. Make sure that only the people who need them have access to such equipment.

- Rope off potentially hazardous areas. People have an amazing capacity to walk into the danger zone, completely oblivious of the risks involved. Tape off or barricade any areas, such as a ditch, loose boards, or an overhead structure in the process of construction.
- Store potentially hazardous chemicals or substances in safe and secure locations. Make sure they are clearly labeled as dangerous.

Cutting losses before they happen has a two-fold benefit. One, you make your property safer for you and your tenants, avoiding accidents, injuries, and lawsuits. Two, your forward-thinking actions could earn you a significant price break on the cost of your insurance. Check with your agent now, and continue checking as you make more improvements.

Granted, you can't eliminate all risk. We don't live in that kind of world. No matter how thorough your initial survey, bricks will still loosen, concrete will crack, wiring will fray, and other problems will crop up. That's why you should make risk surveys a regular part of your operations. Even if you can't eliminate all risk, you can find and repair most situations before they become nasty, costly, and embarrassing. Remember, a single lawsuit has the potential of wiping you and your business out of existence.

> Cutting losses before they happen has a two-fold benefit.

For more information on this topic, visit our Web site at www.businesstown.com

Worrying about Taxes

Chapter 20

someone once said that the art of taxation consists in so plucking the goose as to obtain the largest possible amount of feathers with the smallest possible amount of hissing. This chapter explains what a lot of that hissing is about and even offers a few suggestions on how to hold onto a few of your financial "feathers." Taxation is a serious matter and a costly one. It's essential that you understand the subject very well.

City Taxes

Charles Dudley Warner once said, "The thing generally raised on city land is taxes." Regardless of the city, the harvest of taxes is always a bumper crop. As noted earlier in this book, governments love to govern, and one of the most common acts of government is to raise

Tax Terminology

It's always important in business to understand precisely what each of the common terms related to taxes really means and how it should be used. When it comes to taxation, knowledge is essential. A simple misunderstanding or misuse of a word or phrase could have serious consequences. Here are a few taxation-related terms you'll run across your real-estate dealings:

A **tax credit** is a reduction against the income tax payment. Tax credits that may be available to you include rehabilitation tax credits for historic or older buildings and for some low-income housing.

A **tax deduction** can be used to reduce taxable income. For example, if the taxable income on your property is $100,000, but you can claim $25,000 in deductions, your taxable income would be $75,000.

Tax deductible refers to an expense that can be used to reduce taxable income. Usually, *ad valorem* taxes and interest are deductible for all types of property. Depreciation, repairs, maintenance, and other necessary expenses are tax deductible for income property.

A **tax lien** is a debt attached to a property for the owner's failure to pay taxes, whether they are city or county taxes, estate, income, payroll, sales, or school taxes.

A **tax map** is an official document detailing the location, dimensions, and other pertinent information regarding a parcel of land subject to property taxes. These are considered public records and are generally found in bound volumes at the local tax office.

taxes. Cities attempt to raise revenue any way they can. Sometimes the creativity of these bureaucrats is amazing—and more often than not, it will affect you and your business.

Taxes That Look Like Taxes

You will encounter many different types of city taxes, and you might be surprised to discover that a lot of taxes aren't clearly identified as such. Let's look at the taxes that are obvious first. Here's a list of taxes that may be applicable in your community. Don't assume that this is a complete list. Different cities and towns collect different types of taxes. Always find out what is appropriate for your community and discover just how creative your local bureaucrats can be.

> Different cities and towns collect different types of taxes.

Building registration fee. Generally, each real-estate property is subject to a building registration fee or another type of annual fee. Building registration fees range from $25 to $50 per year, which doesn't sound like much, and for any given property manager that's true. However, like a salesperson on the road, the city is working on volume. Imagine $25 or more multiplied by every building in town. In cities the size of Chicago and New York, the amount must be staggering. It's got to be a hefty sum even in midsize and smaller markets.

Signage fee. These fees are taxes on the signs, sometimes every sign, in your building. Again, the individual fee may not represent much capital by itself, but multiplied by many signs in many buildings, the city coffers get swollen rather quickly. For today's property manager, more taxes on more things is a real sign of the times.

Transfer tax. This tax is levied when property changes hands. This may be the most significant fee charged by any city. Here's how it works in Chicago. Whenever a property changes hands within the city limits—that is, when it is "transferred"—the city charges a fee of $7.50 for every $1,000 in value of that building. If the building sells for $100,000 the buyer owes the city $750 for the "privilege" of doing business.

> A property manager will certainly have to be responsible for paying sewer and water charges to the city.

Boiler inspection fee. This fee is very similar to building registration fee. It's important that you learn quickly what buildings or what *elements* of a building, such as a boiler, are considered taxable property by your municipality.

Building permit fee. The building permit fee is a very popular tax with city governments and the people who run them. This fee usually equals a percentage of the dollars expected to be invested for improvements to an existing property or for new construction.

Moreover, a property manager will certainly have to be responsible for paying sewer and water charges to the city. And parking lots, parking garages, and parking spaces may be taxed, too. The best way to operate is to assume that *if* something related to your property can be taxed, it *may* be taxed, and follow through with necessary inquiries.

Here's the bottom line when it comes to governments and taxes. Anywhere there is a taxing body, such as a municipal government, there will be people fanatically dedicated to finding more things to tax. The bureaucrats always want new ways to generate revenue. And they're always looking your way.

Taxes by Another Name

City officials are well known for saying one thing while meaning something quite different or for "softening" the effect of a term by using a kinder and gentler one. That's certainly true when it comes to taxes. Still, as Shakespeare observed in *Romeo and Juliet*, a rose by any other name would smell as sweet. No matter what you call them, taxes are still taxes. Here are a few examples of how property managers and landlords are taxed without being "taxed."

The City of Chicago requires decorative cast-iron fencing to separate buildings from the streets in all new townhouse construction. The city also requires the owner to create green outdoor space. This gives the home and the area a nice look, but the loss of square footage becomes the owner's expense. No matter what you call it, this is still a tax on the owner. And, as we all know, that cost is transferred directly to the buyer, which means buyers must pay a higher price for their property.

Chicago has also developed a new and interesting tax called a green fee. When a developer is constructing a building of twelve units or more, he or she has to cough up $2,500 per unit to the city. This money is used to improve the city's parks and green space. You'd think the landlord's efforts toward improving the lifestyle for city residents would be acceptable on its own—but you'd be wrong. The city wants you to pay for making things better, and since it's a "tax," you'd better pay up or you will not get a building permit.

Another way cities tax property owners is by creating height restrictions for "down-zoning" or overlay districts. This in effect is a tax because the restrictions reduce the amount of residential property that can be built in different areas of the city. If landlords can't build as many units as they would like because of those restrictions, their income has been taxed. And who really suffers for the added burden? The renter or the next buyer, because while your land costs remain the same, your income can be dramatically reduced. You don't have to be a rocket scientist to realize that a reduction from twelve units to six means significant loss of revenue and that someone must make up that difference. Again, the consumer takes the hit.

Cities began implementing down zoning to restrict the density of their populations. Or at least that was the stated reason. It is interesting to note that this concern over an increasing population occurred during times when urban populations were shrinking when compared to the population data from the 1950s and 1960s. Is it possible that the concern was over a loss of revenue due to declining rather than increasing population?

In Chicago, the local aldermen have tremendous influence on how these fees are structured and implemented. Granted, these requirements do not require direct payment to the government, but a mandatory fee placed on your property in which your noncompliance will result in penalties and perhaps legal fines and associated costs is still a tax on your income.

> Cities began implementing down zoning to restrict the density of their populations.

State Taxes

The state governments aren't quite as involved in your business as municipalities. Generally, they aren't as aggressive on taxing the physical structures of real estate or administering local zoning requirements, but they get their licks in, too. Transfer taxes and revenue taxes account for the bulk of state real estate taxes. These are due at the end of each year when you pay your income tax. As April 15 arrives, property managers prepare to pay gross or net revenue taxes on income generated by their properties.

States may also impose licensing fees for property owners, but the most common tax comes knocking on your door in the form of an amount based on the revenues you've generated.

Federal Taxes

We all know about the federal income tax. Depending upon the structure of the business entity holding your building (corporation, partnership, etc.), you may have to pay income tax on revenue from this property. As we noted, find a very good accountant and listen to his or her advice. A good accountant will advise you to empty the corporation's checking account prior to the end of the year. You will do this in one of two ways, either by taking the money as income or by spending it. You do this so that you don't pay tax on retained earnings or money that remains in the building account and is carried over to the next calendar year. Do not allow yourself or your corporation to be double-taxed. Listen to your accountant. He or she will know whether it is in your best interests to declare it as income or to invest it in that new roof, new appliances, or repairs to the basement.

Corporate and Investment Groups

As a general rule, taxes are due from the owner of a particular property and not the property itself. This is because profits from the property will be distributed during the year or at the end of it to the person or group that owns it. Ideally, cash will be flowing in from rentals all year long. Some dollars will stay in the account to take care of repairs, maintenance, expenses, and as a reserve, but the majority will be disbursed among the partners. As January 1 arrives, the building will receive an influx of capital so that operations can be maintained at the appropriate levels.

The corporation acts as a conduit, dispersing money to the partners, so there should be no tax consequences to the corporate entity itself after the dispersal. When the partnership ends, the partners will face significant taxes based on their capital gains.

As the term implies, capital gains taxes are taxes placed on the gain in the sale of a capital asset. For example, if a building is purchased for $100,000 and is later sold for $125,000, the $25,000 profit must be reported as a long-term capital gain on the original investment. Capital gains will be distributed to the partners, and the business entity itself will not be paying any type of capital gains tax.

This is known as "pass through." Revenues and capital gains are usually passed through to the partners or individuals or corporations owning shares in the property.

1031 Tax Exchange

The 1031 tax exchange (also mentioned in Chapter 8) offers property owners benefits not found in other types of group investments. Under 1031, prior to accepting money for the sale of a building as profit or capital gain, a property owner may hold that money in an escrow account for up to six months to allow use of that money to purchase another property. Thus, the 1031 law provides an excellent way to defer capital gains.

Each partner in an investment group can designate how their share of the capital gains should be invested in the new property. You do not need the participation of all partners to proceed under the 1031 law.

The Biggest Tax Mistakes People Make

Even the federal government admits that IRS personnel can't understand the U.S. tax code. Sadly, that remarkable admission applies to the government folks who are charged with the task of helping Americans find answers to their tax questions. Because the code is so complex and hard to understand, and because it is always in a

Four Characteristics of a Corporation

How does the federal government decide whether an association of investors is taxable as a partnership? This is an important question. Investors in a partnership pay taxes once because of the flow-through feature of tax law. The investors in the group pay taxes. A corporation is actually taxed twice, once at the corporate level and then again as the individual members pay taxes on their income from that corporation. How the Internal Revenue Service defines an association is therefore a significant financial matter for the investors in that association.

The IRS has devised a four-part test to aid its personnel in making this determination. The organization examines four characteristics of a corporation. These characteristics are limited liability, a central management system, continuity of life, and free transferability of ownership interest. If the group under evaluation has three out of four of these characteristics, it is deemed to be a corporation.

state of change, it is important that you, and especially your accountant, pay attention to detail and stay on top of your tax situation. Mistakes can be painful and embarrassing, and can get you into serious legal problems.

Tax Evasion

By far the biggest tax mistake you can make is refusing to pay. Hotel magnate Leona Helmsley once said, "Taxes are only for the poor." Her time in prison proved just how wrong a supposedly intelligent person can be when it comes to tax law. Taxes are for everybody. The government sees tax evasion as a serious crime, and it will prosecute accordingly.

Outside of the fact that tax evasion is morally and legally wrong, it's just not worth the risk. Some misguided individuals think they'll give tax evasion a whirl, believing the worst that could happen would be a brief stay in one of those pleasant white-collar country-club style prisons. What could be so rough about that, eh? If you're even toying with such thoughts, do some serious study about what really goes on in one of those "country clubs." You'll be shocked—ideally, shocked back into common sense. A prison is no place to build a career in property management.

Penalties can be extremely painful. For example, if you underpay a part of your taxes due to a mistake or sloppy bookkeeping, your penalty will probably be 5 percent added to the entire unpaid amount. Fraud is the willful evasion of your tax payments. If your records are found to be fraudulent, that penalty jumps to 50 percent. Also, there is no statute of limitations on fraud. If they so desire, the IRS can go back through every return you've ever filed. The right thing to do is clear. Grit your teeth, control your temper, and pay your taxes.

A Poor Choice of Accountants

Much of the success of your business depends upon sound accounting procedures, especially when filing tax returns. Real-estate transactions require the services of a sophisticated and real-estate-savvy accountant. Someone who doesn't know the business well, regardless of experience or reputation in other areas, can create serious damage to your financial health. Keeping tabs on such changes

Defer Profit to Reduce Taxes

You have a property and you've made improvements. The economy is good and it has appreciated. You can sell for X number of dollars more than you've invested. Then, you can take all that money and invest in bigger and better things, right? Of course not. When you sell, the government will take some of that profit in the form of taxes. So much might be taxed that the sale may not be worthwhile. That's why it's essential to figure your taxes and actual profits before you go through with the sale. Your financial picture might actually be better if you hold on to your property.

In this situation, the two key questions to ask are these:

1. How much of my profit will be eliminated through taxation?
2. How can I structure the sale so as to limit taxation as much as possible?

One useful technique is to defer some of that profit. See if you can extend the payments over several years instead of taking them all in a single year. You can't be taxed on profit you haven't earned.

requires dedication, commitment to customer service, and a certain level of financial real-estate sophistication.

Failure to Accept Responsibility

Regardless of your accountant's efforts, when you sign the tax forms you become responsible for the information on those forms. You must be fully informed as to what is on that document, and you must understand it before you put ink to paper with your signature. If you don't understand something, it is essential that you ask your accountant for an explanation. And be sure you understand the explanation. The old adage "Ignorance of the law is no excuse" most certainly applies to your tax returns.

Go over all your tax returns carefully with your accountant before you sign. No matter what mistakes your accountant makes, if there are problems you are the one who will pay the fine and do the time.

> If you don't understand something, it is essential that you ask your accountant for an explanation.

Assuming Tax Shelters Save Taxes

Many people believe this and head out to jump under the nearest shelter. Actually, most shelters don't save a penny in taxes. They are designed only to defer tax payments. It's a good idea to double-check any tax shelter that is being promoted only for its tax benefits. Most shelters structured that way are not very good investments at all. A good shelter will be designed as a sound investment in the first place, with the tax sheltering benefits as a bonus to the overall program. Unless you are in the 50-percent tax bracket, you probably won't see much real benefit to a tax shelter.

Panicking at an Audit

Panic leads to mistakes, sometimes dumb mistakes, that can get you into far more trouble than the original cause for the audit. The first thing to do upon getting notified of an audit or the possibility of an audit is to remain calm. Immediately contact your accountant and perhaps your lawyer for sound advice as to the proper way to proceed while fully protecting your rights. Be fully prepared to answer IRS questions. Get your documents (and your act) together.

Real-Estate
Tax Benefits

The tax picture isn't all negative. Real estate provides opportunities for tax benefits as well. For example, you may write off some of your expenses, such as maintenance and repair materials and supplies, wages for your maintenance and repair personnel, insurance premiums, leasing commissions, property taxes, interest on borrowed money, and other miscellaneous expenses.

You may be able to take investment tax credits on income-generating tangible property. You might also be able to charge for depreciation on capital costs and improvements made on your property. Both these benefits are called noncash charges. The amounts will be based on the full value of your property, which allows you to benefit from leveraged tax write-offs.

Historic buildings, properties in deteriorating neighborhoods, and some other types of buildings are eligible for some property tax abatements and other tax savings.

Many tax benefits exist, provided you meet certain guidelines. The savings could justify the time and energy invested in checking them out.

Most audits are generated by simple mistakes in arithmetic, minor discrepancies, or misunderstandings. Many so-called audits are conducted by mail. They aren't true audits, but can cause considerable panic. Stay calm. Respond to the questions accurately and the situation just might be resolved via the U.S. Postal Service rather than the U.S. court system.

Even if you're called in for an audit at the IRS offices, chances are you're there just to answer a few questions about minor details. Errors in accounting do happen, and both you and the IRS representatives want to settle the matter as quickly and as easily as possible. The person to be audited will be informed of the specific areas of concern by letter. Bring all records that have been requested to the meeting.

It is recommended that you do not bring any additional records. Do not answer any questions about areas not specifically mentioned in the IRS letter. The relevant documents you have brought must be reviewed before others are requested. Don't give anyone the opportunity to go on a "fishing expedition" through your company's financial records. If you do, then they will.

During an audit, maintain your professionalism. Do not show any hostility or resentment. Be thoroughly prepared, and have all your documents ready and in order. Many times the IRS agent will determine that pursuing a case just isn't worth the investment of government time, money, and manpower. Sloppy records or evasive attitudes invite further scrutiny.

The best way to prevent an audit is to act as if you are going to get one when filling out your tax forms. Assume the best, but plan for the worst. The more organized you and your business records are throughout the year, the better your chances of coming out on top if the audit materializes.

Arguing a Disallowed Deduction Previously Allowed

You take a deduction that you've been taking for years, but for some reason this year that deduction is disallowed. You should fight it, right? Wrong. You may put yourself in harm's way. The IRS can easily decide to disallow all of those previous deductions, too.

Remember, they're not bound by a statute of limitations. Neither are they bound by their own errors concerning your previous returns. You could find yourself in a general examination of your returns going back many years.

Sometimes it's better to take the hit, keep quiet, and get on about your business. This situation calls for just such a response.

Fighting City Hall

"You can't sue city hall" is an old and well-proven maxim, and it applies to the federal government taxation too. You can't sue the federal government over your tax situation. Federal Tort Claims Act, which gives citizens the right to sue their government, is not applicable in tax cases. It's a waste of time, energy, and money and is a big mistake if you even try.

> You can't sue the federal government over your tax situation.

Chapter 21

Legal Concerns

A nything can become a legal issue. In other words, whatever small issue you believe won't hurt you can most certainly come back to stir up one of your worst nightmares. It could be almost anything. The leaky roof on your building, the walls, your wiring, plumbing, the sidewalk outside, the snow over which you have absolutely no control, even your own words spoken in the utmost honesty and sincerity. That's why you need sound, experienced legal advice, to protect yourself if any of these problems come up.

Pay Attention to Everything

Since anything can become a serious legal issue, pay attention to everything. While you probably can't short-circuit all your problems, you can eliminate many of them by paying attention to the normal details of your business. That roof doesn't have to leak. If it does spring a small waterfall, you can rush over to take care of your tenants as fast as possible—as you know you should. Anybody can sue over anything. But if you did all you could to fix the leak within a reasonable amount of time, the judge will probably smile upon you rather than the tenant.

Still, relying on a judge is risky. Some judges tend to always see the tenant as the victim in such situations, while others tend to side with the businesspeople of the community. You can be blessed or cursed by the luck of the draw. Why take chances? Avoid the situation altogether by taking care of any situations that could create legal problems.

The basic rule of survival here isn't very complicated: Take care of business. If there is a leak in a roof, fix it. If the wiring, plumbing, or sidewalk needs repair, then repair it. If a tenant needs "stroking," then invest the time to express your concern, your understanding, and your willingness to address the problem as soon as possible. Some people are chronic complainers, some are "lawsuit crazy," and others just like to stir up trouble. You will encounter your fair share of all types, but generally most people who have a problem are happy to have that problem solved quickly. When you do that, you eliminate a tremendous amount of potential grief.

A Reality Check

Coolidge's Law, a cousin of Murphy's Law, states that anytime you don't want something, you get it. For example, if you don't want commercial zoning next to your residential rental properties, rest assured that some city councilman is out there, working on a proposal for just such rezoning. If you don't want another city tax, you can be sure that there's a group of legislators saying, "You know, we could increase revenues if we just . . . " If you don't want any community hassles over your proposed bed-and-breakfast business in that rehab, you can bet your bottom dollar that someone is organizing a protest to the appropriate governing board to get rid of your operation.

There's no better reason than Coolidge's Law to get involved in the law and law-making processes of your industry. One of the best places to start is the legal or government relations committee of your local trade association. Get involved, or face a lot of situations you don't want.

Handle Legal Matters Immediately

If you do get into trouble or into a sticky situation, the best thing you can do is to talk immediately to other knowledgeable people in the business. Keep talking to them and asking for advice as the situation develops. Success in real estate, as with any business, is built on a daily battle to overcome obstacles.

When a situation develops, react to it. Don't ignore it hoping that it will go away. Problems left unattended have a nasty ability to get far worse. Join local business groups and trade associations in your community. Form alliances, and build a network of experienced friends and associates who can help you in a time of need.

Arbitrate Before You Litigate

Someone once noted that four out of five potential litigants will settle their disputes the first day they come together, if you will put the idea of arbitration into their heads. Too many tenants and too many property managers in today's society automatically jump into the courts to settle disputes. Sometimes the tiniest, least significant matters turn into long, costly, and even embarrassing court cases.

Of course, there is a time and place for lawyers and court proceedings, when nothing else will solve the problem, but don't assume you have to take that step to resolve every dispute. If only out of self-interest, it's always a good idea to make an attempt to work out a troublesome situation before ending up in the daily news.

Consider the cost in legal fees, court fees, lost revenue, additional lost expenses (if you lose the case), and the significant costs of your own lost time. If an open attitude, concern to resolve the situation, and a genuine effort to do so doesn't do the job, the courts will always be there as a back-up plan. Do your best to make them your last resort.

Property Issues Can Become Legal Issues

It's quite popular in our society these days for tenants, lawyers, and action groups to come after landlords. It's as if every situation

When Good Tenants Go Bad

Even the best maintained buildings develop problems. Thirty seconds after you inspect a wall and leave the property, the paint starts peeling and crumbles to the ground, the toilet stops flushing, or the thermostat gets stuck at 85 degrees—in the middle of the summer. If tenants become upset with you, they can dial up city hall to complain to the building inspector. Once you get an angry or nitpicky or career-building inspector on your hands, you may find yourself with a stack of citations. These citations may all be minor—overgrown grass, for example—but they can add up and head skyward, and so will the charges and penalties. Your repair bills and probably your blood pressure will likely follow.

requires a bad guy. Since the landlord is perceived to be in the power position, he or she must be that bad guy. Look at all those Westerns. For the most part, who were the bad guys? They were the greedy landowners trying to keep those poor settlers off the fruited plain and the purple mountain majesties. Think about it. Who was the villain in *Silverado? Pale Rider? A Fistful of Dollars? Riders of the Purple Sage?* Those celluloid battles about brave tenants fighting powerful property owners have inspired a lot of litigation.

Okay. There were (and are) robber barons out there, but for every evil, powerful, lawbreaking businessperson, there were (and are) hundreds of decent, hard-working, law-abiding entrepreneurs. So, let's get past the Hollywood images and look at every situation on a case-by-case basis.

Property management is an environment enmeshed in local, state, and federal laws and regulations. You've got to watch your every step—every step of the way. Right or wrong, there are people out there "gunning" for you regardless of what you do. Sadly, this is just the business environment in which we live. Not to comply with the law is foolish thinking and bad business.

Repair Only What Needs Repair

Imagine how tough and frightening it must be to walk a high wire in the circus. In real estate, property managers have their own "thin line" to walk and sometimes you have to walk it on tiptoes the whole way. You always want to take the best care possible of your buildings and your tenants. That's obvious, but what isn't so obvious is a game some tenants play called "Let's bring out the landlord."

When most folks have a problem, say a broken window, they call and expect you to fix it right away, and that's fine. It's the right thing to do, and fast action on tenant complaints is only good business. However, never do more than you are required to do. Sometimes, it's useful to remember that no good deed goes unpunished. How can that be?

Well, if you fix the broken window and then stay to fix other things around the apartment, things you weren't asked to fix, tenants

> Never do more than you are required to do.

will begin to expect a lot of those little extras all the time. A moment of kindness can turn into a lease-long series of phone calls to bring out the landlord. A lot of those calls will be costly in terms of your time and building expenses.

Nonlegal Influences

The law is a funny thing in the very serious sense that its definition is often in the eye of the beholder—or the inspector. The regulations often require interpretation, and it's the inspector's job to interpret them. If you're working with someone who is cooperating with you to allow you to mow the grass, paint the wall, or fix the cracked window within a reasonable time frame, you're okay. (So are your tenants and your building.) But if you're working with someone trying to build a reputation, or believes he or she is the great protector of the downtrodden, or who just had a fight with a spouse, you could be in for some major citations on minor problems.

Nonlegal influences can affect your business and your property, too. Local groups of all stripes can call for and sometimes get restrictions on property ownership. In Chicago, there is something called an "Alley Access Letter." This is a letter that an alderman must provide to someone who's doing a new development or renovation where there must be access to the property for parking or deliveries. This alley access letter technically isn't even a legal matter—it isn't even a permit, though it must be attached to the building permit. Access to alleys in Chicago is not unlimited, so if you're seeking a building permit, you must also seek out this letter.

Your failure to explore fully this aspect of your business can have costly consequences. Let's say you bought property in Chicago in the hopes of starting your own small business, such as a car wash or auto shop. This requires access to the alley so your customers can come in and out. That's obvious, but the "alley access letter" isn't so obvious. Many people have discovered that they can't get their business license without it. Suddenly you discover that your small business will be quite small indeed. In fact, it will be nonexistent.

> Nonlegal influences can affect your business and your property.

Tenant Responsibilities

We hear a lot of talk in the media about the responsibilities of land-lords and property managers. But tenants have responsibilities to the landlord and to the property, too, and they include the following:

- Maintaining a safe and clean apartment (or other dwelling).
- Maintaining all landlord-provided appliances in good working order.
- Properly disposing of all trash and garbage.
- Properly using electrical and plumbing fixtures and making sure that they are kept clean and safe. If damaged, the tenant should report the problem to the property manager at once (because it is the manager's responsibility to maintain them).
- Making sure guests respect the property and appliances of the landlord.
- Controlling the noise level so that other tenants or neighbors are not disturbed.
- Allowing the landlord to inspect the property upon his or her reasonable request. (Usually, a twenty-four-hour notice is required.)

> Tenants need to understand that they cannot allow friends or relatives to stay with them for extended periods of time without notifying the landlord or property manager and adding the names of the new tenants to the lease.

The tenants also need to understand that they cannot allow friends or relatives to stay with them for extended periods of time without notifying the landlord or property manager and adding the names of the new tenants to the lease.

Following the simple rules should allow for a positive relationship between tenant and landlord, one in which everyone's rights are respected and protected. If the tenant does not follow these rules, he or she might be subject to losing the security deposit, facing a court proceeding, or even getting evicted.

Entry Rights to Your Property

As a landlord or property manager, you have the right to enter your property, but it is not an absolute right—it's a compromise between the landlord's right to know what's going on and have access to the property and the tenant's right to privacy. After all, the apartment or house must be inspected periodically for repair and maintenance problems, and those repairs must be carried out. Both parties want this and should understand the need for periodic inspections.

All rights and restrictions on entry should be spelled out in the lease agreement. If not, the landlord may claim the right to enter whenever he or she pleases. Most agreements stipulate "reasonable" entry. This means the landlord can't just drop in every other day and snoop around. Also, there's usually a notification time, such as a period of twenty-four hours, before entry can be made. Entry is always permissible if the property manger legitimately feels that there is an emergency, such as a fire. And, clearly, a landlord can enter on the spot if the tenant gives permission.

The landlord may need to enter the property for the purpose of showing it to prospective tenants who may move in when the current

Warranty of Implied Habitability

This is a legal term meaning that any place you rent should be habitable. It's a powerful tenant's right, even if it's left unspecified in the lease. The law means that you have the responsibility of ensuring that your property meets the minimum set of standards for health and safety.

A tenant living anywhere in the country has the right to expect the following:

- Compliance with all building codes.
- A safe and clean dwelling.
- Stable walls, floors, and ceilings.
- Appropriate and functioning heating and cooling systems.
- Working plumbing and electrical wiring.
- Safe drinking water and proper sanitation facilities.
- Secure windows and doors.
- Adequate light and ventilation.
- Proper repair and maintenance.

This warranty is based on a recognized idea that in America anyone seeking to rent a place to live has the right to have certain expectations and services that are covered by their rental payments. This right applies equally to the smallest apartment in the dingiest part of town and to the most upscale rental property in the country.

occupant's lease expires. A landlord may also enter without permission if he or she believes the tenant has abandoned the property.

You cannot legally enter a tenant's apartment or house if the tenant does not grant you access—up to a point. If the tenant repeatedly denies entry to the landlord with no justifiable reason, he or she may then legally enter anyway. The landlord will have to handle this professionally and appear at a reasonable hour of the day. As always, rules and regulations vary by community, so it's a good idea to determine your rights and limits in your specific area before you go knocking on any doors.

> You cannot legally enter a tenant's apartment or house if the tenant does not grant you access—up to a point.

Legal Issues Related to Eviction

A landlord or property manager only has three basic reasons for evicting tenants:

1. A missed payment of rent.
2. A violation of the leasing agreement, such as keeping a pet when pets are prohibited.
3. The property has been vacated by the tenant for more than half of the rental period without notification of the landlord or property manager.

No one may be evicted on the grounds of race, nationality, religion, marital status, because they have children, or for any other reasons deemed discriminatory.

Once you have determined that you have grounds for eviction, you must notify the tenant of the problem and that it must be corrected by a stipulated time. Seven to ten days is generally considered enough time to correct a given situation. Your notification should be in writing.

If the tenant corrects the situation, all is well and good. If not, you have to follow up by filing a claim at the county court. The tenant will receive a copy of the complaint plus a summons to appear before the judge. You cannot force your tenant from the property under the authority of the complaint. You'll have to go through the court procedures.

You and your tenant will receive a notice of the hearing at a specified date. The tenant has the right to protest your eviction proceedings by filing an answer with the court. Usually, he or she must file this answer within five working days. The tenant will be required to deposit any outstanding rent money with the clerk of court until the proceedings are concluded.

If your tenant ignores the proceedings, the judge is permitted to issue a final judgment so that the sheriff can evict the tenant. Should the tenant fail to make the court date, eviction is automatic. Depending upon what state you live in, you may even be able to recoup court costs, legal fees, and your rent payments. The court will allow your tenant a reasonable amount of time to leave the property, at which time you may change the locks. You may also attach a lien on the tenant's possessions as payment or partial payment for money owed.

A New Legal Option

A new idea in providing legal services has appeared on the national horizon in recent years, and it's an option you should examine. Firms like the Pre-Paid Legal Services company have replaced fee-for-service billing with a flat monthly fee that the client pays regardless of whether any service was done that month. If you are interested, contact the prepaid legal services companies in your area for detailed information as to how they can help your property management business.

> In a traditional lawyer-client relationship, you pay your attorney or legal firm when you need them.

You're a Member, Not a Client

Here is how it works. In a traditional lawyer-client relationship, you pay your attorney or legal firm when you need them. For example, if there's an accident on your property, you call your lawyer. He or she works to resolve the situation, sends you an invoice with charges calculated per hour spent on your case, and you pay the bill. If you don't use your lawyer's services, you don't need to pay anything—until the next need arrives.

In the prepaid legal world, you join an organization. Other members of the organization are lawyers and legal firms who are the providers of legal services. Provider law firms can be located throughout your community, region, state, or the nation. Each month you pay an agreed-upon membership fee. When that accident or any other incident requiring legal services arises, you simply make a phone call (probably toll-free) to the organization. You'll be put in contact with one of the provider law firms and the case will be assigned to one of that firm's attorneys. In essence, the prepaid legal company becomes the client of the provider law firm. In many cases, the company can be that firm's largest client, which should place the prepaid members in a good position to get excellent service.

The case is generally handled without any costs because you have already paid for legal services with your monthly fees. However, this may not always be the case, because your agreement with the prepaid legal services company may or may not have certain stipulations about additional charges. Clearly, you should be informed up front and in writing about such conditions. When interviewing one

The Privileges of Membership

Several years ago one of the nation's leading credit card companies promoted itself through advertising that touted "the benefits of membership." It seems that many of these prepaid legal services companies really do offer significant benefits to members of the organization. Different companies will offer a different array of services, but as a rule you can expect your prepayments to cover such services as the following:

- Lawsuits.
- Buying and selling property.
- Disputes over property lines.
- Contract reviews.
- Reviews of legal papers and documents.
- Legal consultation.
- Warranty issues.

- Tenant issues.
- Bankruptcy counsel.
- Legal questions relating to small businesses.
- Letter writing and notifications.
- Will preparations and updates.
- Traffic tickets.

Again, services may vary from company to company. Different states will have varying regulations on what law firms can and can't do. You should make it your responsibility to find out precisely what services will and will not be covered by your membership.

of these companies, be sure to ask about any services that will not be covered by that monthly payment. The legal world is already full of surprises. You don't need any more, especially at a time when something goes wrong.

An Accident Jump-Starts an Industry

The prepaid legal services concept was set in motion about thirty years ago after the man who later founded the first of these companies was in an automobile accident. The accident wasn't his fault and he believed he was fully covered. Still, he needed legal services to help him argue his case, and the legal bills kept piling up. He must have wondered, "There's got to be a better, less expensive way than all these hourly rates!" This unexpected situation generated the spark that created a new legal industry.

The idea has caught on. Pre-Paid Legal Services was recently ranked twelfth on the *Forbes* magazine list of Top 200 Small Businesses. *Money* magazine ranked it the thirteenth hottest company in America. *Fortune* magazine recognized it as one of the nation's fastest growing companies. This bit of statistics illustrates that the concept has certainly caught the favorable attention of the nation's business community. Similar companies in your market are certainly options you should at least explore.

Research the Agency and Lawyers

Always do your homework before signing with any prepaid legal services company. Check out the organization thoroughly and ask for references. In particular, follow through with the following:

- Find out if the prepaid organization is asking for a long-term commitment or whether you can you sign up on a more favorable month-to-month basis.
- Determine the organization's policy for handling situations in which you are not satisfied with the services of the assigned law firm, should that occur.
- Inquire about the procedure for changing provider law firms in the case that you and the firm do not prove to be a good match.

Always do your homework before signing with any prepaid legal services company.

Good Information Is Good Business

It's important to make contacts with people who know local regulations, for example, members of neighborhood associations or builders clubs. They can provide you with indispensable and financially beneficial information. Whether or not you're a "people person," get out there and use the invaluable resource of your network. Contacts pay off in real dollars and cents.

For example, there is a little-known law in Chicago that requires the city to pay for trash pickup of tenant-heated properties. Information about this law isn't broadcast through the mass media. The landlord who does not know about this law will always be paying good money for a service that could have been provided for free. Lack of knowledge is lack of power, which translates directly into lack of cash. Good legal information makes for good business.

If you do sign on with a particular organization, then be sure to take the same hard look at the provider firm that they will match you up with. In particular, check the following:

- Whether both the assigned lawyer and the firm he or she represents have extensive experience with real-estate law. If the firm is new, you should receive some proof as to why you should place your business needs in their hands.
- Whether the law firm is in good standing with the local bar association and the Better Business Bureau.
- Whether the provider firm has a top rating from the prepaid legal services organization.
- Whether you feel comfortable and confident with the firm's personnel, who should be professional, courteous, and interested in your situation.

The world is constantly changing, and our legal system is no exception. Today, property managers and landlords have more legal options available than ever before. The traditional fee-for-service law firms are still there to serve your needs, but new opportunities, such as the prepaid legal services companies, are making their mark as well, some of them on a national scale. The point here is that you have options. Explore all of them and determine which makes the most sense for your real-estate needs.

Chapter 22

Contracts: Reading the Fine Print

Motion-picture tycoon Samuel Goldwyn is credited with saying, "A man's word is his bond," which is an excellent philosophy that you should embrace *for yourself*. Give your word and keep it every time, even if it's occasionally painful. Unfortunately, you can't count on the other guy to embrace the same philosophy. A verbal agreement isn't enforceable unless it is put into writing. That writing is called a contract.

This brings us back to Mr. Goldwyn, who also quipped: "A verbal contract isn't worth the paper it's written on." Although Goldwyn may not have fully understood his English there, he clearly knew something about business and the importance of the written contract.

Contracts are an integral element of property management. You can't get along in this business without them. The purpose of the contract is to allow two parties to make a formal agreement, where both sides understand exactly what is and what is not being agreed upon.

Contract Elements

A smart property manager invests the time to really understand the elements that make up a contract. Each contract is unique, but there are a number of elements common to most. Generally, when property changes hands—whether it's for business or personal use—you need to create a contract between buyer and seller. This contract should state the following information:

- The definition of the property for sale.
- The price of the property.
- The terms of the sale.

Names, Addresses, and Phone Numbers

The first part of the contract is the seller's name. This is usually followed by the word "to" on a separate line. Beneath "to" you find the seller's information. This is followed by the address of the property. If the property for sale is a condominium, the contract will note the unit number here.

The Down Payment

The seller's name and contact information is usually followed by a clause dealing with the amount of money put down to acquire the property. The actual amount could be any mutually agreed-upon figure, specified as a particular dollar amount or a particular percentage of the total price.

Mortgage and Financing Terms

This section describes the mortgage the buyer is getting and the terms of that mortgage. For example, if you are obtaining a mortgage for 80 percent of the price, the specific amount of the mortgage or this percentage number will be noted here. Also noted will be the interest rate the buyer is trying to obtain, the amortization schedule, the balloon period, and the amount of time the lender will require for full payback of the amount of money owed.

Most contracts prepared by real-estate boards will provide a number of options in the mortgage contingency paragraph. For example, one option could be "buyer will pay cash." If this option is taken, the previous paragraph relating to the mortgage would be irrelevant and would be deleted.

Another paragraph may list the seller's financing options or terms of a purchase money note, the document used when engaged in seller financing.

Date of Possession

This section notes the specific date the new owner will legally take possession of this property. The date is a negotiable item. Generally the buyer takes possession when the deed transfers and money has been paid to the seller. In some rare cases a buyer can take possession before the closing.

A common clause for the "owner's use and occupancy" is sometimes inserted here. This was used in one of Mark's recent contracts. The seller wanted the money quickly, but needed some extra time to box up, throw away, and cart off all the material on the property. An "owner's use and occupancy" clause was added to the contract. According to this clause, Mark would have a holdback equal to

> The date is a negotiable item.

$8,000. (A holdback is money that will be paid, but not until certain events have occurred.) The contract also stipulated that the seller would have thirty days after the sale had taken place to move out. Following that period Mark would charge $200 a day for any additional time needed by the seller. In this case, the seller took an extra two days, so Mark was paid an additional $400 for the seller's use and occupancy.

Now, you may think $400 is a tidy sum for doing nothing, and it is. But also consider that Mark had to delay bringing in his renovation crew by two days, which had a ripple effect throughout his entire operations. In that context, the sum was far from tidy.

Attorney Approval Clause

This clause is inserted to allow the buyer's lawyer sufficient time to review the contract. Do take this clause seriously. As previously noted, the use of a savvy real-estate lawyer is essential.

Inspection Period Clause

> This section provides a period during which the buyer can have the property inspected.

Similar to the attorney-approval clause, this section provides a period during which the buyer can have the property inspected. This too is essential. As knowledgeable and as experienced as you may be, your eye is still untrained. The buyer always needs to have a professional give the property a thorough "once over." To pass on this clause is to pass on common sense.

Closing Date

Closing occurs on the actual date that the seller delivers the deed and the buyer pays for the property. It is the day that the transfer of ownership of the property referenced in the contract takes place.

The Need for Legalese

Legalese is that incredibly dense accumulation of terms, definitions, and statements that drive people who are not attorneys up the wall.

Lawyers will tell you that this type of wording and language is necessary for the protection of the parties involved, but many businesspeople don't see a need for it at all. They know a contract can be simple. The seller will provide a legal description and a free and clear title to the buyer within a specified time. The buyer will pay a specified amount for the property referenced in the contract. Property will be exchanged for money. The seller walks away with a check and a smile, and the buyer is free to do whatever he or she pleases with the new property.

Unfortunately, just because something can be simple doesn't mean it will be. The days of doing business on a paper napkin are long gone. Now such matters as the intent of the seller or the implied meaning of statements require written contracts. Lawyers do the writing, and therefore we have and will continue to have contracts filled to the brim with legalese. Don't despair. The more you deal with contracts and work with your lawyer, the more you'll understand—because each time you see something you don't understand, don't be afraid to ask for an explanation, or, in some cases, a translation. If you keep asking, you'll soon pick it up, which will make your job much easier.

Boilerplate Is Part of the Structure

The contract's boilerplate includes the standard items that aren't subject to negotiation, the resulting accumulation of all that legalese drawn up to protect the buyer and seller. Like the metal boilerplate used to construct a ship, the contract boilerplate is attached to the basic structure to make it "float." There are numerous matters that must be included in a contract to assure protection of the buyer and seller. If the boilerplate items are written in twelve-point type, they will take up pages of paper; sometimes, they may be condensed into smaller type, which you've probably heard of as the "fine print" or "boiler print," since it requires significantly fewer pages.

There are two types of lawyers. One kind likes to use fine print, and the other kind does not. It seems that many lawyers feel a need to justify their hourly rate. Producing volumes of paper in a contract

Use Plain English

A word of caution: Be very wary of using legalese yourself. It's a language of specifics and legal terminology, applied toward specific legal purposes, but it is not designed for efficient business communication. Trying to use something you don't really understand can cause a lot of confusion. You could come off looking like a dolt.

Worse, if there's any confusion arising out of the contract, the party responsible for creating that confusion is more likely to be held accountable. You could write yourself into a legal trap without knowing it—until the judge rules for the other side. If you're not a lawyer, speak and write in basic English.

fills some of that need. Furthermore, the large volume of paperwork in large-print contracts will often scare the buyer or seller more than the fine print. However, it's really up to you to pick the type of boilerplate you prefer to use, depending on what feels most comfortable.

Don't Do It Yourself

There is an old saying that an attorney who represents himself has a fool for a client. There is wisdom in that statement, and it applies to property management as well as to any business.

As you buy and sell property, gaining more and more experience in real estate, you'll come to rely on a somewhat standard contract form. You'll be comfortable with its contents, its language, and

Independent Contractor/Employee Contracts

Sometimes landlords and property managers try to turn employees into independent contractors to avoid paying taxes. This is unwise and can result in significantly costly penalties. No matter how you structure your agreement, an employee is an employee, and an independent contractor is an independent contractor. If the situation is in a "gray area," how can you tell which is which?

There are a number of general tests, one of which is fairly hard-and-fast. Let's start there. If the property manager dictates the nature of the job and the way that job is to be performed, then the hired person is probably an employee. The latitude generally given an independent contractor is missing.

On the other hand, independent contractors may be identified by the following characteristics:

- A business or contractor's license.
- Payment of self-employment taxes and making their own deductions.
- Assuming legal liability for their work.
- The ability to keep their own hours.
- The ability to leave the job site of their own free will.
- An area of specialization, such as plumbing or electrical work.
- A written or verbal contract for the work to be performed for the property manager.
- Carrying their own insurance.
- Working with their own tools, machinery, equipment, and suppliers.
- Advertising, promotion, and/or publicizing their work for hire.
- Identification, letterhead stationery, and business cards.

its protection. A day will come when you decide that you are perfectly capable of drafting your own contract. Perhaps you'll be in a hurry and don't want to "waste" time with your attorney, or maybe you'll be trying to save a buck. On that day, don't take your own advice. Go see your lawyer.

All contracts should be created with professional input from attorneys who understand the technicalities of real-estate law. To do otherwise is to shoot yourself in the foot. Imagine that on the day after closing a deal you discover you've left out something in your contract. By "saving" a few hundred bucks in legal fees, you may have set yourself up for years of unnecessary expenses.

You can probably find generic contracts at your local real-estate board. These are quite good as far as they go. But remember, every contract you draw up should be unique. The template documents are good only as a base or skeleton of the deal. Use them as a starting point and adapt them as necessary to each negotiation. Make sure your attorney reviews your changes.

Do-it-yourself is fine and fun when it comes to home repairs. When it comes to real estate, do-it-yourself becomes do-it-*to*-yourself.

> All contracts should be created with professional input from attorneys who understand the technicalities of real-estate law.

Contract Negotiations

Before you can sign a contract, you have to have a negotiation. Sometimes you'll be involved in a whole series of meetings. A contract can't be executed until the negotiation phase is completed.

Know Your Limits

This is the key element in all of your negotiations. Before entering into any negotiation, you must have a specific dollar figure that you will not exceed, which is called your top end. Go in without a limit, and you could easily get caught up in a frenzied negotiation, let your emotions rule your mind, and end up agreeing to something you'll later regret. Think about the happy executives buying a Tommy Crown property in the film *The Thomas Crown Affair* (either version). The deal is concluded. Cigars are brought out and the executives start glowing in their success. Thomas Crown walks out and

When It's Not Right for You

Walk away. While working on this book, Mark did exactly that. He was considering the purchase of a six-unit building in a well-known neighborhood in Lincoln Park, North Chicago. The building was in a good location, and Mark knew it wouldn't be on the market very long. This purchase required an urgent decision.

Mark decided to walk away. After investing the time to examine potential rents and the likely return on his investment, he decided the wise move was to pass. Keep in mind, the building was still a good purchase, but for someone else—there was no "upside potential" there for Mark.

When buying property, Mark looks for value and opportunity. In this case, the physical condition of the building was okay, but the rents were at their limit. The building lacked opportunity. It would have been an expensive building. Had it been available at a cheap price with below-market rents, he'd have grabbed it. But as the offer stood, it just didn't seem like the right deal for Mark.

pauses at the door to say, "You paid too much." You really want to avoid being on the bad end of a deal like that.

Give a Little, Get a Lot

Sometimes small gestures make big things happen. Everyone likes to win, and a smart negotiator always has a small victory or two he or she can offer the other party. It's called a "gimme," something you don't have to give up but are willing to sacrifice to make the deal work. You can find any number of "gimmes" in any building or any negotiation. Have some ready to offer if you need to jump-start the process or if you think the other party needs to win a little more to feel good about the agreement.

Here's just one example of how the process can work. When buying commercial property, it is the seller's responsibility to provide you with an environmental audit. Make sure that the seller follows through with this obligation. The environmental audit is designed to discover if there are any environmental problems associated with the site. For example, it's important to know if there are any chemical wastes buried beneath your property. The cost of cleanup and the associated regulatory costs could be substantial, so you want to know this before buying the property.

The cost of an environmental audit varies from market to market, but they generally run around $1,000. Now, in a purchase amounting to hundreds of thousands of dollars, a thousand really isn't much by comparison. That makes it a great "gimme." Put it in your pocket and wait to see if you need to use it. Your contract may include a list of seller responsibilities, including an audit that shows the property is clear of any environmental concerns. If the seller balks at this or some other items, you can offer to absorb the cost, thus giving the seller a small victory. With that victory in the seller's pocket, he or she will be less likely to balk on other matters, perhaps even more substantial ones.

There are countless items like this in every deal. Find a few you'll be willing to absorb, and have them ready to offer when and if the need arises. Again, remember the main rules of negotiation: Seek a win/win agreement, have fun, and carry that enjoyment on to the next negotiating table.

Be Willing to Walk Away

If the deal isn't right, even if it is a good one, you have to have the guts, business sense, and willingness to walk away from it. There are always good deals to be found, so it's wise to wait for the good deal that is also the right deal for you.

You must be willing and able to leave a room during the negotiation; otherwise, you success in negotiation will diminish over time. Real estate really is a free market. Everybody negotiates, and that's expected. No one pays the "sticker price" in buying property. It is to your advantage to negotiate wisely, but keep in mind you need to allow the other guy to come out a winner, too. Regardless of how tough the negotiation may be, you're not trying to crush the enemy. You goal is to structure an agreement where both sides sincerely believe they won. It's the win/win approach.

Reading the Other Party

Develop your personal radar so that you can quickly start picking up those subtle signals that the other side may be ready to conclude the negotiations. This skill gives you the upper hand and may show you the proper moment to offer that last "gimme" to close the deal. Here are a few signs that things are about to wrap up:

- Your negotiations move from areas of disagreement to areas of agreement.
- Body language is more open than closed. For example, open arms with palms up is a much better sign than someone sitting with his or her arms and legs crossed.
- The other side begins to discuss final arrangements.
- Both parties are in considerably more agreement on major issues than when the discussions began.
- You're invited to a social occasion, a sure sign that the deal is on the way to becoming a "done deal."
- Your opposite number starts making notes. It's a good idea for you to reinforce this positive behavior by doing the same.
- You start to hear comments like "I think we're almost there" or "this is beginning to look good."

> No one pays the "sticker price" in buying property.

Breaking a Contract

No one enters a contract with the idea of not going through with it, but there are times when you may be faced with making that decision. It's a good idea to know the positive and negative consequences of such a decision before that time arrives.

If You Are the Buyer

Consider a quote from Joseph Joubert, a French philosopher: "Never cut what you can untie." Breaking a contract doesn't have to be a hostile, unpleasant, stomach-churning experience. If you are the buyer, you have two good windows of opportunity to realize that you should consider breaking your contract. These are the attorney approval period and the inspection period, which are standard in real

Negotiation Tips

Negotiating a contract is a bit of science and a bit of art. It's learned over time and comes via direct experience. Here are a few key tips that can give you an edge in those early efforts.

1. Build an edge for yourself in your negotiating sessions. Try to conduct them on your own "turf," in your office or office complex. If that's not possible, insist on a neutral site where neither side has a home court advantage. If at all possible, avoid negotiating on the other party's "turf."
2. If negotiations stall or get derailed, walk out. Sudden and unexpected changes can shake up a meeting and create positive results. You have to do this correctly. Stand up without notice and say that things are just going nowhere. Suggest a break and then walk out of the room before anyone can agree, disagree, or mumble "say what?" Remember, you're not trying to be obstinate. You just want to get things moving. When you feel it's the right time or when you've been asked to return, be prepared with a new idea or a new slant for the negotiation process.
3. When you want to play the "gimmes," give them up slowly, one at a time. It's important for the other party to feel that he or she has worked for it. It makes their victory all the more sweet, which will translate into a sweet deal for you.

Again, you want to aim for a win/win situation. You need to get what you want, of course, but it's also in your own best interest to let the other party walk away with that same feeling of success.

estate contracts. These are the times you get to see what you are really buying.

Your money will not go "hard" (become nonrefundable) until you have satisfied at least three or four items in the contract. These are the following:

- Your attorney approval period.
- Your inspection period.
- Your environmental audit period.
- Your mortgage contingency.

Once these dates expire, you will probably be required to increase the amount of your earnest money payment. You will also be required to acknowledge that by not protesting any of these items, you are moving forward in the process. You're in effect saying "Everything's okay, let's proceed."

If a seller does not deliver what is promised, clearly the buyer has the right to break the contract. However, realize that in breaking a contract you may forfeit your earnest money. The seller is allowed to keep it because of your default.

When a buyer breaks a contract, he or she obviously ruins the day for the seller. Standard boilerplate in the contract will stipulate the seller's recourse, usually retention of the earnest money. The seller usually doesn't have the right to pursue the buyer for any damages beyond the earnest money. This makes sense for all concerned. The seller still owns the property and he or she has been compensated for time loss.

If the Seller Breaks the Contract

Sellers usually break contracts for one reason: Someone else is willing to pay more money for the property on sale. There is a legal phrase in real-estate law referred to as "specific performance." It means the seller has to fulfill the obligation in the contract. He or she has to honor the signature on that contract, which promises to deliver a specific property on a specific date and for a specific price.

No two properties are alike and that gives the buyer an edge. You can't go out and find another property that's identical to the

Mark Your Deadlines

Obviously, it is imperative that you know as much as you can as early as you can. Note possible conditions in your contract that will cause you to bail out. These could be such things as finding material or environmental defects in the property, misrepresentations by the seller, or your inability to get adequate financing.

You can also ask for extensions if you believe you need more time. This is a common practice. For example, perhaps a snowstorm knocked out the computers in a bank or lending institution, and they were not able to prepare all your financial documents within the timeframe that you had worked out. Through no fault of the buyer or seller, there's a major hitch in the agreement, so ask for an extension—it is preferable to canceling the contract altogether.

one in the contract. You've got your heart set on it and there's no way you can find an exact replacement. The buyer entered the agreement on good faith, and the courts will allow him or her to pursue the seller. Under the law, the seller carries a greater burden on breaking a contract than the buyer.

Breaking a contract in the hopes of getting a better deal can really backfire on a seller. There are uncounted examples of sellers backing out of a deal to get a better price, only to have that new deal fall through. Many times the seller is stuck with the property and may even see its value drop as the economy falters. There is only one way for a seller to break a contract in one, clean stroke: to buy out the other party's contract.

Contract Stipulations for Attorney Fees

Most rental contracts include a provision for the tenant to pay legal/attorney fees should the landlord win a legal dispute with the tenant. Using such a clause is not a hard and fast rule, however. In some situations it's to your advantage. In others, you'll probably want to take a pass.

You should consider a number of factors before making that decision. If you know that your tenant will not be able to raise the cash necessary to pay for your legal costs in the event that you win the court case, then this clause will be useless. Also, consider the legal attitudes in your community. If most of the judges tend to grant awards to tenants most of the time, the cards may be stacked against you. So, why bother?

On the other hand, if your tenants tend to be individuals or families with disposable income, you might want to include that clause. Consider the legal climate, too. If judges seem to render fair judgments, you should at least have a fifty-fifty chance, provided your case is valid and you have the necessary proof.

> If you know that your tenant will not be able to raise the cash necessary to pay for your legal costs in the event that you win the court case, then this clause will be useless.

For more information on this topic, visit our Web site at www.businesstown.com

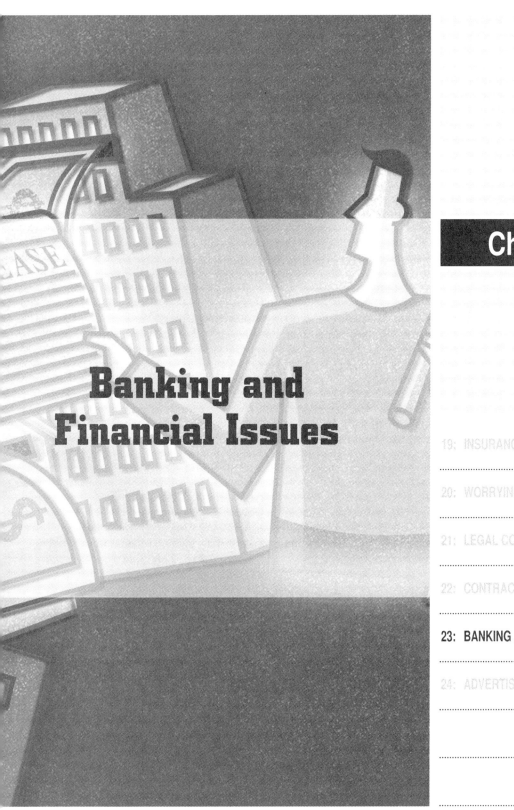

Banking and Financial Issues

Chapter 23

A mbrose Bierce wrote that money is of no advantage except when we part with it. Of course, you have to have money before you can even think of letting it go. Real-estate transactions see lots of money changing hands, and that means you will need to rely upon the services and capital resources of banks and other financial institutions.

Loans and Banks

A real-estate closing is only as good as the money you can borrow to make it happen. As discussed in Chapter 18, your business is more likely to grow and prosper with the service of a good banker. It is important to have an established relationship with a bank. This institution will have your financial records on hand, will have seen how you conduct yourself and your business, and will be in a position to green-light a loan.

Of course, your banker might just as easily red-light that loan. That's why it's good to have a working relationship with more than one bank. On any given day, one banker might say no, but another down the street might gladly give an enthusiastic yes to your project.

You might approach your banker with a variety of acquisitions: single-family dwellings, multi-unit apartments, commercial property, large apartment complexes, shopping centers, and other types of real estate. Each type of acquisition has its own particular financial complexities. Different banks and bankers will have different areas of expertise, and you'll want to pick and choose the best one for each of your projects. You'll be like the team leader in *Mission Impossible*. As every project comes up, you'll take out your list of banking assets and select the best for your next mission.

Financial Relationships

Business is relationships and a good relationship with several bankers will only make your business life easier. Being in a position to have a good line of credit available or just to have a good financial mind to consult and kick around ideas is of great help. Start building those relationships early. Don't wait until you need one.

Here's an example of how even very short-term banking relationships can make the difference between closing a deal and losing one. In 1987, two weeks after the stock market crash, Mark was involved in auctioning ninety-seven condominiums the Gateway Towers Condominium Complex in Pittsburgh, Pennsylvania, for a national financial institution. The mortgage broker assigned to the project clearly was not a local; she was from Colorado Springs. She took the deposits and loan applications for mortgages, but she couldn't deliver. Mark didn't hear about the problems until January 1, 1988. He was told that the purchasers of the condominiums would not be able to get the financing they needed. An avalanche from the Rockies was about to destroy Mark's real-estate commissions.

The only way to get those commissions was to make sure that all those loans closed. He grabbed a guide for all the banks in Pittsburgh, got on the telephone, and started making relationships. This took time and effort, but he found enough bankers willing to listen to his ideas and then to get on board with the project. Mark spread out each mortgage throughout the city's entire banking and savings and loan community, successfully completing the project and getting those sales commissions. The point is lending is local.

Comparison Shop

You compare prices at the grocery store, the building supply shop, and the automobile dealership, don't you? Why shouldn't you do the same when shopping for a bank? Keep in mind that you'll be shopping more for relationships than for money. If you compare rates from one bank to the next, you won't find too much difference among them. Interest rates will vary very little, if at all, because when the Federal Reserve raises or lowers rates, the cost of money changes at about the same rate, which is applicable to all banks across the country. Banks from Connecticut to California will be charging about the same for the use of that money.

You will find some variables. Some banks may charge points, fees to be paid up front for borrowing their money. Other banks may impose prepayment penalties on loans. (Banks make their money off the interest they charge over time. If you pay off the loan early, you

Consult Your Banker

One good way to build and maintain a strong relationship with each of your bankers is to have a lunch or dinner every quarter to talk business. This isn't a time for schmoozing, back-slapping, or an excuse to tell each other what terrific businesspeople you are. The meeting should be friendly, but all business.

A meeting every three months is ideal in terms of timing, because neither party feels as if he or she is being imposed upon. Additionally, enough time has passed for situations, people, and things to have changed. You can update each other on victories, losses, and changes in your respective industries.

Discuss serious business matters. Describe options you're considering, problems you're having, opportunities or potential difficulties on the business horizon, and any other matters you consider appropriate. Give your bankers the opportunity to provide you excellent service by working with them all the way, but if things aren't panning out, you should feel justified to move on.

cut off many of those earning years and they'll want you to pay for the privilege.)

Family and Friend Loans

As a general rule, this procedure has tremendous potential to create problems. Sadly, business problems can spread back into your personal relationships. Many a family or group of friends has been split and even destroyed over arguments about a shared business. Think back in your experience and you'll surely remember some family that was shattered in an unnecessary battle over money.

Having obligations to friends and family can work, but you have to set it up right. This means that you have to treat these

Banking Services You Need

Someone offered this description of lending institutions: "Banks do not raise or lower interest rates depending upon how they feel about it. A bank buys money like a grocer buys bananas—and then adds on salaries and rent and sells the product." In other words, a bank is a business. That means the bank's goal is to earn a profit. To ensure those profits, a bank should work hard to achieve high marks for customer satisfaction. From the property manager's perspective, here are a few banking services that should make you a satisfied customer:

- A bank should offer a property manager maximum interest with a minimal deposit or required balance. (Shop around!)

- You should be able to avoid a fee or additional charges for writing checks. (You'll be writing a lot of checks as a landlord.)

- Services, such as check printing, should be charged at minimum rates and shouldn't be considered profit centers by your bank.

- Rent checks shouldn't be held until they clear the tenants' bank account.

- You should be provided with overdraft protection. (Some of your tenants *will* send you checks with insufficient funds backing them.)

- And, although it's not a requirement, someone at some time should say, "We appreciate your business."

If your bank doesn't offer all or most of these services, perhaps it's time to look for customer satisfaction at another institution.

arrangements as business. Treat the contract or the organization you form just as you would treat a business relationship with any other people. Involve the lawyers and the accountants. More than that, make clear statements that this business will be conducted as a business. Let everyone know up front that the rules will not be bent just because the partners have personal relationships.

Take care of all the paperwork properly. Remember Sam Goldwyn's advice that a verbal contract isn't worth the paper it's written on. Successful personal relationships don't necessarily or automatically translate into successful working relationships in business.

Your friends and family partners need to realize that they will be expected to ante up their share of the investment, and they'll also be required to keep up their end of the bargain throughout the life of the arrangement. You are giving these folks the opportunity of investing in one of your projects, and they should respect the privilege. Why do we use the word "privilege"? Because the term is accurate. Their commitment is simply writing a check. You are the one who researched the market, pounded the pavements, and found the opportunity. You will be the one whose hard work and due diligence will be the force that makes the deal work. This doesn't discredit the value of their money, but it does give proper credit to your brainpower and commitment to the project.

When friends and family sit around a table to discuss a vacation choice, everyone should have a equal voice. But democracy doesn't always work as well in business. Certainly, a leader should take advice and counsel from all concerned, but when someone has to make a decision, some *one* should have that task. If the group can't live with this way of conducting business, the project is probably doomed to failure.

> Successful personal relationships don't necessarily or automatically translate into successful working relationships in business.

Out-of-Market Financing

Your local needs should be met by your network of bankers in your community or region. However, they may or may not be interested in financing property out of their community, which means you may need to look elsewhere.

When seeking outside financing, go to the bank or financial institution nearest the property you want to buy. Start practicing relationship banking and apply for a loan. The folks there should know the community and the market's strengths and weaknesses, and they should have a good idea as to whether or not the property is a good purchase. They'll also provide information telling you what you must do to receive financing in that market. This relationship will prove to be a valuable one if you decide to purchase property in that market again.

Applying for a Loan

Applying for a loan is a process, and it can be an intimidating one for the first time or two you experience it. Handling this process is a business skill, and you'll pick it up with practice. This section will give you some valuable tips to make the practice less painful.

Dress for the Part

We live in an era of relaxed dress codes or even no dress code at all. Many businesses now have a casual-dress Friday policy. Walk through the office of an average company, and you'll see people dressed as if heading out for a day of leisure. Some of the nation's most influential executives hold news conferences while wearing sports shirts and slacks. We definitely live in a dress-down business world.

Banks are an exception. It's still a suit-and-tie world, and if you want to succeed in it, you'd best play by the rules. First impressions are extremely important, and that's especially true when you're asking someone to trust you with a few hundred thousand dollars. When you dress the part, you're sending a message: "I know the rules. I know how to play this game and win. I'm someone you can do business with."

Know Your Facts and Figures

A good impression is important, but that's just the start. The way you project yourself and succeed in real estate is what will garner the respect of others, including bankers. You have to have something

> Banks are an exception. It's still a suit-and-tie world.

substantial behind your suit-and-tie window dressing. The bank wants to know if you are a man or woman of substance.

Think like a Boy Scout, and be prepared. You can't afford sloppiness in dress, and you certainly can't afford sloppiness in your presentation. Enter the bank with a prepared portfolio. Have a well-considered and detailed plan of action for your project. "Uh, I'm lookin' at that property over at First and Main" just won't get you much attention. On the other hand, a presentation beginning with "I'd like to purchase the Wilson Building at First and Main. The cost is $100,000 and I'd like to borrow $80,000. Here's my plan for turning it into a . . . " will get your meeting off to a good start.

In order for you to pull this off, you have to know exactly what you're going to do and how you're going to do it. Think every step through, and organize a complete, coherent presentation. The more prepared you are in your presentation, with materials to back up your claims, the closer you are to the money you are applying for.

Begin with Senior Loan Officers

Your first call will be to a senior banking official in the loan department. During the loan application process, you will begin working your way down the corporate ladder to deal with the people who do the actual legwork.

The loan officer will send you a loan package. You'll be required to complete all the forms, describe the property you want to buy, and provide a credit report and additional financial information. The more prepared you are, the quicker you'll get a response, and you do want a quick response, even if your proposal is rejected. You're better off knowing that you don't have the loan as early as possible, so that you can move on to the next banker on your list.

Preparing the material for the loan package is solely your responsibility. You have to provide all the facts and figures. Don't depend upon the bank or the seller to do this work or provide information for you.

> The more prepared you are, the quicker you'll get a response, and you do want a quick response, even if your proposal is rejected.

Be Prepared for Tough Questions

Once you've provided the documentation and paid a fee, the bank will require that a certified appraiser inspect the property. After the inspection, the appraiser will send the bank a written report on the physical condition of the property and verify the accuracy of leases and expenses. The appraisal has to be in the file before the bank will consider the application. This objective, third-party look at the property in question carries a lot of weight with the loan committee.

Be prepared for a meeting to discuss your purchase with the appraiser. A lot of questions will come your way, and you'd better be prepared to answer them in depth and with confidence. Here are a few samples of the types of questions you'll be asked:

- Do you have plans to renovate the property?
- Will you be putting additional dollars, or "deep pockets," in the renovation?
- Are you counting on the present value or the post-renovation value? For instance, Mark is in the process of buying a six-unit apartment building for $550,000—today's value. He will invest approximately $20,000 per apartment in renovations, increasing the building's value to $670,000 or more (its post-renovation value), depending upon the rental income.
- Where is the down payment coming from?
- Do you have a construction budget?
- What are comparable rents in the area?
- What history do you have with projects similar to this one?

The process can be nerve-wracking, but in time you will get used to it and the process will become easier. Remember, these folks are not your enemies. They're just trying to take care of their clients' interests, which may turn out to be your interests too.

The Loan Committee

The next step is for the loan committee to review all the paperwork. They look at a lot of factors, including equity, how much you want to borrow, and how much the bank risks in making the loan. Real estate loans usually are for 75–80 percent of the purchase price of the property. This leaves the bank with a 20–25 percent cushion

They look at a lot of factors, including equity, how much you want to borrow, and how much the bank risks in making the loan.

should you default on the loan. The bank also has the value of the property in the event of a default.

Once the loan is approved, the bank usually takes about another two weeks to complete all the loan documentation. This paperwork is your commitment to pay back the money you borrow. The property isn't yours until the loan is paid off. The debt is secured by the real estate. The bank's loan documentation will require your personal guarantee that if the loan defaults and you take a hike, you will be found and held personally responsible for all fees and fines resulting from the default.

Most bank loan documents are not negotiable. There's lots of standard boilerplate designed to protect the institution in the event of a default. It is important that you fully understand those documents and the ramifications of your financial commitment to your lending institution.

How to Make a Bad Impression

Some landlords and property managers are always having problems raising financing for their projects. They're always griping about the unfairness of banks and lending institutions. Before this happens to you, take a few moments to look at the world through the eyes of someone lending money to people in real estate. When you make your approach, will he or she see someone who is polite, organized, and businesslike? Or someone like the five characters listed below?

1. **The Blue-Plate Specialist.** This individual just phones the bank and asks for the loan rate of the day, an attitude that often sends loan officers up the proverbial wall. Loan rates vary. Someone who can afford a 20 or 30 percent deposit will most likely get a more favorable rate than someone who can only deposit 5 percent. If the caller has poor credit, his or her loan rate will be higher than someone with a good rating. That's just the way business works. A lending institution can't quote an accurate rate until they've researched the person

> Take a few moments to look at the world through the eyes of someone lending money to people in real estate.

and the project needing the loan. Professionals in property management should know that and act accordingly.

2. **The Tap Dancer.** When a loan officer asks about a person's credit rating, he or she will get one of these two answers: the truth, as in "I'm in good shape," or something far less than the truth: "I might have a tiny problem here and there." The second answer is called "tap dancing." The applicant keeps moving, hoping not to get pinned down about an inflated income statement, denial of credit problems, or minimizing the effects of major loans on the monthly income. The applicant can't get away with this because the lending institution has too many ways and too many resources of information. Save the dancing shoes for Saturday night, and go with the answer number one.

3. **The Clock Watcher.** Real-estate deals take place in periods measured by weeks and months, not days and hours. A landlord or property manager with an unrealistic attitude of the time involved in making things happen won't see much happening at all. As a rule, any transaction will take at least thirty days, possibly more. Stay off the clock, but keep an eye on the calendar.

4. **The Floater.** When the bank lends money, a rate is locked in for a specific time period (usually thirty, forty-five, or sixty days). Regardless of the fluctuations of the market, which will cause the rates to go up and down, that rate is guaranteed to the borrower. Sometimes, landlords try to "float." That is, they'll sign the loan agreement, but will not accept the lock on the rate, hoping that the market with drop and they'll be able to take advantage of the lower rate. If the rate rises, however, they recant, and demand the rate at the time the agreement was signed. They'll demand it, but they won't get it. In such cases, the floater ends up high and dry.

5. **The "Buttah."** Too many people in real estate hear only what they want to hear when making agreements with loan officers. Weeks later, the property manager finds himself or herself saying such things as, "But I thought you said . . . but, I distinctly heard you say . . . but, I thought you meant . . ."

> When the bank lends money, a rate is locked in for a specific time period (usually thirty, forty-five, or sixty days).

When you're dealing with tens of thousands of dollars or even hundreds of thousands of dollars, don't you think it prudent to really listen to the person and institution making that loan?

Have Deep Pockets

"Deep pockets" refers to your cash reserves. It's your ability to use your own money to fund your project or building when there's no cash flow. Always seek out properties with the prospects of a good cash flow. That way you won't have to reach down into those deep pockets unless you really need the extra funds.

Cash flow can be a form of deep pockets. If you have a number of good properties, each producing a good income, that cash flow can temporarily support a new acquisition. Your operating expenses can be covered while you renovate and lease out the new property.

Open Separate Banking Accounts

It's a bad idea to mix up your personal accounts or other business accounts with your real-estate accounts. You should have at least one bank account specifically set aside for your real-estate accounts. Obviously, you can have more—some landlords open an account for each building they own. How many you actually use will depend upon the size of your holdings, your accounting experience, or your desire for convenience. In any case, make sure you keep accurate records of all income and all expenses for each account.

The bank will insist on a name for the account. This is the name your tenants will write on their rental checks. A company name isn't all that important in real estate in terms of attracting business, but you still need one. It can be as simple as your name followed by the word "Properties" or "Real Estate."

If you select a name that doesn't involve your personal name, such as Acme Apartments, you might have to file a fictitious name statement at the bank, and the bank will probably charge you a filing fee. If the name Acme Apartments is important, say for name recognition and marketing reasons, you can still avoid the fictitious name paperwork and fees. Simply insert your name as part of the business. "John Smith's Acme Apartments" would do the job.

Again, using cash flow as your deep pockets is only a temporary measure and should never be considered as a long-term means of doing business.

Your pockets can never be deep enough, and the unknown is always out there, ready to strike. Unexpected expenses or new real-estate taxes can appear out of the blue. You'd better be able to handle them, and the way you do that is by having cash reserves—deep pockets.

Picking Your Pocket

Regardless of the true depth of your pockets or how much actual cash is down there, somebody out there wants to pick them. Just as you'll find in other industries, real estate has its share of scams and schemes. The scam artists prey on your gullibility and also on your desire to be a trusting "nice guy" who believes in the honesty of his fellow human beings.

A smart property manager approaches every situation with an open, yet skeptical eye. This is not to suggest that you should fingerprint and blood-test everyone with whom you do business. Just be businesslike in all your dealings. As President Ronald Reagan was fond of saying, "Trust, but verify."

Beware the Contractor

You now know how to take care of your finances with your banker. But there is another area where you need to be financially astute—in your dealings with contractors. Unless you are fully capable of taking care of maintenance and repair yourself and unless you want to spend the time to do all that work on your own, this aspect of your business is pretty much out of your control. The do-it-yourself route may be fine when you're starting out and only have one small property, but that's not the way to build a successful business in property management. You have much bigger and more complicated chores to attend to.

Most certainly, there are plenty of honest, hard-working, and dependable contractors out there, but there are cheats, crooks, and

> A smart property manager approaches every situation with an open, yet skeptical eye.

cons as well. Up front, you can't tell the difference, so it's best to practice sound business principles with everyone. You can move on to handshake deals or "do what you think best and bill me later" after you have already established a good working relationship with your contractor, after the contractor has already proven himself or herself. Even then, you'd be wise to be wary. Times and people change. Contractors (and anyone else) can become addicted to gambling or alcohol and drugs, or they can just decide to chuck it all and run off to Tahiti with a secretary. That's their own business—provided they don't do it with your money.

One of the surest ways to overspend, which is to say lose money, is by failing to monitor your maintenance and repair expenditures. Even if you run a tight ship in your accounting procedures, there are ways people can cheat you out of your money. A careless moment or a slip into sloppy procedures can provide a huge window of opportunity for the scam artist, who can't wait to get to you through a weak spot in your operations.

Get Multiple Bids

The best way to avoid getting ripped off is to shop around. This applies to everything from bricks to business cards to bankers. When it comes to contractors, you have to be extremely careful to make sure you get real value in labor and materials for the money you spend. Find those contractors who do good work and who honor their commitments. Continue working with them as long as they continue to provide you with excellent work. Even then, get multiple bids on any major repair and maintenance work. If a contractor is having a bad month or saving up for that trip to Tahiti, you may find your charges are a lot higher than for previous work of a similar nature. After all, the cost of piña coladas are going up every day.

Although you can try to get a lower bid from other contractors, be aware that a lower price may mean a lower quality of service. If the numbers are too low, you can expect problems. Basically, the job will never be completed. Here is why. If the bid is too low, that means the company can't make a profit. The contractor will insist on upfront money and/or partial payments, and then will find any

> Find those contractors who do good work and who honor their commitments. Continue working with them as long as they continue to provide you with excellent work.

number of reasons to stall the project so that the company makes a profit—at your expense. In this case, making a profit isn't the same as earning a profit. You'll be forced into getting a lien release from the contractor or finding someone else to do the work. Not getting the job done or major delays in getting the job done can be far more costly than paying a higher price to begin with.

Beware Ghost Wages

Many of your suppliers will be working on hourly rates. Painters, plumbers, electricians, and yard maintenance people, among others, work this way. So do scam artists who create ghost payrolls. That means they log hours not really worked, hours that you get to pay for. There are two ways of doing this. One is to simply bill fifteen hours for a ten-hour job. The other is to bill for workmen who were never on the job—phantoms on the payroll.

Don't sweat the small stuff. You'll rarely, if ever, catch the electrician, carpenter, or other contractor who works an hour and charges for two. Small losses are just part of the cost of doing business. However, when it comes to major projects, such behavior can run up your costs to astronomical heights. And if the work is shoddy, you'll have to pay to have it repaired or redone later on. You have to monitor such projects as closely as possible. It's difficult for a contractor to charge you for the work of three laborers when you've been out to the job site regularly and have seen only two. They'll have a hard time justifying ten hours of labor when you've seen them arrive at eight in the morning and you've waved them goodbye at four in the afternoon.

Every Dollar Counts

In discussing the federal budget, Senator Everett Dirksen coined the phrase, "A billion here, a billion there—pretty soon it adds up to real money." Well, your expenses aren't likely to be in the billions, but if you don't carefully watch the dollars you do have, you stand a good chance of losing a lot of them. Whether you're dealing with bankers or bricklayers, lose a little here, lose a little there, and pretty soon it adds up to some very real money indeed. This is your money. Make it your responsibility.

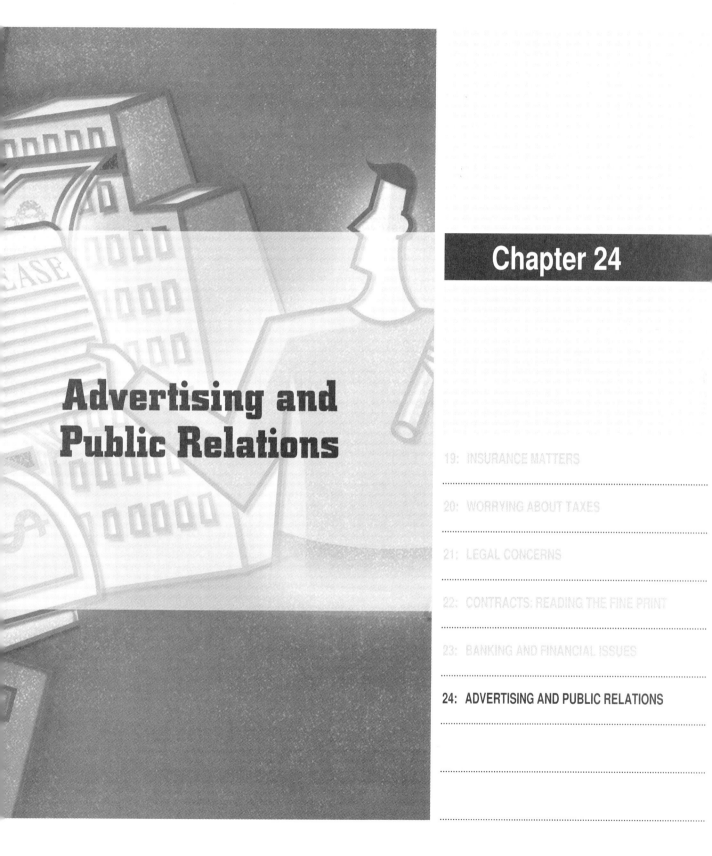

Chapter 24

Advertising and Public Relations

A s a property manager, you will certainly need some basic
information about advertising and public relations, valuable
resources that should be put to use only after careful planning and evaluation. This chapter is a brief overview of the resources
available to most markets in some form.

It's important to remember that each market is unique. What
applies in Brownsville, Texas, may not make any sense at all in
Bangor, Maine. For example, talk radio may be the best medium of
radio advertising in some markets while country and western radio
stations dominate some others. Daily newspapers are a natural vehicle, but in some markets the weekly papers and even the free "shoppers" serve as a better, more efficient vehicle.

Putting the Information out There

If you need to get information out to the public, you should develop
a written advertising and public relations plan. It doesn't have to be
complex. In fact, the simpler the better. The following three questions will be key to developing your plan.

What Is Your Market?

What group or groups contain most of your tenants or prospective tenants? Are you in a college town with a lot of young people
who would make good tenants, or are you in or near a retirement
community? Get as specific as you can about what your prospective
tenant group. Develop a profile of your typical tenant. Include such
data as age, sex, race, employment, college attended, income levels,
and so on. This profile will allow you to make an intelligent decision
about the second question.

Which Vehicles Reach This Market?

You can get accurate data on the market served from the individual media representative. Various organizations provide this service for the nation's media, and they are available to your local
advertising media. Many of your media decisions will be amazingly

simple. If you're located in a small town with just one weekly newspaper, that's your medium. If your market is college students, you'll probably not reach very many of them through the golden oldies station featuring "warm and wavering" big band hits of the 1920s. On the other hand, if your market is retirees, that station might be the ideal venue. The point is to get accurate information about the markets served and to make a rational decision about which ones to investigate and eventually bet your advertising dollar on. This brings us to question number three.

Can I Afford It?

Advertising rates range from the affordable to the completely outrageous. If you just can't afford the media that best reaches your market, then you might have to settle for a medium with a smaller audience. The key to your advertising success will be repetition. An

Conduct a SWOT Analysis

Before conducting any type of marketing, advertising, or public relations, you need to know how well you stack up in the marketplace. A great tool is the SWOT analysis. SWOT stands for "strengths, weaknesses, opportunities, and threats."

Strengths are internal factors over which you can exercise total or at least a degree of control. For example, your team could be composed of the finest property managers in the state.

Weaknesses are also internal. For example, you could have the best team, but the public could be totally unaware of that fact. There's some direction for your advertising program right there.

Opportunities are external factors. You can't control the arrival of an opportunity, but you can exploit it. For instance, if a major property, such as an industrial park, is getting into trouble because of weak property management, your advertising and marketing efforts promoting the strength of your team is the exploitation of an opportunity.

Threats also come from without. A failing economy or increased competition are examples of threats.

The information you obtain from the SWOT analysis will be of tremendous benefit in directing and fine-tuning your promotional efforts.

old rule of thumb says that advertisement audiences don't even recognize seeing, hearing, or reading an ad until they have been exposed to it six times. Find a medium or a combination where you can afford regular advertising, and stick with your strategy.

One last word on media purchases. As a general rule, match your advertising investments to your sales curve. For example, if your tenants go apartment-hunting at the end of summer, that's when you want to run your advertising. If early summer is a traditionally slow time for your rentals, there's little value in investing money to pull up the curve. Better save and invest when the most prospects are around.

> It's important to consider your advertising strategy, or the "pitch" you are making to your prospects.

Your Advertising Strategy

It's important to consider your advertising strategy, or the "pitch" you are making to your prospects. What do you have to offer that your competitors do not? Why should a member of the target audience want to rent from your company? What motivates the buying decision? Give it a little thought, and you'll come up with a number of benefits and advantages.

This may not be much of a consideration if your advertising is limited to "1 rm riv view call 555-5555" in the local classifieds. But even in such short copy advertising, you should promote benefits important to your prospect. Would that one room with a river view seem more appealing to a potential renter promoted as a newly renovated apartment or as one close to the college, downtown, or major traffic arteries? Regardless of an apartment's benefits in your eyes, promote what's important in the eyes of the prospective renter. What do your prospective tenants want and need, and how can you provide it? Now let's take a quick tour of your advertising media choices.

Television Ads

Television advertising was at one time so powerful that merchants actually helped sell products by simply inserting in other advertising the phrase, "as advertised on television." Times have changed, but "the tube" can still be an effective option for some landlords and property managers. However, consider these two points. First, television is probably too expensive a vehicle because the actual cost of the ads can be quite high. And secondly, television advertising will reach many more people that necessary, many of whom won't be your ideal prospects. This is called waste circulation. Even if a lot of people are reached by the message, they aren't customers and can do you no good (though they can waste your time and tie up your answering machine).

However, you can avoid high fees and the channels viewed by the general public. Cable and satellite television have opened up many markets, and in some cases the prices per ad are comparable to radio station prices. These companies often provide production services at low rates to attract advertisers. Furthermore, some public-access channels have a very limited audience that you might consider as your potential tenant pool.

Advertising Potential May Be There

Radio and television advertising is probably not effective for selling property, but in some major markets it must be working because you see some of this type of advertising on a continuing bases. Take a look at your local market, ask other real-estate advertisers for their opinions and experience, and then make up your mind on your own.

Radio Commercials

Radio offers many, many options through its many formats. You can purchase advertising on all news, rock, golden oldies, rap, gospel, country and western, ethnic, new age, and other radio stations. This variety can force you into some tough decisions, but it has its advantages. The targeting of the market served is often narrow enough for effective use by landlords and property managers. Evaluate the target audience in terms of who it is and how many of them are being reached, and whether the medium is cost-effective for your business on a regular basis.

Magazines and Newspapers

Depending upon the size of your market, you may have any number of magazines from which to choose, such as city magazines, entertainment magazines, Chamber of Commerce publications, and business groups pamphlets. Again, always consider your market. It may be prestigious to advertise in a "slick" four-color publication, but make sure it effectively reaches your target audience. City or local commerce-related publications may be a good choice for selling some properties or even promoting certain apartment complexes.

Many cities have smaller weekly or monthly magazines known as "shoppers" or "savers." These may prove to be good vehicles for promoting individual apartments or complexes. One potential problem is learning the exact circulation. A paid circulation magazine has a clear idea of who is buying it from the subscriber list and from vendor sales. Smaller magazines may be given out freely at stands around town, and so it's often difficult to tell who is reading them.

Another useful medium, the newspaper, has been and will probably remain the backbone of advertising rental properties and properties for sale. These ads are organized in a special section of the classifieds, usually titled Real Estate. Because people who are looking for a place to live will usually start their search with the real-estate section of their newspaper, this medium of advertising is hard to beat.

The real-estate section is generally segmented by the type of property offered, rentals, sales, commercial properties, and so on. Often these sections will include news and information about the local real-estate market to help drum up readership. You should make an effort to get yourself and your business covered in this section. Your advertising can be in the form of the traditional classified ad, that "1 rm riv view" format, or you can choose to use display advertising, which lets you put borders around your ad, run illustrations or photos, and use different fonts. It's more expensive, but a display ad attracts more attention. Again, this is a matter of your needs versus your budget.

> Another useful medium, the newspaper, has been and will probably remain the backbone of advertising rental properties and properties for sale.

News Releases

While not really a paid advertising vehicle, a news release is an excellent way to promote yourself, your business, and your property. Getting favorable publicity is almost like getting free advertising—but to come out on top in this game you have to work at it.

Make it as easy as possible for the editor to select your story. Media are inundated with news releases every day; many of these news releases are poorly prepared and some are "puff" pieces, items of no real news worthiness. Editors develop an eye for people who constantly bombard them with non-news news, and these so-called press releases end up in the "round file" beneath the editors' desks. To avoid this, always make sure your release contains real news.

Write your release in simple language and avoid jargon or fancy words. Present the information in descending order of importance, with the most important news element at the top. Don't pad the news release with irrelevant information. That's a sure way to provoke an editor's ire. Always double-check your spelling and grammar. Include necessary contact information, like your name and phone number.

If you want the news to go out immediately, "slug" your document with "For Immediate Release." If you want the publication to hold it for a few days, slug it with "For Release on _____ " (fill in the appropriate date).

You can usually gain a slight edge if you hand-deliver your release to the appropriate editor, generally the city editor or the business news editor. That simple act puts a face to the name on the release. Hand delivery makes your document stand out more in the editor's mind, too. Provided your release is genuine news, that act alone could earn you the coverage. Remember, the editor has limited space available, and many of the stories on his or her desk appear to be of equal news value. Make sure yours stands out. Hand delivery also gives you the opportunity to make friends or at least friendly contact with the editor and news staff. Who knows, when they need information or a quote for a real-estate story, you might just move to the top of their to-call list.

> Hand delivery makes your document stand out more.

For more information on this topic, visit our Web site at www.businesstown.com

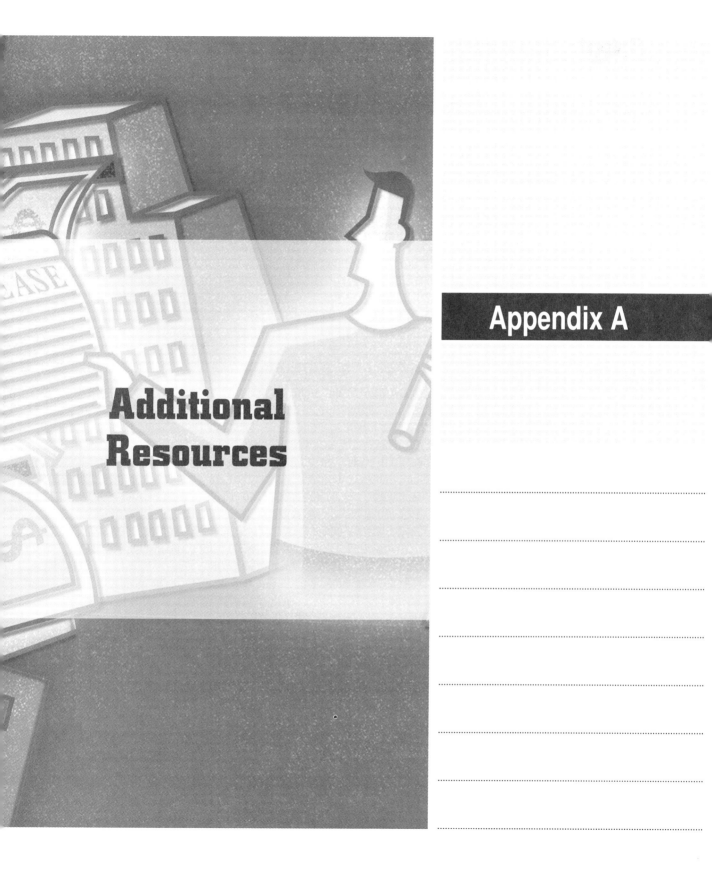

Appendix A

Additional Resources

When it comes to property management, advice and counsel are available from a remarkably varied number of sources. Today, in part due to the expansion and popularity of the Internet, the property manager in even the smallest of communities has access to worldwide resources. Friends and associates in real estate or related businesses can provide valuable information. Most communities have a number of business groups and clubs that will welcome your membership and participation. Professional organizations can be of particular aid and comfort. So, in many cases, your problem isn't how to find the resources you need, but to select which one best suits your particular needs.

The Power of Networking

From the earliest days of mankind, people have come together for protection, mutual support, and to become friends and associates. That's certainly true of people in real estate. Networking is a major factor in keeping this industry going. You should be an active part of at least one professional network, preferably many networks. Take a look at your neighborhood associations and community groups. Talk to people who belong to these groups to learn more about the benefits of joining. Make sure you conduct a thorough investigation; someone who may have gotten a "crossed wire" with an organization may try to get a little payback by badmouthing the group. Check out the facts (and the people) for yourself.

Any group is made up of different people who have various ideas and beliefs to offer, which can be extremely valuable in generating new solutions to different problems in the industry. You'll probably make a few friends and quite a few valuable associates along the way. Group dynamics vary, so attend a few meetings to get a feel for the organization before you actually join. Make sure that the organization fits your needs and that you fit the organization. You'll want to be a contributing member, not just someone who pays dues and shows up for a monthly helping of chicken and peas.

Your Real Estate Board

An excellent place to begin your search is at your local real-estate board. This organization is a great resource for finding out what's going on, building network connections, and keeping in tune with happenings in the local industry. The office staff should be up to speed on what organizations are in the area. They may also have information about the formation of new groups.

Check Local Schools

Visit nearby universities, colleges, community colleges, and even the trade schools. Many of them offer courses, seminars, and lectures designed to serve the educational needs of the professional communities, and real estate is no exception. These resources can increase your knowledge of your business, but they also provide numerous opportunities to meet colleagues and to create and build your network.

Read the Newspapers

An obvious source of information about the local real-estate market is the real-estate section of your local newspaper. Newspapers have a lot more than advertising to offer. Reading the real-estate section can give you a good impression of the value of local properties,

Continue Your Education

Attend the regular (usually monthly) meetings of your local property managers association. It's easy to arrange an invitation, and the exposure to what's going on in your business will be invaluable. Associations and business groups often conduct or arrange for professional lectures, seminars, and business-related courses. These are great opportunities to stay informed on changes in the markets, new trends in management, and the latest technologies. The associations and the courses offered are also great places to network.

If you're a young person in school just considering getting involved in property management, think about investing a little of your pregraduation time in learning more about the business directly. It would be a very good idea for you to get a part-time job in a real-estate management firm or a company involved in real estate. Even work in the evenings or on weekends will give you a valuable and expanded view of what might be in your future. You can answer calls, go on tours and presentations, learn about dealing with customers and government officials, and so on. It's a great way to get your feet wet and to be paid for it at the same time.

Continue that education once you're in the business. One of the best means is to build your own scrapbook about the industry and your market. Clip newspaper and magazine articles and pull information from the Internet. You can even clip ads from other firms to use as idea starters for your own efforts. Keeping a scrapbook is an easy way to create a historical record on your community. You will find it a valuable resource.

Earn Your Real-Estate License

A real-estate license marks you as a professional, as someone who cares about his or her business, properties, and clients. A license will open up entire new worlds of information and opportunities. The insight you'll gain will be invaluable. By joining your state's mailing list, you'll be kept up-to-date and informed about new rules and regulations, changes in the old ones, and pending legislation. When you join your local real-estate board, you'll also receive current information about these issues and about changes and updates on matters in your community.

You'll apply for your license through your state. Each state is different and some regulations will make provisions to license real-estate professionals, such as people actively involved in leasing, renting, or managing properties. Some states even have specific licensing for property managers.

how pricing is fluctuating, which markets are hot and which ones might be going soft, who your competitors are and what they are doing, property availabilities, and a host of other information.

Surf the Net

The Internet is perhaps the fastest-growing source of news and information in the world, and its capabilities are increasing at such a quick pace that it's practically impossible to track. If you have access to the World Wide Web, you should most certainly take advantage of this resource. Search for organizations and brokers in your area with whom you might want to network. Brokers are particularly helpful because they are already "wired" to the needs of the community and are great sources of information.

The Internet is also a great source of educational material, and some institutions are already offering courses online. Be aware of two major concerns when you visit any Web site. One, there may be a charge for access. More than likely, you'll be provided with some information to get your attention and then will be required to pay a fee to continue. Two, anybody can post any type of information on a Web site. You're pretty safe with the official sites of recognized and worthy organizations, but there are people who are more than willing to put out false information to cause trouble, create confusion, or just because they don't know any better. Again, let the buyer beware.

Join Professional Associations

The real-estate industry is rich in professional organizations. The abbreviations for these groups sometimes look like a bunch of letters from a spilled bowl of alphabet soup. For example, there's CPM and CCIM, CRE and SIOR, and a number of acronyms that stand for organizations related to real estate. Explore the benefits of membership in one or more of these organizations. Joining will open the doors to a wealth of information, membership benefits, and valuable contacts within your industry. Take a look and then see which area of this alphabet soup is to your taste.

Counselors of Real Estate (CRE)

The CRE was established in 1953 to serve the needs, locally and nationally, of the nation's property advisors. Currently, the organization serves more than 1,000 members around the world. According to their Web site, the CRE seeks to support leaders in the real-estate industry by providing valuable information, facilitating professional development, providing an opportunity for professional communication and networking.

To contact the CRE, see the following contact information:

Counselors of Real Estate
430 N. Michigan Ave.
Chicago, IL 60611-4089
(312) 329-8427
info@cre.org
www.cre.org

The CRE promotes a strict code of ethics and standards of professional practice. Membership is by invitation only, and is granted as recognition of outstanding performance in the industry. Applicants are judged on a number of criteria. They must do the following:

- Provide valuable real-estate counseling services to clients and/or employers.
- Hold a senior position in a firm.
- Be recognized for excellence.
- Must have knowledge, integrity, and judgment.
- Have at least ten years of experience in real estate (at least three in counseling).
- Meet all basic membership requirements.

> The CRE promotes a strict code of ethics and standards of professional practice.

Society of Industrial and Office Realtors (SIOR)

This group boasts some powerful statistics. During 2001 members reported an average of $27.5 million per person in dollar volume with a cumulative value for the entire membership of $57.1

billion; more than 60,000 transactions; members selling or leasing an average of 1.2 million square feet per person with a cumulative total of 2.4 billion square feet sold or leased.

The society has more than 2,000 members located in twenty-five countries on six continents. Members of SIOR specialize primarily in industrial, office, sales-management, and advisory areas.

The society promotes a number of member benefits. Among them are the following:

- SIOR designation, which signifies a high level of competence and achievement in the industry.
- Prestige of membership in an exclusive organization.
- Networking opportunities with like-minded individuals and corporations throughout North America and the world. Members reported 450 cooperative transactions with other members in 2001. These networking efforts were valued at $854 million in 24.5 million square feet of space.
- Information and education through programs, seminars, conventions, publications, and e-mail. The society's Web site allows members unlimited access to comparative statistics, which covers 130 markets.
- The society's quarterly magazine.
- Continuing education through courses, seminars, and publications.
- Assistance with members' public relations efforts.
- Mediation and arbitration to resolve conflicts in business.

For more information, visit SIOR's Web site at *www.sior.com*.

Institute of Real Estate Management (IREM)

Founded more than sixty-five years ago, IREM is a professional organization committed to serving the educational, marketing, and advocacy needs of the nation's property managers. Its goal is to enhance and support members' professional competence so they can access new markets, clients, and tenants and provide the quality of service that will retain them.

> IREM is a professional organization committed to serving the educational, marketing, and advocacy needs of the nation's property managers.

The organization provides education, research, analysis, publications, career development, and networking opportunities for property managers, property management firms, and people in related fields such managers and owners of office buildings, retail properties, industrial properties, corporate real-estate holdings, conventionally financed and government assisted multi-family dwellings, homeowners associations, mobile home parks, and single-family dwellings.

Traditional classroom courses in real-estate management are taught by instructors who hold the Certified Property Manager designation. Home study and online courses are also available. These courses stress real-world skills and include such topics as asset management, legal issues, risk management, ethics, maintenance and operations, marketing, leasing, financial operations, accounting, business development, and management of human resources. Additionally, IREM offers customized on-line training for corporations, organizations, and even government agencies.

Earning Additional Professional Designations

The real estate industry is very conscious about promoting and maintaining high standards of business conduct. That's why business cards and letterhead sometimes appear to have fallen into a bowl of alphabet soup. Those extra letters represent extra work, extra effort, and extra commitment to professionalism. For example, the Institute of Real Estate Management provides the opportunity for its members to earn a number of professional designations. These are the following:

- Certified Property Manager (CPM), which covers all types of properties. It is designed exclusively for property and asset managers.

- Accredited Residential Manager (ARM) certification applies to managers of traditional apartment dwellings, federally-assisted housing, condominiums, homeowner associations, single-family dwellings, and mobile home parks.

- Accredited Manager Organization (AMO) was created to serve the needs of real estate management firms. Currently there are more than six hundred accredited firms throughout North America.

IREM provides its members with a line of real-estate management books, research reports, monographs, periodicals, and standard business forms which focus on such key areas as management of commercial, residential, general property, and management companies. Its publication, *Journal of Property Management*, addresses current trends, legislation, case studies and analysis, and thoughts and comments of industry professionals.

The contact information for IREM follows:

Institute of Real Estate Management
430 N. Michigan Ave.
Chicago, IL 60611-4090
(800) 837-0706
custserv@irem.org

Realtors Land Institute (RLI)

RLI is an affiliate of the National Association of Realtors. Its focus is on five key areas of land brokerage: (1) farms and ranches, (2) undeveloped land, (3) transitional and development land, (4) subdivisions and wholesale lots, and (5) site selection and assemblage of land parcels. The organization was founded in 1954 under the name Farm Brokers.

The RLI goal is to connect real estate professionals interested in enhancing their competence in areas related to land, including land brokerage, agribusiness, land management, planning, development, land appraisal, acquisitions, and other related subjects. Members may earn the Accredited Land Consultant (ALC) designation.

RLI services include:

- Identifying members as land specialists within the real estate industry.
- Developing and maintaining professional standards.
- Promoting professional expertise through continuing education.
- Awarding the ALC designation to those meeting the requirements.
- Recommendations on public policy affecting land use.

> RLI is an affiliate of the National Association of Realtors.

- Advocacy of wise land use and the reasonable rights and privileges of private land ownership.
- Marketing efforts to enhance the business environment of its members.

For more information, contact RLI:

Realtors Land Institute
430 N. Michigan Ave.
Chicago, IL 60611
(800) 441-LAND
rli@realtors.org

Certified Property Manager (CPM)

Certified Property Manager designation is awarded by the Institute of Real Estate management, which is associated with the National Association of Realtors, and you should definitely consider this as a follow-up step to getting your real estate license. Once you earn your CPM, you'll have the opportunity to attend professional classes, seminars, and lectures targeted to your specific business needs.

Certified Commercial Investment Member (CCIM)

Achieving your CCIM, often called the "Ph.D. of commercial real estate," will place you within an organization of approximately 7,000 people who own, invest, or use commercial real estate. Only 6 percent of the nation's estimated 125,000 commercial real-estate professionals have the CCIM designation. Members include property managers, landlords, brokers, investment counselors, leasing professionals, asset managers, appraisers, developers, corporate real-estate executives, commercial lenders, bankers, attorneys, and other professionals in related fields. Those holding the CCIM designation generate more than $54 billion yearly through approximately 60,000 transactions.

The designation was established in 1954 by the California Association of Realtors. It was adopted by the National Association of Realtors in 1967 and became an NAR affiliate in 1991.

> Members include property managers, landlords, brokers, investment counselors, leasing professionals, asset managers, appraisers, developers, corporate real-estate executives, commercial lenders, bankers, attorneys, and other professionals in related fields.

Contact Mark

Coauthor of this book, Mark Weiss, whose experiences in property management and real estate have been invaluable in writing this book, can also serve as your resource for additional information. His contact information follows:

Mark B. Weiss, CCIM
Mark B. Weiss Real Estate
    Brokerage
2442 N. Lincoln Ave.
Chicago, IL 60614
(773) 871-1818
www.markbweissre.com

The point of getting involved is not the membership in an organization, but the CCIM designation you earn. The course of study covers the basics of the commercial real-estate industry, including the following areas of study:

- Financial analysis
- Market analysis
- User decision analysis
- Investment analysis

As they say on the game shows, "and that's not all." Following completion of the course, candidates for the CCIM have to submit a professional resume to the CCIM Institute for evaluation. The resume must document a number of closed transactions and/or consultations in commercial real-estate transactions. And there's still more. The candidates must then take an exam. The goal of the Institute is to create commercial real-estate professionals who have appropriate "book learning" combined with real-world experience. Additional training is also available through elective courses.

The CCIM Institute doesn't consider the earning of its designation the end of the road. Continuing education in the field of commercial real estate is encouraged and promoted. Founded in 1969 as an affiliate of the National Association of Realtors, the CCIM Institute is dedicated to improving commercial real-estate practices through education and networking among its members. The group is organized into regions and local chapters in the United States and Canada. Additionally, the CCIM Institute has strong ties with other national and international real estate organizations. Among them are the International Real Estate Federation (FIABCI) and the International Property Market (MIPIM).

To get in touch with CCIM Institute, use the following contact information:

CCIM Institute
430 N. Michigan Ave., 8th Floor
Chicago, IL 60611-4092
(800) 621-7027
pr@ccim.com

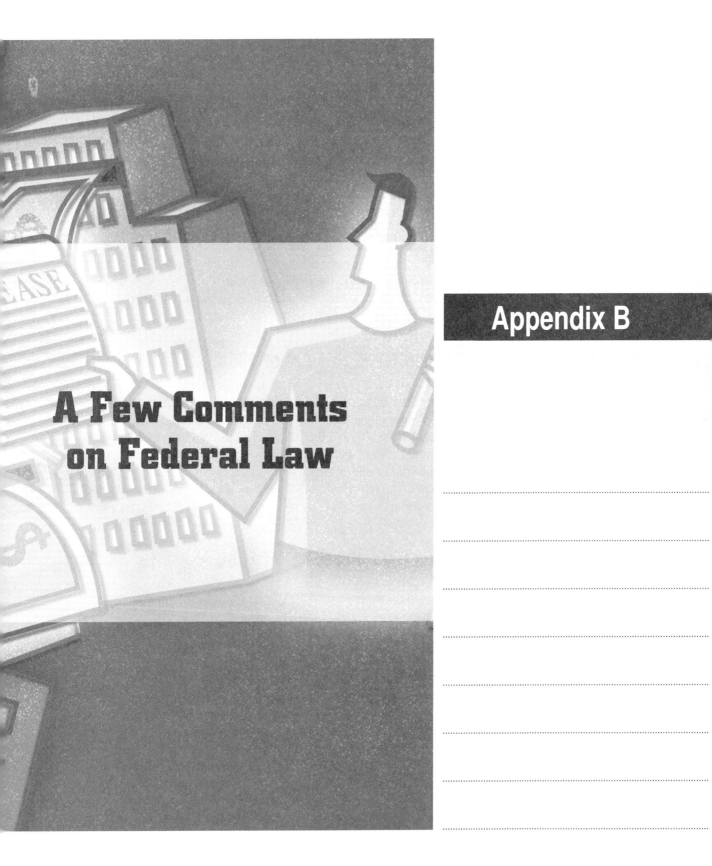

A Few Comments on Federal Law

Appendix B

This appendix is a brief overview of some key points of federal law relating to property management. It should not replace further study and research, which you should conduct in order to get a more in-depth understanding of the laws applicable to your own concerns. Furthermore, be sure you continue to consult your attorney on legal matters. The law is never "set in stone." It is an ever-changing entity; every day, new laws appear on the books and many laws are either revised or dropped entirely. The consequences of ignoring the provisions under which you and your business operate can be severe, and claiming ignorance is never an option.

> The consequences of ignoring the provisions under which you and your business operate can be severe, and claiming ignorance is never an option.

The Civil Rights Act of 1866

While the legal concept of fair housing for all was not born during the times of the American Revolution, it is nevertheless deeply embedded in our history. Shortly after the Civil War, the U.S. Supreme Court ruled that all citizens had the same rights to inherit, purchase, lease, sell, hold, and convey real estate. This act is a major foundation stone in the legal concept of fair housing in the United States. The court has upheld this decision throughout the intervening years.

The Civil Rights Act of 1964

This act prohibited discrimination in programs receiving assistance from the federal government and set the stage for another major anti-discrimination act four years later.

Title VIII of the Civil Rights Act of 1968

More popularly known as the Fair Housing Act, this law extended the protections of earlier acts to additional categories of people and to additional situations. A landlord or property manager is not permitted to discriminate in selling, renting, or financing property because of an individual or family's race, color, religion, national origin, sex, family status, or physical or mental handicap. These conditions are absolute. You are prohibited from doing the following on the basis of any of the above categories:

- Refuse to show, rent, or even negotiate a property.
- Insert discriminatory clauses into your leasing agreements.
- Discriminate in your advertising or promotional programs.
- Refuse to show a property by saying it is not available when it actually is available.
- Interfere in any way with someone's fair exercise of their rights under the act. This coverage extends protection to the sale and rental of raw land.

Equal Credit Opportunity Act

Originally brought about in 1974 as a means of opening credit opportunities to women, this act has been amended in 1976 to include other groups. Today, no one can be prevented from getting a financial loan on the basis of his or her race, color, religion, national origin, sex, marital status, age, or because of receiving income from public assistance. The law applies to applications for leasing an apartment or house because rent is considered a means of extending credit to an individual or family.

> The law applies to applications for leasing an apartment or house because rent is considered a means of extending credit to an individual or family.

Fair Credit Reporting Act

This act directly affects property management because managers and landlords use credit information to evaluate the credit worthiness of prospective tenants. The act assures both the landlord and the tenant that the credit information reported is accurate. FCRA provides for regulation of agencies that report on consumer credit, on persons and organizations using those reports, and on businesses and individuals who provide data to consumer reporting agencies.

Americans with Disabilities Act

If you are engaged in private business, but with facilities accessed by the public, such as a hotel or resort, your business activities are covered by the ADA. Effective since the early 1990s, the act prohibits discrimination based on an individual's disability. It applies to public accommodations, transportation, state and local government services, and other categories. There are two key areas for property managers and landlords.

1. You can't discriminate in employment. Of course, common sense must prevail. For example, you wouldn't be expected to hire a blind person to roof your two-story apartment. The wheelchair-bound office manger is another case entirely.
2. Your property must be made accessible to disabled persons whenever such changes or modifications are practical.

Also note that the ADA covers both physical and mental disabilities.

> Your property must be made accessible to disabled persons whenever such changes or modifications are practical.

Uniform Residential Landlord and Tenant Act

Established in the early 1970s, this act creates standards for the relationship between a landlord or property manager and the tenants occupying the property. Each state has its own form of the act and stipulations vary from state to state. Here are some highlights:

- You can't draft a clause in your lease eliminating or restricting a tenant's rights under the act. Even if the tenant signs such a lease, the clause(s) will have no legal effect.
- You can't raise a tenant's rent or impose anything that could be considered punishment because that person has filed a complaint against you to a governing body.
- A tenant has tenancy from "period to period," that is, month-to-month or week-to-week, according to the terms of the lease. Exceptions are permitted under the act.
- Should a court find a lease or a portion of a lease to be grossly unfair, it may choose to refrain from enforcing the unfair clause or clauses. Additionally, it states that the landlord and tenant should inspect the rented property together within five days of the rental. Overall conditions, appliances,

and furnishings should be examined during the inspection. An inventory should be drafted and signed, and each party should keep a copy.

- Most disagreements between landlord and tenant arise from disputes over return or the lack thereof of a security deposit. While there is considerable variation from state to state, a landlord may usually deduct the cost of damages, repairs, or unpaid rent from a deposit provided he or she provides documentation and, if applicable, a receipt. Generally, the security deposit is considered a financial resource for covering possible damages and repairs and cannot be used as payment for the final month's rent.

- A lease can be considered valid even if unsigned if either of the parties pays or accepts a rental payment.

- The landlord has the responsibility for maintaining a safe and habitable property.

- A landlord or property manager may enter his or her property for inspection, for regular maintenance, for repairs, to make improvements, or to show the unit to prospective tenants. With the exception of emergencies, entries must be reasonable and with suitable prior notice.

- Unless the landlord approves, a tenant cannot operate a business from the property. Tenants are required to live according to all applicable laws and regulations in the community. They are expected to be reasonable in the use of the rental unit, its furnishings, and its appliances, and to respect the rights of other tenants. Violations may give the landlord or property manager cause to demand compliance and, upon a tenant's refusal to cooperate, seek termination of the lease and even seek compensation for damages, repairs, and legal costs related to the situation.

- A tenant who abandons his or her rental property may still be responsible for payment of unpaid rent.

- If a tenant makes a reasonable request, say to repair a broken water pipe, you must make a good faith effort toward the necessary repair. If not, the tenant may give notice and terminate the lease. He or she may also be due any prepaid rent,

> A tenant who abandons his or her rental property may still be responsible for payment of unpaid rent.

the security deposit, and may have the right to sue for damages and legal costs.

- If the rental unit is rendered uninhabitable, a tenant may give notice and then terminate the lease. If only part of the unit is uninhabitable, the tenant may have the right to deduct a portion of the rent as compensation for the loss of its use.

Again, there is considerable variation in the application of these laws from state to state. Use this list only as a general guideline as to what type of situations are covered by the act. Check your own state laws for the precise stipulations applicable to your business.

The Sherman Anti-Trust Act of 1890

This is another one of those "golden oldies," an act that applies to a variety of situations. In terms of real estate, this act prohibits tampering with prices in setting real-estate commissions, fees for rentals, or expenses in maintaining property. The intent here is to assure choice in the marketplace for the consumer. Simple communication among property managers about the amounts they are charging for rents and related costs may be considered criminal. There are civil and criminal penalties for conviction of price fixing, and they can be severe.

Occupational Safety and Health Act

This 1974 measure created OSHA, an organization that promotes and enforces safety and health measures for workers. OSHA may conduct research, inspect property, and conduct health- and safety-related investigations. Employers must keep accurate and in-depth records of injuries and illnesses experienced by workers.

Senior Citizens Housing Act

This 1962 act authorizes loan programs for low-rent apartments offered to individuals age sixty-two and older. It also provides for loans to create facilities for recreation.

> Simple communication among property managers about the amounts they are charging for rents and related costs may be considered criminal.

Real Estate Settlement Procedures Act

RESPA was created in 1974 and amended in 1975. It is designed to make purchasing a home easier by regulating lending practices, closing procedures, and settlement procedures in mortgages related to a federal agency. RESPA also reduces certain costs and challenges related to buying a home.

Condominium and Cooperative Abuse Relief Act

This act was created in 1980 to minimize the potentially harmful effects on the low-income, moderate-income, the elderly, and handicapped people from conversions to co-ops and condos. Other provisions concern the application of fairness to the creation of co-ops and condos.

There Are Plenty of Laws out There

There are more laws and regulations that may or may not have a significant impact on you and your real-estate business. Ever heard of the Black Lung Revenues Act of 1981? How about the Coastal Zone Management Act of 1972? Or the National Flood Insurance Act of 1968? The Magnuson-Moss Warranty Act of 1975? The National Historic Preservation Act of 1966? The Veterans' Housing Benefits Act of 1978?

These and the other acts, laws, and regulations relating to real estate are all written in government and attorney "legalese" and may appear rather incomprehensible. Yet, they can be valuable sources of support or, if violated, a road to costly penalties and even time behind bars.

Contact your landlord and property manager's associations, chambers of commerce, and business groups for printed information, audio and video tapes, seminars and courses, personal advice and counsels, and other forms of insight in plain English. And always, always, always invest in consultations with your attorney.

> There are more laws and regulations that may or may not have a significant impact on you and your real-estate business.

Property Management Forms

The following are several forms that have proven valuable to Mark in his work as landlord and property manager. You may also find them helpful. Note that you might find it necessary to adapt them to fit your individual business needs.

Lease Rider

Tenant(s): _____

_____

Address: _____

_____

This rider is made part of and is incorporated into the Lease dated _____

between Weiss Real Estate Brokerage, Inc. and _____

1. RIDER OR LEASE PROVISIONS AND ALTERATIONS
No representations or agreements made by building or management company personnel which alter the terms of the Lease or Rider are effective unless in writing. In the event of a conflict between the Lease and the Rider, the terms and provisions of the Rider shall prevail.

2. RENT PAYMENT POLICY
All rent payments are due in the office of Mark B. Weiss Real Estate Brokerage, Inc., on or before the first day of each month. Rent will be considered late if it is received after the fifth of the month. A late fee will be charged pursuant to terms of the lease.

3. NSF CHECKS
The tenant agrees to pay a charge of $25.00 for each NSF check.

4. FIVE-DAY NOTICES
Any tenant whose rent is not received by the fifth of the month will receive a five-day notice to pay the rent and late fee or to vacate the premises.

5. LOCK CHANGING
This property is keyed to a Master System by the lessor. The tenant agrees that he/she will not use any other locksmith other than that locksmith employed by the lessor to maintain the present system. Thus if the tenant loses the key, he/she must notify the

lessor and use the appropriate locksmith. The tenant is responsible for all fees related to new locks or keys if the lock to the unit or the property requires changes due to the tenant's negligence or loss thereof.

6. LOST KEYS

Any keys that are lost or broken by the tenant will be replaced by the lessor at the cost of $5.00 per key. If the tenant is locked out of the apartment and requires Mark B. Weiss Real Estate Brokerage, Inc. to provide access into the apartment, the tenant shall pay $50.00 to the lessor at the time of service.

7. UTILITIES

The tenant agrees to be solely responsible for all applicable utility charges such as cooking gas, heat, electricity, and telephone service and installation. The tenant assumes responsibility to promptly pay all such charges during the tenancy. The tenant also agrees to notify utility companies when moving in or out.

8. PETS

If written consent is given to lessee to have a pet, the pet must be taken to and from the building by the rear stairway only. Pet droppings are to be picked up by the animal's owner and disposed of properly.

9. LAUNDRY FACILITY

The tenant agrees to clean up any dirt, lint, and any other debris or garbage that he/she causes to be in the laundry room after using it. As the building already has a laundry facility provided by the lessor, the tenant agrees not to install any other washers, dryers, or laundry machines, in the apartment, the laundry facility, or any other part of the property.

10. GARBAGE REMOVAL

It is the tenant's responsibility to remove all garbage and place it in the property receptacles provided in the rear of the building. Garbage must be placed in securely fastened plastic bags.

11. STORAGE

The tenant must store all items in the designated storage areas. Storage of any item is not permitted in the common areas of the building.

12. DECK AND BACK PORCH

The tenants agree not to have parties or large gatherings on the back porch or deck.

13. DECORATING

No material changes shall be made to the apartment without written consent of the landlord. This includes interior decorating such as painting and wallpapering. The tenant shall not affix anything to kitchen cabinets, appliances, or vanities.

14. SMOKE DETECTORS

It is the tenant's responsibility to regularly test and maintain the smoke detectors installed by the landlord. Removal of smoke detectors will be charged at $20.00 each.

15. DISTURBANCES

No noise or music shall be permitted at any time which in any way disturbs other building occupants. In the event of complaints from neighbor and/or janitor, the tenant will be subject to eviction procedures as set forth by local ordinance.

16. APARTMENT UPKEEP

During the winter months, the tenant will lower and close all storm windows in the unit.

The tenant will install a shower curtain for the purpose of protecting the walls which surround the tub.

The tenant is responsible for changing and replacing light bulbs. The landlord will not provide shades for the unit.

The tenant shall use a cutting board and agrees not to cut directly on the counter tops.

The tenant is responsible for any damages.

17. EXCESSIVE MAINTENANCE

Charges for excessive maintenance above and beyond normal wear and tear will be charged to the tenant and become payable each month at the rate of $30.00 per hour.

18. PROBLEMS AND COMPLAINTS

All problems and complaints such as electrical, plumbing, disturbances, damages, or nuisances should be reported to the lessor as soon as possible.

19. PROPERTY DAMAGE

Any damage to the apartment caused by the lessee and repaired by the lessor during the term of the lease will be charged to the lessee. Broken windows, glass doors, and carpentry work will be assessed and charged at the current local rate for the necessary labor and supplies. The lessee will be presented with a bill which is payable with the subsequent month's rent.

20. LEASE TERMINATION

Beginning ninety days prior to the end of the lease term, the landlord may show the apartment for rent as often as necessary with reasonable notice to the tenant.

21. STIPULATIONS UPON LEASE TERMINATION

Upon termination of the lease, the entire apartment, including kitchen range, refrigerator, microwave, bathrooms, closets, and cabinets shall be cleaned by the tenant. The refrigerator is to be defrosted, the plug pulled, and the door left open.

The carpeting must be free of stains, blemishes, and holes.

All debris and rubbish must be placed in proper rubbish containers.

All personal belongings shall be removed from the unit and storage spaces and all keys shall be returned to the rental office.

In the event that any of the foregoing has not been performed by the lessee, the following specific cleaning and replacement charges will be immediately due from the lessee to the lessor:

> Refrigerator cleaning:. $75.00
> Range/oven cleaning: $75.00
> Cabinet/counter cleaning:. $25.00
> Apartment/building/nail key replacement: $20.00
> Light bulb replacement:. . . . . $2.00 each
> Trash removal/excessive cleaning: . . . . $15.00 per hour
> Decorating/maintenance: . . . . $20.00 per hour
> Carpet cleaning: $200.00

22. MOVE OUT

The tenant agrees to move in/out via the rear entrance only. The tenant agrees to pay for any and all damages caused to, but not limited to, any of the following: stairwells, stairs, landings, railings, porches, walls, flooring, ceilings, doors, and gates.

The tenant agrees to be completely moved out by midnight of the last day of the lease. The tenant agrees to pay two times the proration of the current monthly rent for each day of occupancy after the last day of the lease. Occupancy for any part of a day will be charged at the rate determined above for a full day.

23. SECURITY DEPOSIT

The tenants will not use their security deposit to pay for the final month of rent in their lease term.

24. RENTERS INSURANCE

Lessee agrees to have renters insurance in place prior to moving into the apartment. In the insurance policy the lessee will name the lessor as an additional insured.

I/We have read the above Lease Rider and will abide by these terms. We recognized the fact that each individual assumes responsibility for the full rent amount for the stated lease term.

Lessee: _____

Date: _____

Lessee: _____

Date: _____

Lessee: _____

Date: _____

Lessor: MARK B. WEISS REAL ESATE BROKERAGE, INC.

Date: _____

Rental Agency Letter

The following is a letter Mark uses for working with leasing agents laying out policies for rentals. It is recommended that you follow these procedures whenever dealing with leasing agents or agencies.

To all apartment Leasing Agencies,

Mark, B. Weiss Real Estate Brokerage welcomes working with leasing agencies for our apartment rentals. The commission rate that will be paid to the leasing agent is equal to one-half month's rent, not to exceed $1,000.00.

The following terms apply to all leasing companies based on the procedures used by Mark B. Weiss Real Estate Brokerage. The credit verification form to be used will be provided by the office of Mark B. Weiss Real Estate, at the cost of $25.00 per applicant. The leasing agency/real estate company may do a prequalifying credit check if they wish, but all applicants must be qualified by our office, and approval will only be given based on our own credit check. Along with the credit check form, we will provide you with our rental application. These are the first two forms for the rental process that are to be competed and returned to our office.

All lease forms are to be obtained from the office of Mark B. Weiss Real Estate, as they are our specific forms and riders. These leases and specific lease riders are subject to change, so please check with our office prior to renting an apartment.

We will provide you with samples of the lease and lease rider and encourage you to share them with applicants. After we check credit history and verify application information, a representative from Mark B. Weiss Real Estate Brokerage will contact you with either acceptance or nonacceptance of the applicant.

Accepted applicants will set up an appointment either to fill out the lease and lease rider at our office, located at 2442 N. Lincoln Avenue, 2nd Floor, in Chicago.

Our lease terms are as follows: A security deposit of one month's rent is required for all leases. In addition, there is a $50.00 per person key deposit that is refundable at the end of the lease, when the keys are returned to us. If pets are permitted (please ask regarding this policy for each specific unit), there is an additional deposit of one-half month's rent. The first month's rent is to be paid when the keys are picked up by the tenants, prior to moving in.

All monies are to be paid to Mark B. Weiss Real Estate Brokerage, including security deposits, key deposits, credit check fees, and first month's rent. Mark B Weiss Real Estate

Brokerage will pay the leasing agent commission from the deposit received when the first month's rent is paid. At the time of the lease signing, the complete security deposit, key deposit, and any additional applicable deposits must be paid to Mark B. Weiss Real Estate Brokerage.

It is important that you realize you are renting our apartments as they are shown. We understand that your applicants may desire certain amenities that are not present in the apartments that you show. Although we are in the business of renting apartments, it is not our preference to make specific changes and additions to our rental units each time a new lease is signed. Therefore, we would appreciate it if you keep in mind that it is our intention to rent the apartments with the current amenities respective to each apartment. Thank you for your interest in leasing our apartments, and we forward to working with you in the future.

I/we agree to the terms of this agreement in the process of renting apartments for properties owned and managed by Mark B. Weiss Real Estate Brokerage, Inc.

_____   _____
Licensed Rental Agent   Date

_____   _____
Agent for Mark B. Weiss Real Estate Brokerage   Date

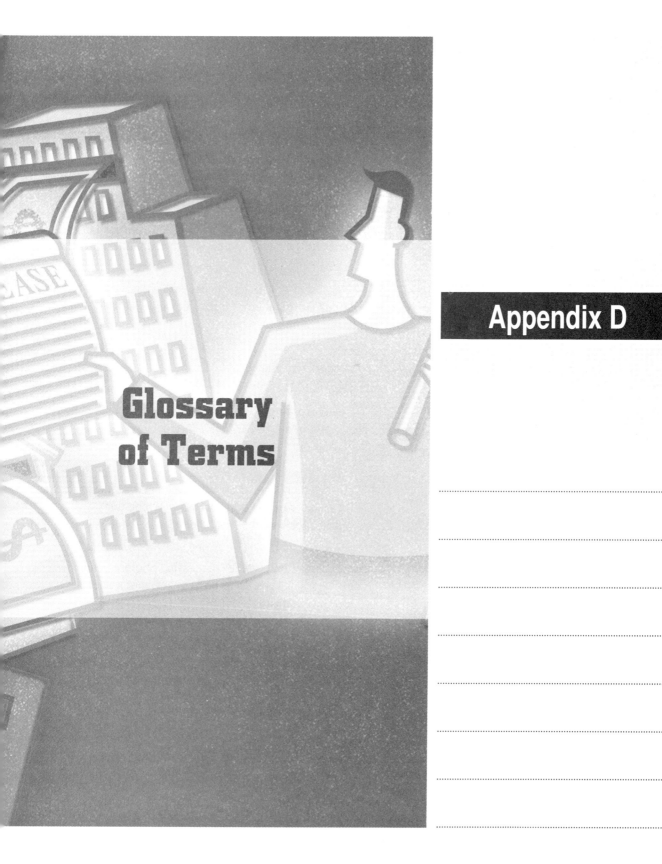

Glossary
of Terms

AAA tenants

tenants with the highest credit rating, as determined by a national credit-rating service.

abandonment

the release of a claim or a right in a piece of property with the intention of terminating ownership.

abnormal sale

a sale atypical in the context of the market, which may occur because of undue pressure on either the buyer or the seller, or for some other reason.

absentee ownership

ownership of a property in which the owner does not physically reside.

absorption rate

the percent of total real-estate space of a particular type that can be sold or leased in a local market.

abstract of title

a history of the ownership of a parcel of land listing transfer of title, rights, and liabilities.

accelerated depreciation

a method of depreciation for income tax purposes, which increases the write-off at a rate higher than under straight-line depreciation.

acceleration clause

states that upon default all of the principal installments come due immediately.

access

the right to enter and leave property.

accessibility

the ease with which one can enter and leave a property.

accrual

accumulation.

accrued depreciation

a decrease of utility or value of a property over time.

acquisition

the process by which property ownership is achieved.

acquisition cost

total cost of purchasing an asset, which includes closing costs and other transaction expenses added to the selling price.

acre

a measure of land equal to 43,560 square feet.

actual authority

a power that a principal has expressly conferred upon an agent or any power that is incidental or necessary to carry out the express power.

actual eviction

the violation of any material breach of covenants by the landlord or any other act which wrongfully deprives the tenant of the possession of the premises.

adjusted cost basis

the value of property for accounting purposes, equal to the original costs plus costs of any improvements less depreciation.

adjustments

in the market-data approach to value, these are the additions and subtractions which are made to account for differences between market-comparable properties and the subject properties being appraised.

ad valorem

"based on value" (from Latin). Most local governments levy an *ad valorem* tax on property.

GLOSSARY OF TERMS

advance
used in construction financing to provide the builder with working capital.

adverse possession
a method of acquiring original title to property by open, notorious, and hostile possession for a statutory period of time; also referred to as prescription.

affidavit of title
a sworn statement by a seller that no defects other than those stated in a contract or deed exist in the title being conveyed.

after-tax cash flow
cash throw-off plus tax savings or minus tax liability of a project.

agency
a relationship in which one party (the principal) authorizes another party (the agent) to act as the principal's representative.

agent
one who acts for and in place of a principal for the purpose of affecting the principal's legal relations with third persons.

agreement of sale
a contract between a purchaser and seller that draws up the terms and conditions of that sale; also known as a sales contract.

agricultural property
an unimproved property available for farming.

air rights
the right to occupy, use, and control the space above a particular property.

alienation
the transfer of title from one person to another.

alienation clause
a mortgage provision that requires full payment of the debt upon the transfer of title to the property.

ALTA title policy
a standard title insurance policy with expanded coverage.

amortization
prorated repayment of a debt. In a level payment mortgage, this is the portion of the debt service that reduces the principal.

amortized loan
a financial debt that is paid off over a period of time by a series of periodic payments. A loan may be fully amortized or partially amortized, in which case it requires a balloon payment to satisfy the debt at the end of the term.

anchor tenant
a well-known commercial business, such as a chain store or department store, used as the primary tenant in a shopping center.

annual
yearly.

annual percentage rate (APR)
the yearly cost of credit.

apportionment
a division of expenses and charges between buyer and seller at the date of closing; normally, the seller pays for expenses up to and including the day of closing.

appraisal
a procedure employed by a disinterested professional to estimate the value of a piece of property.

appraisal report
submitted by the appraiser to support the opinion of value.

appreciation
a positive growth in market value of a property or asset.

appurtenance
any right or privilege which belongs to and passes with the property.

arrears
not on time; late in making payments or completing work.

"as is"
a phrase which disclaims any promises or warranties—a person purchasing real estate "as is" takes it in exactly the condition in which it is found.

assessed value
the value of the property as determined by the tax assessor for the purpose of setting the property tax.

assessor
a tax official who carries out the assessment (that is, determines the assessed value of property).

assignee
the person receiving a contractual benefit or right.

assignment
(1) the means by which a person transfers contract rights; (2) occurs when the lessee parts with the entire estate, retaining no interest.

assignor
the person transferring a contractual right or benefit.

assumption fee
a lender's fee charged to the buyer who takes title to property by assuming an existing mortgage.

assumption of mortgage
a transfer of mortgage obligation to the purchaser who becomes personally liable on any deficiencies occurring in a foreclosure sale with the original borrower being secondarily liable.

authorization to sell
another name for the listing agreement, entered into by the seller and broker, determining the rights and responsibilities of each.

balloon payment
the remaining balance at maturity on a loan that has not been completely repaid through periodic payments. Once paid, the outstanding balance is zero.

base rent
in percentage leases, this amount is the minimum due to the landlord.

basis
the "original" value of property established by the IRS and used in calculations for income tax purposes.

basis point
there are 100 basis points in 1 percentage point.

beneficial interest
an equitable title in property.

beneficiary
(1) the lender under a deed of trust; (2) the investor in a REIT.

bilateral contract
a contract that communicates mutual promises and binds two parties to certain actions.

bill of sale

a document used to transform ownership of personal property.

blanket mortgage

a mortgage that covers more than one piece of real estate.

boot

in federal taxation, cash or something else of value given in the exchange of two properties when the value of one is less than the value of the other.

broker

a person acting as an intermediary for another and who, for a fee, offers to perform certain functions; examples are real-estate brokers and mortgage brokers.

building code

ordinances passed by local governments which specify minimum standards of construction for new buildings and major additions or renovations.

building permit

a permission of the local government to carry out construction or remodeling on a property; it must be obtained by the builder before the work is begun.

capital

(1) in economics, a factor of production which includes all physical resources except for land; (2) in finance, a sum of money.

capital gains

the taxable profit realized from the sale of property.

capital-gains tax

a tax on profits of a qualified capital asset.

capitalization

used in the income approach to value. To capitalize income means to convert future income to present (current) value.

capitalization rate

the rate of interest considered to be a reasonable return on investment, given the risk.

cash flow

the sum of money generated from income producing property after all operating expenses and mortgage payments have been made.

caveat emptor

"let the buyer beware."

certificate of title

a document that states the quality of title the seller possesses; it is issued by the title examiner.

chattel

items of personal property, such as furniture, appliances, and lighting fixtures, that are not permanently affixed to the property and do not pass on to the new owner after the property's sale.

closed mortgage

a mortgage that cannot be prepaid before maturity.

closing

the concluding meeting of all concerned parties for the purpose of transferring title to a property.

closing costs

the expenses incurred and paid at the time of settlement on the transfer of property.

closing statement

a prepared statement indicating debits and credits due upon closing.

cloud on title

any defect in the title to property, such as a lien, a claim, or a judgment.

commercial bank

the largest financial intermediary directly involved in the financing of real estate; the primary real estate activity of commercial banks involves short-term loans.

commercial property

income property zoned for such uses as office buildings or service facilities.

commission

(1) amount due as fee for broker's performance, usually a percentage of sales price; (2) in government, a board empowered to act.

commitment letter

a promise received from a lender to supply financing if certain conditions are met.

comparable

a recently sold comparable property that is used in the market data approach.

comparable sales approach

see **market data approach**.

comparative analysis

a method of appraising property in which the selling price of similar properties are used as the basis for estimating the value of the subject property.

comparative square-foot method

a technique to estimate reproduction or replacement cost which measures the total square footage or cubic footage and multiplies this total by the current cost per square foot.

comparison method

a technique for deriving a capitalization rate that determines how much more an investor has to be compensated for a particular real-estate investment in comparison to an "ideal" real-estate investment.

compound interest

interest paid on interest, in addition to being paid on the original principal.

condemnation

the process of exercising eminent domain through court action.

conditional sale contract

a contract for the sale of personal property in which title is retained by the seller until the conditions of the contract have been met.

condominium

a legal form of ownership which involves a separation of property into individual ownership elements and common ownership elements.

consideration

anything of value offered to induce someone to enter into a contractual agreement.

construction loan

a mortgage loan that provides the funds necessary for the building or construction of a real-estate project.

constructive eviction

occurs when the landlord's failure to maintain a property's standard living conditions renders the property unlivable for the tenant.

constructive notice

the knowledge that the law presumes a person has about a particular fact irrespective of whether the person knows about the fact or not.

Consumer Price Index (CPI)

an index prepared by the Bureau of Labor Statistics to measure changes in price levels of a predetermined mix of consumer goods and services.

conventional mortgage

a loan made without any government agency guaranteeing or insuring the mortgage.

conveyance

the transfer of title to land from one party to another.

cooperative

a form of property ownership in which a corporation is established to hold title in property and to lease the property to shareholders in the corporation.

cost approach

a method of estimating value based on the economic principle of substitution; the value of a building cannot be greater than the cost of purchasing a similar site and constructing a building of equal utility.

cost basis

the value of property for accounting purposes, equal to the original price plus all acquisition expenses.

date of appraisal

the date as of which the opinion of value is based.

debit

money owed.

debit coverage ratio

ratio which is calculated by dividing the annual net operating income by the annual debt service of a mortgage loan.

debt financing

the use of borrowed funds to make a real-estate purchase.

debt service

an installment payment that includes both interest and amortization of principal.

declining-balance depreciation

an accelerated depreciation method in which, after the depreciation is taken, the remaining depreciable balance is the base for calculating the subsequent year's depreciation.

decree of foreclosure

a court order that makes a foreclosure effective.

deduction

a legal adjustment to reduce taxable income.

deed

a written instrument, usually under seal, which contains an agreement to transfer some property interest from a grantor to a grantee.

deed in lieu of foreclosure

used by the mortgagor who is in default to convey the property to the mortgagee in order to eliminate the need for a foreclosure.

deed in trust

used to convey property to a trustee in a land trust.

deed of release

given by lien holders, remainder men, or mortgagees to relinquish their claims on the property.

deed of surrender
used to merge a life estate with a reversion or remainder.

deed of trust
a deed to real property, which serves the same purpose as a mortgage, involving three parties instead of two. The third party holds title for the benefit of the lender.

deed restriction
see **restrictive covenant**.

default
the failure to perform a contractual obligation or duty.

deferred interest mortgage
under this mortgage, a lower interest rate and thus a lower monthly mortgage payment is charged. Upon selling the house, the lender receives the deferred interest plus a fee for postponing the interest that would normally have been paid each month.

deficiency judgment
a personal claim based on a judicial order against the debtor. This occurs when a property fails to bring in a price at the foreclosure sale, which covers the mortgage amount.

depreciation
a decrease in value due to physical deterioration, or functional or economic obsolescence.

discounting
the process of adjusting a sum to take into account the time value of money.

discount points
a fee charged by the lender at settlement that results in increasing the lender's effective yield on the

money borrowed. One discount point equals 1 percent of the loan amount.

down payment
the amount paid by the purchaser which when added to the mortgage amount equals the total sales price. At time of closing, the down payment is referred to as equity.

earnest money
a sum of money given to bind an offer of agreement.

easement
a right to limited use of enjoyment by one or more persons in the land of another.

easement appurtenant
an easement created to benefit a particular tract of land.

easement by implication
occurs because of necessity, such as the conveyance of a land-locked property.

easement in gross
a personal right to use the land of another.

economic base analysis
a technique by which a relationship is determined between basic and nonbasic industries to forecast future economic growth in the community.

economic life
the time period over which an improvement to land earns more income than the cost incurred in generating the income.

economic obsolescence
a loss in value due to factors outside the subject property, such as changes in competition or surrounding land use. Also referred to as locational obsolescence.

economic rent

the amount of rental which a building would receive if set by the market (as opposed to contract rent, which is set by the lease).

effective gross income

income received from the property before the deductions for operating expenses.

effective interest rate

the percentage rate of interest actually being paid by a borrower.

eminent domain

the right of government to acquire property for a public purpose after paying just compensation.

encroachment

the extension of some improvement or object across the boundary of an adjoining tract.

encumbrance

any interest in or claim on the land of another that in some manner burdens or diminishes the value of the property.

Environmental Protection Agency (EPA)

the federal agency that oversees and enforces federally enacted minimum standards dealing with environmental protection.

escalation clause

(1) in finance, permits the lender to raise the interest rate upon the occurrence of certain stipulated conditions; (2) in leasing, permits the lessor to raise lease payments upon the occurrence of certain stipulated conditions.

escrow

money or documents held by a third party (escrow agent) until specific conditions of an agreement or contract are met.

escrow account

a trust into which escrow monies are deposited and from which they are disbursed. Both lawyers and real-estate brokers may maintain escrow accounts.

estoppel

the prevention of a person's denying or alleging a fact because it is contrary to a previous denial or affirmation.

exclusive agency listing

a type of agreement in which the owner of a property employs only one real-estate broker for selling the property but retains the right to personally sell and thereby not pay a commission. However, if anyone other than the owner makes the sale, the listing broker is still entitled to the commission stipulated.

exclusive right to sell listing

under this listing arrangement, the broker employed is entitled to a commission no matter who sells the property during the listing period.

Federal Deposit Insurance Corporation (FDIC)

a federal agency established to insure the deposits in member commercial banks.

fiduciary

a person who essentially holds the character of trustee. A fiduciary must carry out the duties in a manner which best serves the interest of the party for whom the fiduciary relationship is establishes.

financing
acquisition of borrowed capital.

first lien
claim with highest priority against property; also known as a senior lien.

first mortgage
a mortgage on real estate in which the lender's rights are superior to the rights of subsequent lenders.

first right of refusal
a provision requiring an owner to allow a specified person or group the first chance to purchase property at a fair market price before it can be offered to a third party. Commonly used in condominiums and cooperatives.

flat lease
a leasing agreement that ensures that the rent payment remains the same throughout the term of the lease.

flexible loan insurance program (FLIP)
a financing technique in which cash is deposited in a pledged, interest-bearing savings account in order to serve as both a cash collateral for the lender and as a source of supplemental payments for the borrower during the first few years of the loan.

floor area ratio (FAR)
a ratio that indicates the relationship between a floor area and land. For example, a 3:1 FAR means that three square feet of floor space may be constructed per one square foot of land—that is, for this parcel of land, you can either construct a three-floor building that covers the entire piece of land, a six-floor building that is built on half of the available land, and so on.

foreclosure
legal proceedings instigated by a lender to deprive a person of ownership rights when mortgage payments have not been held up.

front foot
a property measurement for purposes of valuation, which is measured by the front footage on the street line.

fully amortized mortgage
a method of loan repayment in which the dollar amount of each payment is the same. The first part of each payment is interest and the remainder reduces the principal. Over the life of the mortgage, the outstanding balance is reduced to zero.

functional obsolescence
a loss in value due to conditions within the structure which make the building outdated when compared with a new building.

future interest
a deal that postpones the right of possession, as in the case of eventual reversion of property rights.

gap financing
a loan covering the time period between when the construction loan is due and the conditions set by the permanent lender have not been met.

general warranty deed
contains covenants in which the grantor formally guarantees that good and marketable title is being conveyed.

grandfather clause
creating an exemption from application of a new law due to previously existing circumstances.

grantee
purchaser, the person who is receiving title to property.

grantor
seller, the person who is making conveyance of title or property interest.

GLOSSARY OF TERMS

gross income
see **effective gross income**.

gross income multiplier (GIM)
a method of appraising income-producing property based on a multiple of the annual gross income; also called gross rent multiplier.

gross leasable area
total area on which rent is paid by tenants.

gross lease
a lease in which the landlord, not the tenant, is responsible for property tax, maintenance, repairs, and other operating costs.

gross rent multiplier
see **gross income multiplier**.

ground lease
a lease of land, usually for a long term.

ground rent
a payment made by the tenant under a ground lease.

housing codes
local government codes that specify minimum standards that a dwelling unit must meet.

improved land
any land to which improvements such as roads or buildings have been made.

income approach
a traditional means of appraising property based on the assumption that value is equal to the present worth of future rights to income.

income property
property that generates income for its owner, as, for example, an office building or apartment complex.

increasing and decreasing returns
this economic principle states that the addition of more factors of production will add higher and higher amounts to net income up to a certain point, which is the point where the maximum value of the asset has been reached; any further addition of factors of production will do nothing to increase the value.

incumbrance
see **encumbrance.**

independent contractor
one whose time and efforts are regulated by the individual; independent contractors are not under the direction or control of a larger company.

installment land contract
see **land contract**.

installment sale
a means of deferring the paying of capital gains taxes until the installment payments are actually received.

insurance coverage
the total amount of insurance protection carried.

internal rate of return
equating the work of future benefits to the present worth of the investment; also referred to as discounted cash flow.

land lease
in certain parts of the country, the land under residential real estate is leased through a long-term lease agreement whereby the owner of the land receives periodic rent for the use of the land.

landlord
the owner or lessor of property.

land trust

a device whereby property is transferred to a trustee under a trust agreement.

latent defect

a defect which cannot be discovered by ordinary inspection.

lease

an agreement between a landlord and a tenant that transfers exclusive possession but not ownership of realty for a specified period of time in return for the payment of rent.

leased fee

the landlord's interest in leased property.

leasehold

the interest that the tenant has created by a lease.

lease purchase agreement

an arrangement whereby part of the rent payment is applied to the purchase price and when the prearranged total amount has been paid, title is transferred.

legal description

a written description of a parcel of land that sets its precise location.

lessee

tenant.

lessor

landlord.

leverage

using borrowed capital to finance the purchase of real estate or other assets.

levy

(1) imposition of property tax; (2) in executing on a lien, obtaining money by the sale of property.

license

a personal privilege to go upon the land of another; not considered an interest in land.

licensee

anyone, either a broker or salesperson, licensed to broker real estate.

lien

a legally recognized right to enforce a claim or charge on the property of another for payment of some debt, duty, or obligation.

lienee

the person whose property is burdened by the lien.

like-kind property

property which qualifies for a tax-free exchange.

limited partnership

an entity with a general partner and one or more passive investors, who are known as limited partners.

line of credit

the extent that an individual may borrow from a bank without further need for approval.

listing contract

an employment agreement between an owner and broker defining the duties and rights of both parties.

loan closing

when all conditions have been met, the loan officer disburses funds and authorizes the recording of the mortgage.

loan commitment

a contractual agreement from a lender to finance a certain amount of the purchase price.

loan correspondent

a person who negotiates and services loans for out-of-state lenders.

loan origination fee

a charge incurred by a borrower to cover the administrative costs of the lender in making the loan.

loan processing

steps taken by a lender to complete a loan transaction.

loan-to-value ratio

the relationship between the amount borrowed and the appraised value of the property.

location

(1) a particular surface on the Earth which is defined by legal description; (2) how a particular site relates to a surrounding land use pattern.

locational obsolescence

see **economic obsolescence**.

long term capital gain

the profit realized from the sale or exchange of an asset previously held for more then one year.

market value

the price of a property that the average transaction in a particular market will bring in.

month-to-month tenancy

a one-month lease which is subject to renewal upon the consent of the lessor and the lessee.

mortgage

a legal document that creates a lien upon a piece of property.

mortgage broker

a person who brokers mortgage arrangements between the borrower and the lender, and is compensated by a finder's fee (paid for by the borrower).

mortgage correspondent

a person authorized to represent a financial institution for offering mortgage services in a particular geographic area.

mortgagee

the lending party that receives the mortgage as security for debt.

mortgagee in possession

lender who has taken over property after the mortgagor's inability to continue payments.

mortgagor

the borrowing party that offers the mortgage as security for their debt.

narrative appraisal report

the report that establishes value, compiled by a property appraiser.

net income (net operating income or NOI)

gross income less all operating expenses.

net leasable area

the area of a building in possession of the tenant; it does not include such areas as the lobby of an apartment building.

net lease

a type of lease that may obligate the lessee to pay such costs as property taxes, special assessments, and insurance premiums.

net listing price

a set price that the seller will receive upon sale of property–the balance between net listing price and the actual price of the property is the broker's commission. This practice is prohibited by the licensing law in many states because it sets at odds the interests of the seller and the broker.

nominal interest rate

the rate of interest stated in the contract.

nonrecourse loan

a loan with no personal liability at stake–the sole security for such a loan is the property pledged.

obsolescence

a loss in value due to disrepair or people's behavior patterns and tastes.

occupancy

physical possession of real estate.

occupancy rate

the percentage of the space available for rent that is occupied at a particular time.

offer

a promise conditioned upon some requested-for act or promise.

open-end mortgage

a mortgage containing a clause which allows the mortgagor to borrow additional money without rewriting the mortgage.

open listing agreement

an agreement between an owner and a broker that allows the owner to work with other brokers in order to maximize the chances of selling the property.

open mortgage

a mortgage without a prepayment clause.

operating expenses

expenses incurred through owning and maintaining a property (excluding any debts associates with the property and the property taxes); operating expenses are subtracted from gross income to derive net income.

opinion of title
see **attorney's opinion of title.**

option

a right which is given for consideration to a party (optionee) by property owner (optionor) to purchase or lease property within a specified time at a specified price and terms. An option is irrevocable by the optionee and will not be extinguished by death or insanity of either party.

over-improved land

occurs when the owner combines more factors of production inputs with the land than can be profitably absorbed.

participation mortgage

an agreement between a mortgagee and a mortgagor that provides the lender with a certain percentage of ownership in the project once the lender makes the loan.

partition

the division of real estate held by two or more people that results in each of the parties holding individual or severalty ownership.

percentage lease
the lessor receives a percentage of the gross sales or net profits as the rentals payment for the lease of the property.

personal property
movables which are not annexed to or are part of the land; also referred to as **chattels**.

physical deterioration
the loss in value due to wear and tear of the structure.

physical life
the normal life expectancy of any property or asset.

planned unit development
a type of exception or special use permitted under many modern zoning ordinances that allows a mixture of different land uses or densities; also known as a community unit plan.

plat book
a public record that identifies a geographic section demarked with streets, lots, and other landmarks.

population density
the number of residents per a given geographical area.

prepayment clause
a section in a mortgage note which permits the borrower to pay without penalty the outstanding balance before the due date.

prepayment penalty
the charge levied by the lender for paying off a mortgage prior to its maturity date.

prescriptive easement
an easement obtained by the open, hostile, and continuous use of the property belonging to someone else for the statutory period of time.

present value
the worth in today's dollars of a future income stream and/or reversion at a given discount rate.

primary financing
the loan that has the first priority.

prime rate
the interest rate charged to a lender's AAA customers. This is normally the base from which other interest rates are derived.

procuring cause
the actions by a broker which result in the owner being able to make a sale.

promissory note
the primary legal financing obligation in which the borrower promises to pay back a sum of money borrowed.

purchase and leaseback
the simultaneous buying of property and leasing it back to the seller.

purchase money mortgage
a mortgage given by the seller to the buyer to cover all or part of the sales price.

rate of return
a percentage relationship between the investment price or equity invested and the composite return.

Real Estate Settlement Procedures Act (RESPA)
a law which covers most mortgage loans made to 1-4 unit residential property. It requires the lender to provide the loan applicant with pertinent information so that the borrower can make informed decisions as to which lender will be used to finance the purchase.

redemption period
the right of a mortgagor to make good on the default within a specified time and receive the property back.

refinancing
a description of an extension of the existing financing either through the same lender or through a new financial arrangement.

release clause
a stipulation that, upon the payment of a certain percentage of a loan, certain lots will be removed from the blanket lien held by the lender.

renegotiable rate mortgage
a renegotiated loan where the maturity is fixed (for example, thirty years) but the interest rate, and hence the monthly payment, is renegotiated periodically (for example, every three or five years).

rent concession
a discount lowering the actual cost of a lease to a tenant.

rent control
in certain geographic locations laws have been passed that impose limitations on how much rent can be charged and what percentage increase can be levied by the landlord.

replacement cost
the cost of substituting a similar structure with utility equivalent to the subject property but constructed with modern materials.

right of way
an easement allowing someone to cross over a parcel of land.

sale-leaseback
a technique used by owners of property as a means of raising capital. The process involves the simultaneous selling and leasing back of the property, usually through a net lease.

sales contract
an agreement in which the buyer and seller agree to the terms and conditions of the sale of property.

second mortgage
a mortgage subordinate to a first mortgage; also referred to as a junior mortgage.

security deposit
a sum of money given to assure the performance of an obligation.

setback lines
a requirement in zoning ordinances in which all structures are to be a minimum distance from property lines.

specific performance
an equitable remedy in which the court orders the contract to be performed as agreed to by the parties.

straight-line depreciation
a method of computing depreciation for income tax purposes in which the difference between the original cost and the salvage value is deducted in even installments over the depreciable life of the asset.

strict foreclosure
when a purchaser defaults under a mortgage, the seller acquires title to land and wipes out the mortgagor's equity.

sublease
the transfer of possession from a tenant to another person (a sublessee), with the original lessee retaining the right of reversion.

survey
the process of measuring a parcel of land.

take-out commitment
an agreement by a permanent lender to provide the permanent financing for a real-estate project when a certain event (normally, the completion of the project) occurs.

taxation
the right of government to require contribution from citizens to pay for government services.

tax base
the total tax-assessed value of all real property in a particular jurisdiction.

tax deed
a deed issued when property is sold to satisfy delinquent taxes.

tax-free exchanges
a method of deferring capital gains taxes by exchanging one qualified property for another qualified property.

tax rate
the rate, normally stated in units of $100.00, multiplied by the assessed value of property to determine the amount of the property tax due.

tax roll
located in the public records, the tax roll identifies each parcel of land, the owner of record, and the assessed value of the property.

tax sale
foreclosure of an unpaid tax lien in a public sale.

tax shelter
shielding income or gains from income tax liability.

tenancy
the possession of an estate.

tenancy at sufferance
a tenancy created when one is in wrongful possession of realty, even though the original possession may have been legal.

tenancy in common
a form of concurrent ownership where two or more persons hold separate titles in the same estate.

tenancy in partnership
a multiple form of ownership where the property is held in a lawful business venture.

tenant
the party that has the legal right to occupy the property of a lessor under an agreement to pay rent.

tenement
property held by a tenant.

term mortgage (straight term)
a method of financing in which interest only is paid during the time of the loan. The entire principle is due at maturity, generally in five years or less.

time value of money
based on the idea that since money is assumed to earn interest, a dollar today is considered to be more valuable than a dollar a year from today.

title
the legally recognized evidence of a person's right to own property.

title company
a company that examines the public records to determine the marketability of an owner's title.

title insurance
a policy that protects the insured against loss or damage due to defects in title.

topographic map
map showing elevation changes with contour lines.

topography
a description of surface features of land.

trade fixtures
personal property used in business that has been annexed to real property and is removable by the owner.

trading on the equity
increasing the rate of return on the owner's equity by borrowing part or all of the purchase price at a rate of interest less than the expected rate of return generated on the net income of the property.

trustor
the person who creates a trust and gives the instructions to the trustee; also known as a settlor.

under-improved land
when a parcel of land can profitably absorb more units than are currently being employed.

undisclosed principal
the concealed identity of the person represented by an agent who is dealing with another party on that person's behalf.

undivided interest
the common interest of co-owners that is indistinguishable from each co-owner's individual interest.

uninsurable title
a title that an insurance company refuses to insure due to some present claim or encumbrance.

utility
(1) the usefulness or satisfaction received from a good or service; (2) various services such as electricity, water, and gas.

waiver
the renunciation of a claim or privilege.

warranty
an assurance that defects do not exist.

warranty deed
a deed in which the grantor makes formal assurance as to quality of title.

water table
the distance from ground level to natural groundwater.

wear and tear
the lessening in value of an asset due to ordinary and normal use.

wrap-around mortgage
a junior mortgage that provides an owner additional capital without refinancing the first mortgage.

yield
the interest earned by an investor on the investment.

yield to maturity
the total return to the investor if the investment is held to total term.

zoning
a police power device that allows for legislative division of space into districts and imposition of regulations prescribing use and intensity of use to which land within each designated district may be put.

zoning ordinance
a zoning law passed by a local government that consists of a text of regulations and a map.

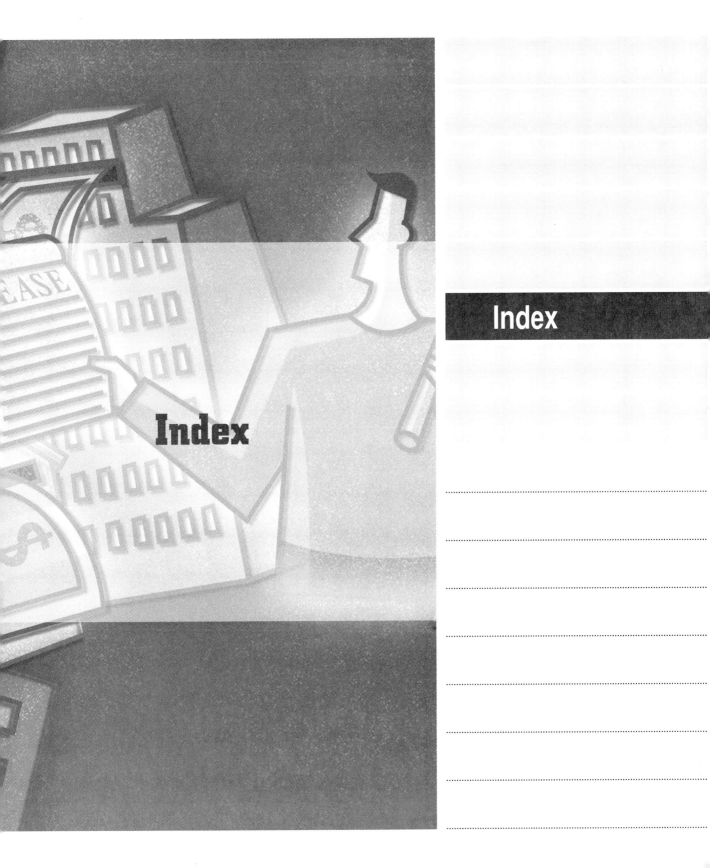

Index

About the Author

Mark B. Weiss began the company bearing his name in 1988. Since then, Mark B. Weiss Real Estate Brokerage, Inc., has taken a prominent role and become well recognized as a leader in the sale of commercial and investment property for financial institutions, private owners, corporations, and trusts, and as a developer of vintage property renovations throughout Chicago's neighborhoods.

A graduate of DePaul University, Mr. Weiss is president of the Lincoln Park Builder's Club; a director of the Chicago Association of Realtors and chairman of the Association's commercial committee; a member and past director of the Illinois C.C.I.M. chapter; a member and past director of the Chicago Real Estate Council; and a member of the National Association of Realtors, the Realtors National Marketing Institute, the Real Estate Investment Association, the National Association of Auctioneers, and the Lincoln Park Chamber of Commerce. Mr. Weiss is a founder and serves on the holding company board of directors of NCB Holdings, the New Century Bank, and Ontario Street Investments.

Mr. Weiss is often appointed a Receiver in Cook and DuPage County and has often been retained as an expert witness in legal cases involving a variety of private, bankruptcy, and disputed real estate matters.

Mr. Weiss has been actively engaged in selling property using the auction method of sale and is well respected locally, as well as nationally, for his successful real estate auction events.

Mr. Weiss often appears on local television programs as a real estate expert for interviews and panel discussions, and has authored books on a variety of real estate topics. He is an instructor for the Latin School of Chicago's "Live and Learn" program.

Mr. Weiss is the chairman of the Mark. B. Weiss Foundation, which annually conducts the "Kindle the Light" scholarship award. The Mark B. Weiss Foundation channels charitable contributions to a variety of worthy causes.

STREETWISE® BOOKS

New for Fall 2002!

**Complete Business Plan
with Software**
$29.95
ISBN 1-58062-798-6

Financing the Small Business
$19.95
ISBN 1-58062-765-X

**Landlording & Property
Management**
$19.95
ISBN 1-58062-766-8

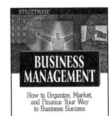

Project Management
$19.95
ISBN 1-58062-770-6

Retirement Planning
$19.95
ISBN 1-58062-772-2

Also Available in the Streetwise Series:

24 Hour MBA
$19.95
ISBN 1-58062-256-9

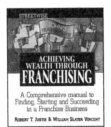

**Achieving Wealth
Through Franchising**
$19.95
ISBN 1-58062-503-7

**Business Letters
w/CD-ROM**
$24.95
ISBN 1-58062-133-3

Business Management
$19.95
ISBN 1-58062-540-1

Complete Business Plan
$19.95
ISBN 1-55850-845-7

**Customer-Focused
Selling**
$19.95
ISBN 1-55850-725-6

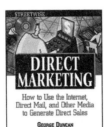

Direct Marketing
$19.95
ISBN 1-58062-439-1

**Do-It-Yourself
Advertising**
$19.95
ISBN 1-55850-727-2

Finance & Accounting
$17.95
ISBN 1-58062-196-1

Get Your Business Online
$19.95
ISBN 1-58062-368-9

Adams Streetwise® books for growing your business

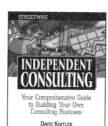

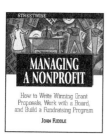

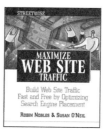

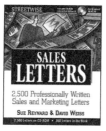
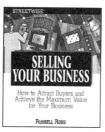

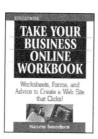

FIND MORE ON THIS TOPIC BY VISITING
BusinessTown.com
The Web's big site for growing businesses!

- ☑ **Separate channels on all aspects of starting and running a business**

- ☑ **Lots of info on how to do business online**

- ☑ **1,000+ pages of savvy business advice**

- ☑ **Complete Web guide to thousands of useful business sites**

- ☑ **Free e-mail newsletter**

- ☑ **Question and answer forums, and more!**

businesstown.com